The U.S. Army War College
Military Education in a Democracy

The U.S. Army War College

Military Education in a Democracy

JUDITH HICKS STIEHM

TEMPLE UNIVERSITY PRESS
Philadelphia

Temple University Press, Philadelphia 19122
Copyright © 2002 by Temple University
All rights reserved
Published 2002
Printed in the United States of America

⊛ The paper used in this publication meets the requirements of the
American National Standard for Information Sciences—Permanence
of Paper for Printed Library Materials, ANSI Z39.48-1984

Library of Congress Cataloging-in-Publication Data

Stiehm, Judith.
    The U.S. Army War College : military education in a democracy / Judith Hicks
Stiehm
        p.   cm.
    Includes bibliographical references and index.
    ISBN 1-56639-959-9 (cloth : alk. paper) — ISBN 1-56639-960-2 (pbk. : alk. paper)
        1. Army War College (U.S.)   2. Military education—United States.   I. Title.

    U413 .S75 2002
    355'.0071'173–dc21   2001057467

Contents

Photographs follow page 100

Acknowledgments

THREE PEOPLE provided me with the access to write this book and never made suggestions or questioned its direction, although they must have held their breath now and then. They were Richard A. Chilcoat, then commandant of the U.S. Army War College; Robert Brace, then the dean of academic affairs; and Karl Farris, then the director of the Peacekeeping Institute. I thank them and hope they are at least tolerant of the outcome.

I particularly thank Colonel Mike Corbell and the members of Seminar 2, Class of 1997, for their friendship and support, and my colleagues at the Peacekeeping Institute and at the Strategic Studies Institute. They include Tom Adams, Adolf Carlson, Walter Clarke, Bonnie Jezior, Bill Johnsen, Doug Johnson, Dianne Smith , Earl H. Tilford, Jr., and Richard Witherspoon.

Many of the continuing civilian faculty guided me to an understanding of how different their job is from mine at a civilian university. They included Herb Barber, Gary Guertner, Sami G. Hajjar, Herb Harbach, David Jablonsky, and Gabriel Marcella.

Other Army War College colleagues who provided insight include Douglas B. Campbell, Carol Kerr, Jack Madigan, Glenda Nogami, Pat Pond, and Les Rockey.

A number of interviews with knowledgeable outsiders proved invaluable. These included Archie D. Barrett, Paul Cerjan, Bob Cronin, Tommy Glakas, Rosemary Mariner, John McDonald, Robert Natter, Bill Netter, Mark Smith, Murray Williamson, and Robert Wood.

The military is the subject of research for a limited number of civilian academics. Having Peter Feaver, Richard Kohn, and Eliot Cohen to talk to was helpful. And, finally, thanks to a former colleague, Mark Kann.

Those thanked have helped me to avoid errors but will almost certainly disagree with some of my conclusions. Still, we are partners in an important enterprise—that of trying to educate citizens, especially civilians, about our military. An informed public is more likely to have the kind of military it needs, and that military is more likely to enjoy consistent support.

The U.S. Army War College
Military Education in a Democracy

Introduction

Our Guardians

Guardians are the armed citizens, police and military, who protect their unarmed fellow citizens. What is important (and, perhaps, curious) is that although they possess the potential to oppress, guardians instead serve. Why do they do so? How are we guarded from our guardians?[1]

The power of the U.S. military is unparalleled. Its reach is global; its weaponry is expensive and lethal; and at senior levels, officers' salaries and status are substantial. In general, the public and media accord the military respect, for although there are monitors and critics of the military, they are more likely to pay attention to waste and excess than to complain about actual or potential oppression.

One safeguard against oppression is the fact that our military is used almost exclusively outside the United States. Another is the military's division into services—Army, Navy, Air Force, Marines—and these services' further division into active-duty, guard, and reserve components. Rapid rotation of assignments also prevents our guardians from developing independent bases of power. Perhaps the most important factor, though, is the education of our guardians.

Guardian Education

Plato believed that the education of guardians was so important that he devoted most of *The Republic* to a detailed account of what he believed would be their ideal education. In that classic, Plato proposed a program that began in the womb and continued until age fifty. It included physical, intellectual, military, moral, and practical education. It also specified that guardians accept the wisdom and direction of a "philosopher-king" (or kings). The guardians, then, protected the citizenry, but they did not make rules for them. Their role was limited to applying force when and as directed.

1

U.S. military officers also receive a good deal of physical, intellectual, military, moral, and practical education. This begins not in the womb but before induction, at a military academy (West Point, the Naval Academy, the Air Force Academy); through the Reserve Officer Training Corps (ROTC) at a civilian college or university; or at Officer Candidate School (OCS).[2] Specialty training occurs shortly after induction and recurs throughout an officer's career. In about the tenth year of service, an officer who plans to make the military a career attends a command and general staff college that emphasizes the planning and execution of large and complex military operations. In about the twentieth year of service, selected officers attend a war college where they learn to manage even larger operations and to think strategically.

It is important to note that the curriculum at a war college is not solely concerned with the application of force. Officers also learn how military strategy fits into a more inclusive national-security strategy, and they learn how to work with and advise civilian leaders. The war-college year is intended to prepare war fighters and to educate strategists.[3] It melds training and education. It is the subject of this book.

The education of U.S. officers differs from that of Plato's guardians in one important way. Instead of being trained to accept the direction of a philosopher-king who has successfully completed guardian training, demonstrated superior wisdom, and forsworn the pleasures of both private property and family, a U.S. officer is taught to take direction from a civilian commander-in-chief whose authority comes solely from electoral victory. Apart from reaching age thirty-five and being native-born, political success is the only requirement for becoming president and, hence, commander-in-chief. The U.S. commander-in-chief can be ignorant of, or even opposed to, the military. His or her personal and political values and behavior can be antithetical to those of the officer corps. She or he may give orders that officers believe are unethical or unwise. Thus, just as guardians possess a potential to act oppressively, there is also potential for a significant gap between the views of military officers and those of their leaders who may or may not be well informed and judicious.

CIVIL(IAN)–MILITARY RELATIONS

Legally, civilians control the military in the United States.[4] Practically, they have done so, as well. The public does not worry about the military exercising a veto over policy issues; nor does it worry that the military might take over the government.[5] This is true even though militaries elsewhere regularly take political and governmental action—sometimes even in countries that are ostensibly democratic.[6] The phenomena of the armed obeying the unarmed and of the armed obeying directives with which it disagrees and directives that can lead to certain death seem counter-intuitive. That is why this volume will take as a recurring theme the content of military teaching about civil–military relations.

Those relations are most significant at senior levels, where professional interaction between officers and civilian officials is most likely to occur.[7] The senior military leadership has a duty to advise its civilian "masters." Although some critics may think that advising too easily becomes advocacy, or even insistence, advising involves more than staying silent until queried, then answering only what is asked. Further, officers have participated in long-term planning, for example, in weapons procurement. They must anticipate which policies are likely to be developed by civilian leaders—leaders who are not only not yet in office but may not even be regarded as candidates for office. In addition to advising and planning, military officers serve in, or as liaisons to, a number of executive agencies. They serve as attaches to embassies. Again, no sturdy fence separates senior military and civilian officials.[8]

THE WAR COLLEGES

The war colleges are almost invisible institutions, but they are important because they offer the last formal, professional military education given to the officers who form the pool from which generals and most admirals are selected.[9] One of the colleges' important tasks is to take highly successful, disciplined, and focused officers and retool them for "the general."[10] This involves teaching them to recognize the frailty of firmly held beliefs, the limitations on resources, the fickleness of the political, the role of diplomacy and economics in security strategy; it also involves teaching them to weigh the lessons to be learned both from history and from the latest technology. At the war colleges, officers with twenty years of experience learn even more about how to make war. But peace is a part of their curriculum, too.

PEACE

The founder of the Army War College, Elihu Root, said that the Army's purpose was "not to promote war but to preserve peace by intelligent and adequate preparation to repel aggression."[11]

Again, although there is always a good deal of talk about "killing people and breaking things" and about "fighting and winning the nation's wars," the military does not necessarily actually want to do these things. It does believe, though, that strength is a deterrent and hence a means to peace.

Over the past fifty years, the United States has participated in major conflicts in Korea and Vietnam. It has fought a war in the Persian Gulf approved by the U.S. Congress and by the United Nations. It has invaded Panama and Grenada. It has fought proxy wars in Nicaragua and Afghanistan. But the "Big One"—the war with the Soviet Union—was never fought.[12] It was prepared for, but it was deterred. The extent and expense of both sides' preparations led to the coining of the phrase "the Cold War." With the recent dissolution of the Soviet Union, that "war" is over. Peace has broken out. The military, the war colleges, and security specialists are having to retool and rethink. The question is: What do, and what should, soldiers study in the face of peace?

AN OVERVIEW

The first two chapters of this volume set the stage. Chapter 1 discusses the different purposes (missions), programs, and character of the Army's sister war colleges. These are the College of Naval Warfare (commonly referred to as the Naval War College and the first of the war colleges), the Air War College, the Industrial College of the Armed Forces, the National War College (created after World War II and intended to enhance cooperation among the services), and the new (and small) Marine War College. The differences among the services and among these schools are both substantial and significant. Chapter 2 provides a history of the Army War College from its inception to the mid-1980s.

The war colleges are a peculiar hybrid. They share many characteristics with civilian academic institutions: They have libraries and offer both required and elective courses; they feature guest lectures and collect student evaluations; some grant degrees. In other ways, the war colleges are distinctly military—and not just with regard to subject matter. Uniforms are prevalent; days are fully scheduled; and bodies are buff. The vital ingredients of a college are, of course, its students, its faculty, and its administrators. Thus, Chapter 3 takes U.S. Army War College (USAWC) students, a select and experienced group of (about) forty-year-old career officers, as its subject. Chapter 4 deals with USAWC faculty, who are largely active-duty officers and recent war-college students. They are not as schooled as civilian faculty, and instructional demands made on them are more onerous than those made on faculty at civilian institutions. USAWC administrators are the subject of Chapter 9. These include the commandant and his staff. War-college administrators are less autonomous than those in many civilian schools. Thus, the Army Chief of Staff, the Chair of the Joint Chiefs of Staff, and the Secretary of Defense all may conduct reviews and give direction. So may the U.S. Congress. In each of these three chapters, attention will be given to the ways in which the war colleges are like, and the ways in which they are unlike, civilian institutions.

Chapter 5 offers a description of the Carlisle experience, including a chronological account of the events of the school year. Chapters 6–8 analyze the curricula presented to the USAWC's class of 1985; its class of 1990; and a composite of the curricula presented to the classes of 1995, 1996, and 1997.[13] Perhaps reflecting the author's bias, more emphasis has been given to the courses taught by the departments concerned with leadership and strategy than to the courses offered by the department that concentrates on operations.

The concluding chapter pursues three themes. One concerns the tensions that exist within an institution that is both military and academic. The second considers what is taught and learned about civil–military relations at the senior level. The third involves the institution's responsiveness to the end of the Cold War. What happened when strategic thinkers had to abandon their mantra of "Russia, Russia, Russia" and shift to a consideration of the role of the military in peacetime? In 1997, as in 1897, the nation was secure and at peace. In 1997, however, the U.S. possessed a large, standing army stationed all over the globe. Our "defense" had become very "forward."

Peace has not made things easier for the military and the war colleges. In fact, the USAWC's response was to create a new, acronymized mantra, "VUCA, VUCA, VUCA." VUCA is said to describe the new security environment and stands for "volatile, uncertain, complex, and ambiguous." War-college administrators, faculty, and students know that even in peacetime they must attend to strategy, education, and curricula. Pentagon officials know that decisions must be made about weapons and technology. But neither the changed circumstances nor civilian authorities have provided the military much in the way of direction and definition. Being prepared is certainly the military's mission. For what is something of a puzzle.

1   The War Colleges

ALTHOUGH THIS VOLUME focuses on the Army War College at Carlisle, Pennsylvania, senior military leaders are drawn from not one but six war colleges. Thus, it is important to provide an overview of those institutions and note how they differ from one another. One, the National War College, is a joint (multi, with no lead service) school. A second, the Industrial College of the Armed Forces, is also joint, but it also has a significant number of civilian students and faculty. Both are included in the later discussion of war-college curricula. But first, in preparation for an account of the four service war colleges (Army, Naval, Air, Marine Corps),[1] it is worth sketching the ways in which the services differ from one another. Just as "Africa" encompasses nations as different as Tunisia, Kenya, South Africa, and Senegal, so the word "military," which refers to the services collectively, fails to reflect their differences. After a discussion of the missions and cultures of the various services, the curriculum offered at each of the Army's sister war colleges will be reviewed.

SORTING OUT THE SERVICES

Perhaps a story will help to set the stage. Jokes that distinguish the services from one another abound, but one of the most repeated goes as follows:

> Four officers were ordered to "Secure the building." The Naval officer turned out the lights and locked the door. The Army officer laid mines around the perimeter and posted sentries. The Marine officer ordered an assault. The Air Force officer tenured a lease with an option to buy.[2]

Most civilians would recognize the Army officer's green; the Navy officer's black; the Air Force officer's blue; and the Marine officer's red, white, and blue uniforms. Most know the services' different missions. The Army fights on land; the Navy on water; the Air Force in the air (and space); and the Marines from the Halls of Montezuma to the shores of Tripoli. (Specifically, Marines mostly fight in areas where the land meets the sea.) A smaller number of civilians would be prepared to describe the services' different cultures—cultures whose differences have been described as "profound, pervasive, and persistent."[3]

First, it must be remembered that all are "services." Society has given members of the military the special responsibility of taking human life on behalf of society. Also, service members have the duty of risking their lives, and some have the additional duty of sacrificing their lives.[4] Service members, then, are deeply committed to the nation and presumably to its values of liberty, democracy, and the free market—but, perhaps ironically, the cultures of none of the services are particularly free, democratic, or income maximizing. Thus, it could be said that military professionals are people willing to die for values that are not the ones by which they have chosen to live.[5]

In *The Spirit of the Laws*, Montesquieu tried to sum up the central value of different kinds of governments. For instance, he said, the core value of despotism was "fear"; that of a limited monarchy, "honor"; and that of a republic, "*virtú*." Carl Builder tries to do the same for the services by describing their "altar for worship." That of the Navy, he says, is tradition, and one of its strongest traditions is the independence and absolute power of a ship's commander. Builder argues that the Air Force altar is technology, while that of the Army is service to "the nation and its citizens."[6]

The services have internal hierarchies as well as service altars. Within the Navy the carrier-based aviation community (especially tailhookers, pilots who fly on and off carriers) may hold the most clout. (Or they did until their infamous Las Vegas convention, at which female officers were manhandled and the Navy tried to cover up.) Then comes the submarine, and then the surface-warfare community. At the bottom of the hierarchy is mine warfare and support. This structure is quite rigid. Once one has been assigned to a kind of ship or plane in the Navy, one usually sticks with it.[7] In the Air Force, the division and the hierarchy is simpler: There are pilots and non-pilots. There may be some rivalry between bomber (a strategic weapon) and fighter (a tactical weapon) pilots, but there is room for crossover among pilots, and some room for mavericks. The Army also has an apparently simple division: combat and noncombat. The combat branches—infantry, artillery, and armor (sometimes called cavalry and meaning tanks)—are the more honored and risky branches, but Builder believes that Army officers acknowledge branch interdependence and accord one another more mutual respect than is true of the hierarchies of the Navy and Air Force.[8]

The Goldwater–Nichols Act of 1986 was supposed to reduce rivalry and increase cooperation among the services. But competition has not been eliminated. Perhaps the most obvious way competition is displayed is in funding requests to Congress. In the budget arena the services compete head-on—and make rather consistent arguments on their own behalf. The Navy's argument is almost always framed as the need for a certain number of ships. When he was Secretary of the Navy, John F. Lehman, Jr., successfully called for the "600 ship navy." Prodigiously expensive, that number was soon reduced to just 320 ships and 12 carriers. Builder calls the Navy the "hypochondriac of the services" and claims that its arguments rarely vary, no matter who is in charge, who is seen as the enemy, and what advances have been made in technology. In (slight) contrast, the Air Force makes its argument in terms of wings—that is, planes—but the Air Force's numbers are not as stable as the Navy's. To the Air Force, new and more marvelous can outweigh numbers.[9] The Army talks about divisions or "end points" (people) in the Regular (not Guard or Reserve) Army, but its numbers fluctuate greatly between wartime and peacetime, and the Army expects this to happen. Only recently have the Abrams (tank), the Bradley (fighting vehicle), computer technology, and the panels studying the Army of the future brought technology to the fore in the Army's budget discussions. In the past, Army officers' pride has rested more with their soldiers and their skills than with their equipment. The Army's job, the taking and controlling of territory, means that when it is in action, it will always require large numbers of people.

Builder suggests that the Army *knows* it is the core service—that it is indispensable.[10] Moreover, the Army does not just "fight and win the nation's wars." It has long been akin to a handy man who does a variety of requested tasks. Thus, the Army ran the Civilian Conservation Corps (CCC) in the 1930s; its engineers build levees and dams; it responds to natural disasters and to humanitarian emergencies; and it serves in noncombat tasks such as peacekeeping. The fact that the real variety of Army activities is not congruent with the narrow mission of "fighting and winning" is a matter of recurring discussion, and sometimes even of what one might call fretting.

The Air Force knows its firepower is relevant, but its legitimacy as an independent service is sometimes challenged by the fact that 1) the other services also have aviation, and 2) the Air Force cannot win a war alone. In contrast, the Navy's existence as a separate service is measured in centuries. It is sure that when the site of warfare is water (which covers more than 70 percent of Earth), the mission is the Navy's. However, the Navy's significance is contested by the Air Force, which has a greater capacity to move troops, supplies, and equipment rapidly, as well as having enormous firepower.

Overall, the Army's sense of security about its centrality and relevance, combined with its knowledge that all nations have always had armies, may have made it the most willing to act jointly, and even to contemplate unification. The Navy, which is as old as the Army, has great regard for its tradition, its independence, and the independence of its commanders. Since World War II, though, it has had to absorb aviation, nuclear power, and nuclear weapons. It has also found itself in competition with the Air Force for transportation and force projection assignments. The Air Force, the offspring of the Army, does not monopolize flight, but it savors new technology and argues that it provides "decisive" force. It has made much of its role in the Persian Gulf and in Kosovo and Afghanistan, where it used "smart" bombs in urban areas and conventional bombing on the battlefield. But air power has never settled a conflict. In every case, ground troops must take and hold terrain and organize any occupation.

Again, their different missions, histories, and cultures distinguish the services from one another. Builder claims that their differences are reflected even in something as abstract as analysis, where the Air Force is "sophisticated and elegant," the Army is " ingenuous and credulous," and the Navy is "suspicious and pragmatic."[11] Differences among services are also apparent in something as concrete as their war-college curricula.

THE NAVAL WAR COLLEGE

The Naval War College is the oldest (1885) war college and is perceived as the most intellectual, the most academic. Its motto is in Latin, and, unsurprisingly, says "Victory through sea power." Located on an island in historic and scenic Newport, Rhode Island, the Naval War College enrolls students in four different schools: the College of Naval Warfare and the College of Naval Command and Staff (both for U.S. officers and some civilians), and the Naval Command College and the Naval Staff College (for some sixty international officers).[12]

The first president (not commandant) of the Naval War College, Stephen B. Luce, stated its mission: research on war, on statesmanship connected to war, and on the prevention of war.[13] Luce appointed Alfred Thayer Mahan as one of his first four faculty; Mahan promptly published *The Influence of Seapower upon History, 1660–1783*. *The Influence* quickly had a powerful and international influence on military thinking. Soon thereafter Mahan became the president of the college.

The Naval War College developed a reputation for war-gaming as early as 1887. (Its reputation has been sustained.) Closed during World War I, the college spent the years after that war and before World War II preparing (planning) for almost exactly the battles it would, in fact, fight in World War II. It has been said that the only two things not planned for were the attack on Pearl Harbor and the Japanese kamikaze (suicide) pilots.[14] The Naval War College did not close during World War II, although the importance of attendance declined and continued to be low through the Vietnam era.

In the 1970s, the school underwent a dramatic transformation under the direction of Vice Admiral Stansfield Turner. It was then that the three areas of decision-making, strategy, and operations became the central elements of the curriculum. These remain the curriculum core to this day. About the same time, electives were introduced, and the Center for Advanced Research was established. In 1981, the Center for Naval Warfare Studies (CNWS) subsumed the Advanced Research Program for students, the Naval War College Press, and the War Gaming Department, thus drawing together all research programs.

The CNWS emphasizes research. Three departments offer the core curriculum in three blocs, each lasting about three months. The blocs are: National Security Decision Making, Strategy and Policy, and Joint Military Operations. The same subjects are taught by the same departments (but sequenced differently) at the (co-located) Command and Staff School. Both colleges are accredited to confer master of arts degrees in national security and strategic studies.[15] Senior Naval officers have

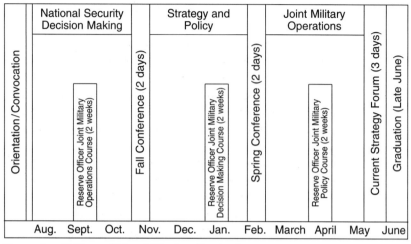

FIGURE 1.   College of Naval Warfare Curriculum.
Source: Naval War College Catalogue 1998–99, 21.

generally attended one of the two Newport schools, but not both. This
has not been true of the other services, which see their command and
staff and war colleges as sequential and each as necessary.

A typical academic year at the Naval War College is shown in
Figure 1.

The National Security Decision Making unit is concerned with the
relationship between military strategy and the national resources, economic, political, and organizational factors that affect military strategy and decision-making dynamics, especially under conditions of
uncertainty.[16] Attention is given to joint and coalition planning and to
the use of reserve as well as regular units in the development of strategy. The unit concludes with a week-long strategy and force-planning
exercise.

Prominent elements of the Strategy and Policy course are the study
of strategists such as Clausewitz, Sun Tzu, Jomini, Corbett, Douhet,
Mao, and, of course, Mahan; examination of historical cases such as the
Peloponnesian War; and case studies of recent wars as well as scenarios for possible future wars. Special attention is given to the match
between military strategy and political objectives, civil–military and
coalition relationships, and assessment of the results of conflicts.[17]

The final third of the core curriculum is devoted to joint military operations and to an examination of law—international, naval, and that of armed conflict. The course proceeds by examining concepts first, then moves to case studies and to application through war-gaming.

A wide range of electives is also offered, from "Negotiation for the Commanding Officer" to "Abraham Lincoln" and "Expeditionary Warfare." One elective is taken each trimester. A small number of students are given permission to omit a trimester elective in order to focus on a research project.

The core is completed by two two-day conferences and a three-day Current Strategy Forum. In recent years, the two conferences have frequently taken professional ethics and the media as their topics. In 1999, though, a conference on civil–military relations was substituted for the media conference. The end-of-year Current Strategy Forum includes a number of civilian participants with a wide variety of experience.

Although the college is in a small town, the class does not have the unity one finds at some of the other schools, because only half the students enter together in the summer trimester. The remainder enter at the beginning of one of the other two trimesters.

Students do extensive reading; they prepare briefings; they write papers; they take exams; and they are graded.[18] The best get honors.[19] The atmosphere is very schoollike.

Approximately a third of the research faculty are civilians. More than 40 percent of the departmental faculty are civilians, and almost all of the civilians have Ph.D.s.[20] Typically, civilian faculty have renewable appointments of one to four years, and military faculty have three-year assignments, the first year of which they spend as students. Seven core faculty have "indefinite" appointments.[21] These factors give the Naval War College faculty more expertise and continuity than is characteristic of the other war colleges.

The Naval War College is recognizably an academic institution, and it is conducted as a college is conducted. It emphasizes that the curriculum is a "thinking curriculum" and that the faculty "owns" the curriculum. Paradoxically, while it is admired, attendance is not required for promotion to admiral. Getting to the top in the Navy still depends on going down to the sea in ships.

THE MARINE CORPS WAR COLLEGE

The Marine Corps does not have an academy of its own. It does not have an ROTC program of its own. It does have a war college of its own—well, sort of. It all began in 1989 with the founding of the Marine Corps University (at Quantico, Virginia), which was given responsibility for all Marine Corps professional military education. Almost at once (1990), the Marine Corps War College was founded and became an integral part of the university.[22]

When the Marine Corps' War College catalogue says the student body is small, it means small. In 1997–98, in fact, there were six Marine, two Navy, two Air Force, and two Army students, for a total of twelve.[23] These twelve students functioned as a unit for a full year—quite the opposite of the Naval War College.

"Academic Freedom" is given an extended discussion at the very beginning of the Catalog (p. 3).[24] Also, all through its descriptive literature the Marine Corps War College emphasizes "original thought," "new ideas," "new concepts," "innovative critical thinking," and the freedom to "seek changes in academic and institutional policies."[25]

The curriculum shown in Figure 2 and the education received by the Marine Corps War College students differ from those of the other colleges. First, not only does everyone do everything together, but the class is peripatetic: Students spend a fair amount of time on the road. For example, they go to Washington, D.C., to see Congress, the Secretary of Defense, and the Joint Chiefs—and to a number of the combatant commands, as well. Also, a substantial part of the curriculum is focused on a variety of peacekeeping missions, activities that the Army also does but seems to be ambivalent about.

Further, everyone studies every region in the Regional Studies segment of the curriculum and attention is given not just to security, but also to economics, politics, and culture.[26] And in General Studies, everyone takes the Executive Speaking Course, Economics, and the Total Quality Leadership class. Each student also prepares a research paper ("of publishable quality"), and that paper is developed in conjunction with a one-week internship in the private or governmental sector.

The goal is "holistic" understanding, and grading is done "holistically"—but competitively. Letter grades are given; only the top three in

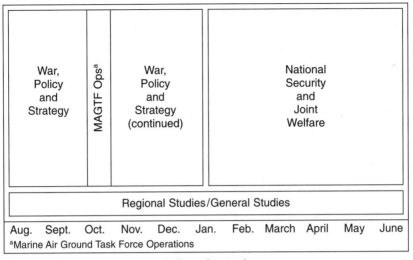

FIGURE 2.   Marine Corps War College Curriculum.
Source: Marine Corps War College Academic Catalogue 1997–98, 4.

each segment can expect to receive an "A." The top two students over-all (of twelve) are designated "Distinguished Graduates."

"Active learning" is central to the program and includes field trips, discussions, tutorials, exercises, and war games. "Active preparation," though, probably understates what is done by the faculty to create the situation for that learning.[27] University faculty would be astounded at the planning that goes into the teaching of most war-college courses. Further, at the end of each course at the Marine War College, a formal review of every element of the course is conducted by an internal com-mittee of seven, including a faculty member, a student, and administrators. Further, an external review is implemented that involves evaluation by alumni, senior Marine leaders, and others who employ the graduates.

Importantly, the first item for student evaluation is "Effectiveness of the College in imparting an atmosphere that fosters creative and open thought," and the second is "Effectiveness of the College in providing an intellectual foundation from which to assess past, present, and future national and military strategies." The Marine Corps wants thinkers from this group.

Again, the Marine Corps is an extraordinarily disciplined and directive institution. It is also highly organized. Its Marine Corps War College Standard Operating Procedures manuals make sure that there are
few sins of omission in spite of staff and faculty turnover.[28] Through this
program, though, it tries to produce a small number of creative, yet
pragmatic senior leaders. Its efforts to achieve "free" thinking in an
"unfree" culture bear careful scrutiny. Does its year of intensity, of
immersion, and of intimacy foster the original, deep, useful thought it
seeks? In *The Laws*, Plato lays out a scheme for the best possible state,
as contrasted with his more utopian *The Republic*. In *The Laws*, he gives
an account of the creation of a small group of highly reliable citizens
who are sent into the world to explore what is done elsewhere and to
consider possible benefits from innovation. The Marine Corps War College does not provide a broad and general education for a large number of senior officers. Like *The Laws*, it invests in only a few, but for that
few it appears to be encouraging intellectual risk-taking and critical
thinking beyond that of its sister schools.

THE AIR WAR COLLEGE

The Army and Navy War Colleges are small installations in historic,
small-town settings. The Marine War College is located on a major
installation, but the class of twelve spends a good deal of its time elsewhere. The Air War College is located on Maxwell Air Force Base in
Montgomery, Alabama. It is located with the Air Command and Staff
College, but the two colleges are not as interrelated as the schools at
Newport, and senior officers tend to attend both schools during their
career.

A typical class numbers about 250, making the student body significantly smaller than that of the Army War College. The Air War College,
too, assigns students to a seminar (but for the whole year), which provides "an optimum balance of diverse backgrounds." Some of the factors that are considered in making seminar assignments are listed—for
example, rated (pilots) or non-rated, Guard or Reserve. Race, ethnicity,
and sex are not listed, but . . .

The Army War College encourages the wearing of civilian clothes. (It
does require jackets and ties, a "uniform" that is more appropriate to
the business world than to a civilian graduate school—well, maybe to

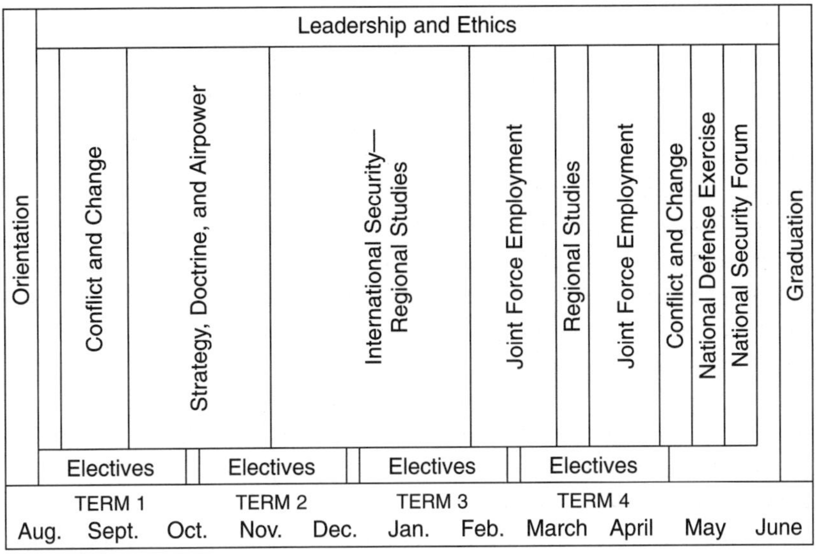

Leadership and Ethics											
Orientation	Conflict and Change	Strategy, Doctrine, and Airpower	International Security—Regional Studies	Joint Force Employment	Regional Studies	Joint Force Employment	Conflict and Change	National Defense Exercise	National Security Forum	Graduation	
	Electives		Electives		Electives		Electives				
	TERM 1		TERM 2		TERM 3		TERM 4				
Aug.	Sept.	Oct.	Nov.	Dec.	Jan.	Feb.	March	April	May	June	

FIGURE 3. Air War College Curriculum.
Source: Air War College Curriculum Catalogue 1997, n.p.

a business school.) Air War College students, by contrast, wear uniforms. Theirs is clearly a military environment.

The Air Force has been teaching "Curriculum 2000" since 1995.[29] Its three key concepts—leadership, strategy, and jointness—are similar to the concepts highlighted at the Naval War College, although "leadership" is substituted for "decision-making." Topics recently added to the curriculum include the effect of downsizing, peace operations, and the continued acceleration of change. Course material is conceived as moving from principles of warfare through process to application. The college's intended product is a "soldier-statesman."[30]

The departmental organization at the Air War College differs from that of the other colleges. It has five departments. One of them is Leadership and Ethics, which teaches a year-long required course (see Figure 3). This course establishes the difference between the certainty of the tactical situation and the uncertainties of the strategic environment. It uses Myers-Briggs Type Indicator (MBTI) and the Strategic Leadership Development Inventory (SLDI) during its unit on individual development. In thinking about leadership in the Air Force, it may be helpful to remember that only those who fly are in combat—and that pilots represent only a small percentage of the force. Thus, most Air Force personnel have civilian-like jobs, and Air Force leadership is more managerial in style than is, for example, Army leadership. Army leaders, two-thirds of whose troops are in combat specialities, emphasize leading by example.

The first core course is offered by the Department of Conflict and Change. It assumes that "not only is war against the United States possible, but indeed, unless human nature has changed, *likely.*" The "prudent scholar/warrior" ought not simply accept the view of "experts" that "there's no threat. So we can down-size, bottom-up review, and convert the U.S. armed forces into a joint collection of armed social workers." An important lesson to be learned is that "the American people need to understand why money is still required to sustain a large military establishment of standing forces [even] when obvious threats are diminished."[31] Other topics include operations other than war; the possibilities of space combat; biological warfare; and study of British strategy in the late nineteenth century, when Britain dominated the world as the United States does today. Motivations are described as "realist" when promoting national interests and "liberal" when directed toward advancing democracy, free trade and enterprise, and human rights.[32]

Strategy, Doctrine, and Air Power are featured in term two. The same strategic thinkers studied at Carlisle and Newport are studied at Maxwell. With "theory" under their belts, students move on to a set of case studies drawn from World War II, the Cold War, and Vietnam, and then to consideration of lessons learned by the different services through the Gulf War.

The third term is offered by the Department of International Security Studies and brings the political, economic, and global to the seminar room. Terrorism, civil–military relations, the media, allies, and the different commands are given attention.

The fourth and final term focuses on Joint Force Employment. It is capped by a two-week war game of two major regional conflicts.

While students march through this curriculum, they also take electives. Some eighty are offered. Also, during their work in Regional Studies, students make a ten-to-twelve-day field trip to one of twelve geographical areas, including Russia, China, and Central Asia. Their trip is preceded by twenty-eight hours of "focused academic preparation" and followed by a four-hour "hot wash" on return.

A set of non-credit electives is also available. These include courses on the media, wellness, executive writing, speed reading, Microsoft Word and PowerPoint, personal finance, and grant writing.

The final event before graduation is the week-long National Security Forum, which is similar to that held at the Army War College. This brings some one hundred guests to discuss issues with students and invited experts. According to its primary stated goal, it "provides the USAF a means to influence community leaders nationwide." Secondary goals are "to demonstrate the capabilities of tomorrow's military leaders" and to show "[Air War College] students current civilian understanding of and support for military issues." Once again, the implicit message seems to be that the Air Force tail needs to wag the civilian dog.

THE NATIONAL WAR COLLEGE

This is one of the two colleges located at Fort McNair in Washington, D.C. Both are components of the National Defense University (NDU) established in 1976.[33] Both are free of a particular identification with any of the four services. Neither is residential. The city bustles with distractions. The experience is quite different from that at the other colleges.

Jointness is all. Only at the National Defense University college do students fulfill all requirements for the Joint Specialty Officer designation. Students who attend the service war colleges must complete a six-week "Phase II" course before receiving that designation.

The presidency of the university rotates among the services. The vice president is an ambassador. At the National War College (NWC), jointness includes working with government agencies, not just the other services. Thus, while 75 percent of the students are military, 25 percent are from the State Department and other federal agencies. The "interagency process" is a central concern.

The faculty is organized into just two departments: Military Strategy and Operations and National Security. The latter includes decision-making, the constitutional order, bureaucratic politics, the media, and the nature of U.S. society. In 1994, the faculty comprised twenty-three military officers (30 percent of whom held Ph.D.s); seventeen civilian professors; and eleven agency representatives.[34] The civilian faculty all

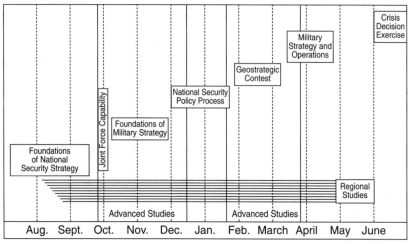

FIGURE 4.   National War College Curriculum.
Source: National Defense University Catalogue 1996–98, 45.

held Ph.D.s, all had taught at major civilian universities, and all but one had worked in the federal government. Two-thirds of the faculty were war college graduates. Fourteen percent were women. A model curriculum is shown in Figure 4.

In the Student Handbook the curriculum's "integrating themes" are spelled out:

- "Policy is often as much an outcome of bureaucratic processes, compromise, and the influence of a dominant personality as it is of a 'rational' calculus."
- "State resources are limited."
- "Ethical norms inform and constrain policy-makers' freedom of action."
- "A national security strategy must identify the interests of the nation ... the challenges to those interests ... and specify the objectives to be met through the use of specific policy instruments, particularly in any use of military force."
- "Instruments of policy must be orchestrated within a cohesive strategy."
- "Military strategy and operations require the development within the Armed Forces of a joint culture."

From the beginning, students study and assess nonviolent instruments of statecraft and consider the resources required and available for any course of action. There is also a brief review of macroeconomics and international economics. In the study of the National Security Policy Process, NWC students give far more attention to the federal government than do students at the other schools. A detailed study of executive agencies, including the National Security Council, is followed by careful study of Congress, then of the political environment itself. The last segment of the core looks at operations—first as an element of conventional deployment and deterrence, and then as a response to a crisis.

At the NWC, regional studies are a year-long process that culminates in a two-week trip to the region studied. Advanced courses are taken concurrently with the core curriculum. Non-credit, elective professional-development courses include Executive Writing, Executive Speaking, and Executive Health. Clearly thinking of oneself as an "executive" is intended as part of the these students' training.

The seminar organization is used, but seminars are shuffled six or seven times during the year as each element of the core is completed.

The Washington, D.C., location makes possible Distinguished Visitors' Day, when some fifty retired generals, admirals, and ambassadors come for lunch and to interact with students. Also, the Distinguished Lecture Program is conducted jointly with the Industrial College of the Armed Forces (ICAF) and other units of the university. In addition, the NDU sponsors four symposia for civilian scholars and other interested civilians each year. Three are on NATO, the Pacific, and Joint Operations; the fourth changes its theme each year.

Not only are the textbooks at the NDU free, but the students may keep them. However, like professors and executives and officers at the other colleges, these potential senior leaders are turned into their own secretaries for a year. The exchange is a laptop computer to have and to hold—and, for some, the chance to learn to use for the first time.

THE INDUSTRIAL COLLEGE OF THE ARMED FORCES

The Industrial College of the Armed Forces is the second college within the National Defense University. Its focus is "the resource component of national power, with emphasis on materiel acquisition and joint

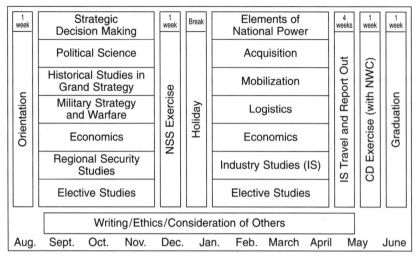

FIGURE 5.   Industrial College of the Armed Forces Framework for Grand Strategy. The concurrent teaching of the courses emphasizes their interrelationship. The midyear exercise requires students to develop an integrated national-security strategy. The Crisis Decision Exercise integrates the entire academic year.
Source: Industrial College of the Armed Forces, Student Handbook, 1997–98, app. A.

logistics." The crucial link here is that of government to industry.[35] Some see this college as the least prestigious, but in some ways it is both the broadest and the most fundamental.

The ICAF core curriculum shares a focus on strategy, decision-making, regional studies, and jointness with its sister schools. Its specialized components, though, include Economics, Logistics and Mobilization, and Industry Studies, in which a seminar group studies one of some eighteen industries in depth. Two elective Advanced Courses are taken each semester, and a research option is open to students. A sample curriculum is shown in Figure 5.

Seminar groups are organized on the distributive model in the first semester. In the second semester, they are based on one's Industry Study Group.

War-gaming and simulation are part of the curriculum. The National Security Strategy Exercise comes in the first semester. The Crisis Decision Exercise near the end of the year is a joint exercise with the NWC.

ICAF is wired. Students are issued laptops, and life is conducted through e-mail. Information dominance is a "thread" woven through the curriculum.[36] On arrival, students receive a CD-ROM with all course syllabi, the CIA World Fact Book, and a variety of other references. At graduation, they receive another CD, which includes the seminars' Industry Study reports.

Social functions at ICAF are much more limited than those at the other colleges, although athletic competition between the two McNair colleges in nine different sports receives a fair amount of notice. Intramural competition exists, too.

The faculty of about eighty is evenly divided between those holding master's degrees and those with doctorates. More than 60 percent of the faculty are civilians; more than two-thirds of these hold doctorates.[37] Nine Agency Chairs bring senior professionals from executive-branch agencies to the college as faculty, usually for a two-year period. Chairs are also appointed by each of the services and by the Chair of the Joint Chiefs of Staff.[38]

The 180 military students are divided roughly into thirds: Army, Air, and Navy/Marines/Coast Guard. Seventy percent will have had recent operational experience, but only a fifth will have had joint experience. There are likely to be some ninety civilians and International Fellows in the class, as well. About a third of the civilians come from the Departments of the Air Force, Army, and Navy. Others come from a range of government agencies, including the National Security Agency, the General Accounting Office, and the Agency for International Development. In 1995–96, both Hughes Aircraft and McDonnell Douglas had students in attendance.

ICAF is unique in the time and energy it devotes to the study of industry. Still, it shares many qualities with its sister schools. The job of its graduates may not be to fight, but it is very much to win the nation's wars.

As will be seen, the Army War College shares many elements of its program with the other war colleges. Although each service school continues to give some emphasis to its special mission, Goldwater-Nichols requirements have led to significant emphasis on joint operations and to some homogenization of the colleges' curricula.[39] Nevertheless, each school differs from the others.

Two are joint schools. One of these, the National War College, gives special attention to the U.S. government, both to its executive agencies and to the U.S. Congress. The expectation is that many senior officers will work closely with civilian officials and that understanding the political arena is important to fulfilling one's duties responsibly as adviser and implementer of national strategy. The other, the Industrial College of the Armed Forces, concentrates on issues of the economy and its potential mobilization. It has more civilian students than the other schools, and each student develops expertise on one sector of the economy.

The Marine War College is small. It is intended to give a small number of officers permission to range and to focus on innovation, creativity, the future. The Naval War College is (and has been) the most conventionally academic of the institutions. Its faculty are said to "own" the curriculum, and pride is taken in its rigor. However, the Navy War College and its Command and Staff College are seen as alternatives to each other, not, as it were, as junior and senior high. In some ways, the Air War College is the most like the Army War College. However, the Air War College responded more directly than the others to critiques made in the Skelton Report—for example, by instituting grading.[40] Also, its student handbook has an air of training officers as Air Force lobbyists and as propagandists/instructors to civilians. Officers from the other services observe that the Air Force is exceptionally successful on Capitol Hill (Congress). Sometimes their observations sound critical; sometimes, envious.

2   A History of the Army War College

AT THE END of the nineteenth century, the work of many Americans was professionalized, including that of teachers and physicians. In large part, this was accomplished by establishing formal educational requirements. In designing higher education, the models used were often German. For example, Johns Hopkins University won its place in educational history by importing the German system of doctoral training, which emphasized the seminar and original research. Our Army was in step. It, too, sought to professionalize through education. The model it chose was Prussian.[1]

Elements of military education developed in early-nineteenth-century Prussia remain central to Army higher education today. These include: 1) the development of detailed battle plans; 2) staff rides and the study of maps; and 3) war games. Another important element of Prussian military education was its Railways Department. The modern equivalent would be the attention given to logistics and "lift," and to the incorporation into military planning of the newest technology.[2] (In the nineteenth century, technology transfer tended to be from the world of business to the military rather than vice versa.) Emphasis was also given to studying history and to preserving the materials needed to write it. One result is that research on almost any army-related topic (this one is no exception) is greatly assisted by the Army's habitual devotion to documentation. Histories done by the other services tend to be leaner.

U.S. interest in higher military education, then, was a late nineteenth-century (post–Civil War) phenomenon.

U.S. HIGHER MILITARY EDUCATION: THE CIVIL WAR TO WORLD WAR I

At the end of President Ulysses S. Grant's second administration (1877), the U.S. Army had fewer than 28,000 soldiers. They were deployed

Much of this narrative is drawn from Harry P. Ball's *Of Responsible Command,* published by the Army War College Alumni Association. This copiously detailed account was last updated in 1994.

principally on the frontier, in harbor defense, or in supply and service bureaus such as the Medical Department and the Corps of Engineers. The Army was clearly a stay-at-home army. Meanwhile, the U.S. Navy was growing from the world's twelfth-largest to its third-largest fleet.[3] This meant the Army experienced a relative decline. The National Guard, supported by allies in state governments and in Congress, also represented competition for the Army. The debate as to the relative value of a unitary, regular army versus one that relied heavily on mobilizing state militias had not (and has not) been fully resolved.[4] Still, meeting the competition led the Army to put improvement high on its post–Civil War agenda. "Progress" was emblematic of civil society of the period; the Army was in step.

During the 1870s and 1880s, pre-commissioning exams and active-duty performance reports were developed. So was active-duty education. Thus, by 1875 the Army's Artillery School at Fort Monroe, Virginia, was offering a two-year course (for some twenty students) that, in addition to artillery, included subjects such as engineering, law, and administration. Soon thereafter, Lieutenant Colonel Emory Upton prepared a report arguing on behalf of a "war school." His argument was that during peacetime, a small force should be trained that would be prepared to "officer" a rapidly developed wartime Army.[5] Upton was soon assigned to Fort Monroe to teach in the Department of Military Art and Science, Military History, and Geography. This gave him the opportunity to explore the appropriate content of a "war-school" curriculum.[6]

Other Army branches decided they needed schooling, too. In 1881, the Army created what would shortly become a two-year school for Infantry and for Cavalry (which still meant horses) at Fort Leavenworth, Kansas. When a third school (for the mounted arms) was established at Fort Riley, Kansas, in 1892, Leavenworth sought to distinguish itself by raising the level and expanding the reach of its analysis to include instruction in topics such as international law and military history.[7]

Army reformers of the era had two primary concerns. One, noted earlier, was the need for a set of well-trained senior officers available to command any newly formed, wartime Army composed largely of men who had, just previously, been civilians. The other was the need for a peacetime senior staff that worked at the strategic level of analysis.[8] Its task would be the development of plans for a wide range of contingencies. Both needs fell under the rubric of "being prepared." Both needs were seen as met by the Prussian system. Prussia, of course, believed it must be ready for an attack at any time by Russia, Austria, or France. What the U.S. Army needed to be ready for was less clear. At the end of the century, though, an enemy did finally materialize: Spain.[9]

The Spanish–American War presented the Army with an immense challenge in mobilization and logistics. Its size was not doubled or tripled; it increased tenfold, to 270,000,[10] in four months. And it was sent in large numbers to Cuba, to Puerto Rico, and to the far distant Philippines (by ship—no planes).

The war against the Spanish was won with little fighting.[11] Still, a postwar study headed by Grenville Dodge, a former Civil War general and a railroader, was severely critical of the Army's planning, logistics, and organizational structure. Further, the Army's Commanding General Nelson A. Miles was both critical and vocal. The person who was assigned the blame for the Army's lack of preparedness was Secretary of War Russell A. Alger.[12] He was soon replaced by Elihu Root. Root would become the "father" of the "war school" first proposed by Upton, and would later become secretary of state and winner of a Nobel Peace Prize.

Root was faced with multiple tasks. These included: 1) repatriating Spanish forces from Cuba; 2) demobilizing almost 150,000 U.S. troops; 3) building a continuing U.S. force of almost 100,000; 4) fighting a long-distance colonial war in the Philippines; 5) providing a colonial administration there; and 6) providing relief following a hurricane in Puerto Rico.[13] None of these tasks had been planned for. Further, even if there had been a strong planning unit, the Army would probably have focused on battle plans, on "winning wars," rather than on such highly varied activities. It is important to remember, then, that fighting is *not* what an army does most of the time, even if it is the unique thing an army does. The variety of peacekeeping and other activities asked of the military in the 1990s was not new.

During his four years as secretary of war, Root focused on improving the efficiency and competence of the Army and on creating a unity of effort under the secretary of war (himself). He emphasized preparation, planning, and a future orientation. To accomplish his goals, Root recommended and took the initial steps toward creating both an Army War College and a War Department General Staff (for planning).[14] The functions of the two institutions and the relationship between them would take time to sort out.

General Order 155 (November 27, 1901) established the Army War College. It also provided for a tiered system of professional education akin to that in existence today. Specifically, it authorized "elementary" (entry-level) instruction on each post, specialized instruction for the different branches, a "General Service and Staff College" at Fort Leavenworth for the best officers from all branches, and a War College at Washington Barracks in Washington, D.C. (now Fort McNair) for the most advanced instruction. The War College was to emphasize doing and problem-solving with peers[15] rather than lectures (except for those by distinguished guests), and would be closely associated with the General Staff. Planning was to include joint operations (with the Navy), and there was to be coordination with the Naval War College, as well.

Graduates of the Army War College expected to receive a senior command or a senior staff assignment after their year of schooling. This was very much a Platonic progression. The intent was that only the best would move to the next level. However, the pyramid did not have a single apex. Joining the General Staff (created in 1903) and commanding troops were quite different assignments and had different implications for the content of the college's curriculum.

In 1903, amid much pomp and blessed personally by President Theodore Roosevelt, the cornerstone for a grand, new War College building by the architectural firm of McKim, Mead and White was laid. At the ceremony, Root described the school's purpose as the study of "national defense, military science and responsible command."[16] In 1904, the first nine students began a seven-month course of study under the direction of the college's president, Tasker H. Bliss.

Bliss served for two years. Such a short assignment is not at all unusual. Rapid rotation of both administrators and faculty is a significant way in which a war college differs from a civilian college (see Table 1). Another important difference is the substantial direction that comes from outside the institution. War Department Order 115 (June 27, 1904) outlined the course of work to be pursued.[17] Such top-down decisions affecting the curriculum would be most unusual in a civilian academic setting.

The eleven students in the class of 1908 were the first to occupy the new building and the first to undertake a full-year curriculum. That curriculum had already changed significantly, evolving from one based on solving problems for the Army (by officers assumed already to be

TABLE 1.   U.S. Army War College Commandants

	From	To
Major-General S. B. M. H Young	1902	1903
Brigadier-General Tasker H. Bliss	1903	1905
Brigadier-General Thomas H. Barry	1905	1907
Brigadier-General W. W. Wotherspoon	1907	1909
Brigadier-General Tasker H. Bliss	1909	1909
Brigadier-General W. W. Wotherspoon	1909	1912
Brigadier-General Albert L. Mills	1912	1912
Brigadier-General William Crozier	1912	1913
Brigadier-General Hunter Liggert	1913	1914
Brigadier-General M. M. Macomb	1914	1916
Brigadier-General Joseph E. Kuhn	1917	1917
classes suspended in World War I (1917–19)		
Major-General James W. McAndrew	1919	1921
Major-General E. F. McGlachlin, Jr.	1921	1923
Major-General Hanson E. Ely	1923	1927
Major-General William D. Connor	1927	1932
Major-General George S. Simonds	1932	1935
Major-General M Malin Craig	1935	1935
Brigadier-General Walter S. Grant	1935	1937
Major-General John L. DeWitt	1937	1939
Brigadier-General Philip B. Peyton	1939	1940
classes suspended in World War II (1940–50)		
Lieutenant-General Joseph M. Swing	1950	1951
Lieutenant-General Edward M. Almond	1951	1952
Major-General James E. Moore	1953	1955
Major-General Clyde D. Eddleman	1955	1955
Major-General Max S. Johnson	1955	1959
Major-General William P. Ennis, Jr.	1959	1960
Major-General Thomas W. Dunn	1960	1962
Major-General William F. Train	1962	1964
Major-General Eugene A. Salet	1964	1967
Major-General William J. McCaffrey	1967	1969
Major-General George S. Eckhardt	1969	1971
Major-General Franklin M. Davis, Jr.	1971	1974
Major-General DeWitt C. Smith, Jr.	1974	1977
Major-General Robert G. Yerks	1977	1978
Major-General DeWitt C. Smith,Jr.	1978	1980
Major-General Jack N. Merritt	1980	1982
Major-General Richard D. Lawrence	1982	1983
Major-General Thomas F. Healy	1983	1985
Major-General James E. Thompson	1985	1987
Major-General Haward D. Graves	1987	1989
Major-General Paul C. Cerjan	1989	1991
Major-General William A. Stofft	1991	1994
Major-General Richard A. Chilcoat	1994	1997
Major-General Robert H. Scales, Jr.	1997	2000
Major-General Robert R. Ivany	2000	—

educated), to one focused on the training of officers in "the military art." The importance and value of historical studies and of original research became a matter of energetic discussion—a discussion that would recur. Also, the practice of having members of the Navy and Marine Corps as faculty and students was begun, as was the practice of holding over some new graduates to serve as faculty the next year. From the class of 1908 through that of 1917, standards for admission and the (military) rank of students were gradually raised. The class of 1917 started late because of a mobilization on the Mexican border; it closed early because the United States had entered the war in Europe, World War I. There was no class of 1918.

War colleges often close during wars—presumably to fight the wars they have planned for. However, war colleges do not necessarily anticipate the wars they actually fight. This happens in part because their planning and preparation create an un-self-fulfilling prophecy. Also, responding to new facts is difficult for any institution, and war colleges are no exception. Thus, by 1915 new global events included a Japanese challenge to China, a civil war in Mexico, and a war in Europe. Still, the War College curriculum planned for the class of 1916 was no different from the one that had been used the year before.[18] In fact, plans for fighting in Europe were not developed until six months after the United States had entered the war. Then they were prepared in France, not by the War College or the General Staff.[19] The institutions intended to guarantee preparation had not been prepared.

The War College as it existed from 1904 to 1917 is sometimes referred to as "the First War College." It had 270 graduates. Fifty-seven percent of the Army graduates became generals.[20]

WORLD WAR I TO WORLD WAR II

"Lessons learned"[21] from World War I, in which the Army grew from 100,000 to 4 million in a matter of months, and in which the fighting was done on the other side of an ocean, were that: 1) mobilization is a national, not a military, affair; 2) skilled staff require training (so much so that even during the war, the Army was setting up new schools to prepare officers and noncommissioned officers in both the United States and France); and 3) many of the new services—for example, Air, Chemical Warfare, and Finance—were here to stay.[22] Thus, in the future, there would be more branches, and more specialization, within the Army.

Postwar goals established for professional military education included rationalizing the tiers of education so their content did not overlap but did cover all necessary topics; synchronizing the schools with rank; providing education to more officers;[23] and ensuring that those in the senior school were able to take into account the capacities, interests, and needs of nonmilitary as well as military institutions.[24] The seniormost leaders, then, were to become more than military experts. Their professional education was intended to prepare them to think about the nation and its needs in a larger, more sophisticated way.

The first postwar commandant, James McAndrew, selected nineteen veterans of the European theater for his faculty. Their curriculum was composed of one big idea: first, to plan a large-scale mobilization by examining each function in detail; then to conduct a war game so that students could test their plan. Finally, they would participate in a field exercise incorporating what they had learned in the two previous steps. The "war" selected for the year's work for the class of 1920 was one against Great Britain and Japan. (It included plans for a defense of Oahu and a possible invasion of Montreal.) At the time, the United States was still occupying Germany's Rhineland and had signed a guarantee with France (later rejected by the Senate), and had forces in Siberia supporting opponents of the Russian Revolution. Still, the habit of seeing our recent ally Great Britain as our major threat continued. Also, all Army planning assumed that in the event of any war, a massive mobilization would be required. Ours was not yet a "standing" army. Nevertheless, in laying out the basis for a national defense strategy in 1920, Congress authorized a Regular Army of 298,000.[25] It provided funding for only 200,000, however, and by 1925 had funded only 137,000. The Army of the United States was defined as including the active-duty Army and two other elements: the National Guard and the Organized Reserve Corps. Although this demonstrated that the idea of a "citizen" army remained popular in Congress, that same Congress did reject the idea of universal (male) military training.

The Army War College continued in its fine new building but with continued uncertainty about, first, its relationship to the General Staff, and second, its mission. That is, was its task the training of future members of the General Staff, the training of senior commanders, or both? As pressure developed to do it all,[26] the nature of the War College experience changed from the solving of "one large problem" collectively, and by the "applicatory method," to a program more like that of a graduate school, in that it included lectures ("Informative Phases") and individual research. Also, as part of a new emphasis on command, the analysis of biography (for example, that of Hannibal) became part of the curriculum. Exams, grades, and theses were not, however, a part of the picture.

As the Army shrank, competition for promotion increased, and officers began to see attendance at the War College as important. Even so, the next commandant, Edward F. McGlachlin, sought increased diversity in the student body. He added Reserve and National Guard officers to the class of Regular Army, Navy, and Marine Corps officer students. He even added civilian students from departments such as State and Commerce.

Overload is a grievous problem in any prescribed educational program, and the War College regularly wrestled with it. At different, times different subjects and experiences were given emphasis, but one year was simply not enough to teach command and field operations and to plan for a major mobilization. The secretary of war's answer was to create a new institution to focus on mobilization—the Army Industrial College. Borrowing methods and materials from the Harvard Business School, the college began offering a one-year program in 1926. It was originally designed to be at the same level as Leavenworth but was the seed for what would become a separate (and joint rather than Army) war college, the Industrial College of the Armed Forces.

An engineer, William D. Connor, became commandant of the Army War College in 1927, with a new mission. The War Department's directive to him explicitly required: 1) instruction in "political, economic and social matters which influence the conduct of war"; and 2) study of the logistics of past wars.[27] Also, the directive implicitly made a distinction between "training" and "instruction." "Training" was said to involve the acquiring of defined skills, whereas "education" involved the enlargement of understanding, judgment, and analytic thought.[28] The last became a specific goal for the college.

The continued tension created by the directives to prepare both staff officers and commanders was cut through by Connor's reconceptualization of the curriculum. He directed that the basis for the curriculum be the study of Clausewitz, whose formulation of the military's task was to prepare for war (largely staff work) and to conduct war (largely command work).[29] This format would be followed for more than a decade, until the Army War College was again suspended—this time by World War II.

During the post–World War I period, history was restored to the curriculum in a course titled "Analytical Studies," which required the answering of detailed, often quantitative, questions. Unfortunately, the Army's Historical Section, which should have supported the course, was in bad odor with senior commanders and had difficulty doing what it considered professional history. In fact, one of its first volumes on World War I so annoyed General of the Army John J. Pershing that it was recalled and suppressed. Further, Chief of Staff Charles P. Summerall directed that no manuscripts on World War I would be published without prior submission and approval.[30] The use of extended maneuvers and war games continued to be an important part of the warcollege curriculum and served both to test plans developed by students and to train them in command.

At the end of the 1920s, President Herbert Hoover was still initiating arms-limitations agreements and, in particular, hoping to achieve agreed-on reductions in land forces (as had already been accomplished for capital ships). In addition, isolationist sentiment in Congress and its commitment to a balanced budget combined with the stock-market crash of 1929 to create budgetary restrictions severe enough that the Army had to make choices. The choices were made by Douglas MacArthur, then chief of staff. The Army would choose personnel over posts (fifty-seven posts were closed) and procurement over modernization (which would have included such things as the mechanization of artillery and the creation of an air force).[31]

Budget cuts continued in the Roosevelt administration, and the Army War College absorbed its share (but not more than its share) of cuts. Turnover continued at the top, with four commandants between 1935 and 1940. During the same period, international events in Europe, Africa, and the Far East (specifically, aggression by Germany, Italy, and Japan) and civil war in Spain led the Army to plan for war even while Congress pursued a policy of neutrality.

Foreign relations and international news became a larger part of the Army War College curriculum in the 1930s, but planning continued to focus on the defense of the continental United States, Alaska, Panama and the Canal Zone—and the Philippines. In 1937, though, one plan proposed for gaming suggested a solution that would involve fighting in Europe. Also, in 1938 the college evolved (secretly) a plan that involved a major overseas expedition in the Western Hemisphere. Specifically, the expedition was to be to Brazil, which had a large population of Germans and Italians.[32] However, even the planning for an expeditionary force did not involve planning for a coalition (with allies) force. The U.S. military expected to fight independently. It had not enjoyed its World War I experience of fighting with allies.

The college's method of learning continued to emphasize group problem-solving, with supplemental lectures mostly by distinguished visitors. The student body comprised fewer than a hundred Regular Army officers, selected by their branches, and ten officers from the Navy and Marine Corps. Air Corps and noncombatant branches were represented among the students, all of whom had to be graduates of a command and general staff school and eligible for assignment to the General Staff. There was also an effort to reduce the age of students. Meeting all these requirements, and at the appropriate time, made admission selective and competitive.[33] Still, the college encouraged cooperation rather than competition among students. Grades and exams, which were seen as stimulating competition, remained taboo.

AFTER WORLD WAR II

The Army War College was suspended in 1940, and Leavenworth became an abbreviated course to train staff officers at the division level. During the war, however, a new school had been created, the Army and Navy Staff College, which offered a twenty-one-week course for colonels and lieutenant-colonels and for their Navy equivalents. This was the first truly joint military school. In 1945, Army Generals Dwight D. Eisenhower and George Marshall agreed that, after the war, it should be elevated to a war college—and that neither the Army War College nor the Naval War College would be needed in the future. Accordingly, Eisenhower turned over the Army's cherished Washington, D.C., building to the new National War College in February 1946. At about the same time, the Industrial College was upgraded to war-college status, and the Armed Forces Staff College, a joint intermediate school, was created. Meanwhile, however, the Navy had not closed its war college during the war, and the Army Air Corps was busily planning a college of its own.

Congress and the president decided on the military's new organization in the National Security Act of 1947. This act did *not* unify the services, as the Army (but not the Navy) had hoped. The act did create the Air Force as a separate unit. It did create a Secretary of Defense. It did (finally) provide a statutory basis for the Joint Chiefs of Staff and provided it with a staff. In addition, it created the National Security Council to bring domestic, foreign, and military policy together, and the Central Intelligence Agency to bring intelligence collection together.

Because Eisenhower's goal of unification was not met, a 1948 recommendation was made that the Army War College be reinstated. (Only a limited number of slots were assigned to the Army by the joint war college. Thus, fewer Army officers had a chance to get a war-college education than did Navy and Air Force officers, who could attend their own war colleges as well as the National War College.) By January 1950, the Army War College had been reestablished, and planning had begun for a fall opening at Leavenworth, with a subsequent move to Carlisle.

The first post-World War II commandant would be Joseph M. Swing; his deputy was Arthur G. Trudeau. In spite of the concurrent outbreak of the Korean War, Swing was given a free hand in selecting his faculty and a class of one hundred students. This was the beginning of the Army's "Third War College," and Swing's charge was to make the college the apex of Army education. Specifically, he sought to make it a "post-graduate school, contemplative in nature and mature in aspect." He proposed to encourage creative and objective thinking and to minimize the distinction between faculty and student.[34] "College," rather than "war," was to be emphasized in the aftermath of the long, global war the nation had just fought.

A new curriculum was in order. The school had been closed for almost a decade, and the world of the 1950s was very different from that of the 1930s. In the first postwar curriculum, the year began with a two-week period of "committee study," a form of instruction in which students learned the committee method while developing possible solutions for current Army personnel problems such as racial segregation and integration, the role of female soldiers, and a new, compulsory thirty-year retirement policy.[35] (Obviously, the group solutions did not solve all problems—or, if they could have, the solutions were not implemented.)

This was followed by a ten-week section on "The Army and National Security." By the time the Army War College reopened, the United States' World War II ally, the Soviet Union, had tested an atomic device and become our Cold War enemy; China had been claimed by the forces of Mao Zedong; Berlin had been blockaded; and we were leading United Nations troops in a war on the Korean peninsula. Further, India and Pakistan were newly independent; the French were facing a number of colonial wars; and the first of what would become a series of Arab–Israeli wars had been fought. Our postwar policy of "containment" (of communism) now called for not only a standing army, but one that would be stationed (and would fight) abroad in large numbers.[36] Army officers, like the American public, had a lot of learning to do if they were to think and act globally. Thus, half of the ten-week "The Army and National Security" course focused on international issues, while the second half studied (U.S.) executive-branch organizations concerned with national security, as well as the organization of the Department of the Army itself. The course included a one-week visit to Washington, D.C. (only one hundred miles from Carlisle, but not the two hours away it is on today's freeways) for a series of high-level briefings. Learning more about and from civilians was claiming more of the curriculum.[37]

During the next nine weeks, the subject was "Current Army Problems." These covered an exceedingly broad range of issues, from training to tactical air support, partisan warfare, and the study of the operational organization of the former German and current Soviet armies.

The whole second half of the year was allocated to "War Planning."[38] This began with area assessments and a global strategic estimate and was followed by a week-long war game. The intent was to illustrate what would be required of a realistic war plan. The course then moved into planning in three sections: 1) Joint War Planning; 2) Army Planning and Mobilization; and 3) Theater Planning. In 1950, a second field trip was added. That year, the students went to the White Sands Proving Grounds and the Sandia Base in New Mexico.[39] In 1951, field trips would go to the Aberdeen Proving Grounds and, for the first time, the United Nations. Finally, each student was assigned a 5,000-word research paper. Both the "conduct of war" and the "command" themes, which had been so central to the pre-World War II college, were deemphasized. The postwar curriculum had more reach but necessarily less depth. It also revealed a new tension: that between wanting to give students time for contemplation and wanting them to assimilate as much material as possible.

Many a new idea was put on the table by Commandant Swing and his deputy. These included adding civilian professors and faculty representatives from the Department of State, creating a civilian advisory group, awarding a graduate degree, and bringing the Office of the Chief of Military History to Carlisle.[40] Their vision clearly saw senior military officers as men of affairs, as participants in the shaping of national policy. A different, narrower view saw officers as skilled professionals who serve their country but do not make policy. These different perceptions continue to co-exist.

In the years 1953–58, the Army War College had six commandants. (Its faculty also turned over at a rapid rate.) However, the Army's larger problems were nuclear weapons and its commander-in-chief, President Dwight D. Eisenhower, who wanted a balanced budget and lower taxes. He believed that the 70 percent of the federal budget spent on defense should be reduced by 25 percent. He also supported a new defense strategy featuring massive retaliation that was based on the Air Force (rather than on the Navy or the Army). The Army faced a reduction from twenty to seventeen divisions. At the same time, it had to consider scenarios involving general and limited nuclear war in addition to "conventional" warfare. This meant learning about new weapons, developing new doctrine, and creating the appropriate organization or organizations.[41]

New Army War College initiatives included another recommendation to hire more civilian faculty in order to increase expertise and continuity and a proposal to publish an academic journal.[42] An Advanced Studies Group of five officers was directed to tackle long-range planning, but with few additional resources and numerous demands for rather pedestrian studies, the Advanced Studies Group and the Army War College found it hard to become "the intellectual center of the Army."

An Individual Studies Program became yet another example of the conflicting pressures the college experienced. Were student research papers produced in the program intended to develop the student? To provide the Army with sound research? Or to provide the college with curriculum materials? And how many faculty were competent to supervise and critique students' efforts?

In 1954, the National Security Seminar was inaugurated. In 1955, it became the end-of-year project that replaced a major war game. The seminar brought a large group of civilians to the Army War College to participate with the students in a review of national strategy for a period of several days. It provided outreach and kept military personnel attuned to (at least some) civilian views.

When Maxwell D. Taylor became chief of staff of the Army in 1955, his concern that the nation needed a national-security strategy and that the military needed a supporting military strategy was reflected in a new Carlisle curriculum. That curriculum was put in place in the fall of 1957. In it, war games and planning waned; strategy and doctrine to support strategy waxed. Student theses continued, and the National Security Seminar prospered. Taylor's program would shape the curriculum for the next decade.[43]

New views about the nation's defense arrived with the Kennedy administration, which opened with the Bay of Pigs fiasco and a confrontation with the Soviet Union over Berlin.[44] First, there was a willingness to spend more on defense. Second, there was acceptance of Taylor's argument that there was a need for a flexible, or graduated, response rather than simply a massive response. This led to an Army buildup. Third, a commitment was made to challenge Soviet-supported wars of liberation—including those in the Congo, Laos, and Vietnam—which in turn meant developing a capacity for counterinsurgency warfare. Fourth, Secretary of Defense Robert McNamara brought a managerial revolution to the Pentagon with integrated (five-year) planning, programming and budgeting. These changes meant even the most experienced officers had a lot to learn.

Commandant Eugene A. Salet brought ideas for further changes. These included upgrading the faculty. Also, he sought to increase stability by recommending that 25 percent of the faculty be quasi-permanent.[45] While he did not seek degree accreditation, he wanted the college to be "worthy" of it. However, Salet's ambitious plans (named Army War College–70) proved hard to implement. Meanwhile, both the Department of Defense and the Department of the Army were making critical noises and considering reviews of the war colleges.

The Department of the Army's Haines Board, a review board, completed its work first. Two of its most important recommendations were: 1) that elective courses be used to prepare some specialists; and 2) that an extension or correspondence program be instituted for nonresident students. Both recommendations were adopted.[46] In addition, the faculty was organized into departments.

By the mid-1960s, a new stimulus required response: the war in Vietnam, a limited but protracted conflict. Again, the Army was sent to fight a kind of war for which neither it nor the civilian population had prepared.[47]

The Vietnam War and After

The Army War College did not close during the Vietnam War,[48] but military strategy again took center stage in the curriculum. Management also moved into the spotlight, and case studies regained popularity. Wargaming all but disappeared; a real war was in progress. The arrangement with George Washington University under which students could earn a master's degree also disappeared, although the program had been popular. The contract with George Washington University had been expensive, but beyond that, a question arose about how students were finding the time to earn civilian academic degrees when they were assigned full time to the college.[49]

The question of class size also emerged. Debate revolved around the issue of "stockage"—of how many active-duty Army War College graduates were needed to staff and command a rapidly expanded Army. In 1967, the number proposed was 2,880. It was calculated that achieving that number would require graduating 312 students a year (up from 205). This meant that the brand-new Carlisle facilities would be too small, the faculty would have to be increased, and family housing would be in short supply. These economic factors, plus an anticipated drawdown after Vietnam, led policymakers to decide against expanding the class, although by the mid-1990s classes would have grown to more than 300 students.

The deficiencies of the Army's performance in Vietnam led Army Chief of Staff General William C. Westmoreland to request a "Professionalism Study" from the college in 1970. This study had a profound impact. It found, first, that many officers did not respect their superiors; and second, that they believed that an unhealthy ethic of "striving for success" had come to characterize the officer corps. (The study was not released until two years after its completion. By, then a number of what were hoped to be corrective actions had been taken.) A companion study, "Leadership for the '70s," found that, although values were "consistent and appropriate," their application was too often wanting.[50] As might be expected, in the next curriculum revision, studies related to leadership (including management), human dimensions of professionalism, and behavioral science were given increased attention. Although national-security issues would remain central, the curriculum would lose its unifying theme of "a national strategy and its supporting military program."[51]

During the Vietnam War, the Army War College had begun providing a panel of faculty and students to discuss that war in public forums. This would evolve into the Current Affairs Panel, an outreach program that was understood as an important way to stay in touch with civilians' views and attitudes. In addition, the U.S. Army Military History Research Collection was established at Carlisle, and the practice of collecting oral histories was begun.

Major-General Franklin M. Davis became commandant of the Army War College in 1971. With the support of Westmoreland, who had directed the college to become "the center of contemporary military thought," he initiated the most thorough review of the college to date. Davis's own charge was that, in addition to being "the [intellectual] center," the college should prepare its students for "professional generalship." He sought a long-term development plan to accomplish these goals.[52]

Davis's view was that the curriculum, the faculty, the methods of evaluation, and the organization of the college were all part of an integrated system and needed to be studied (and changed) simultaneously. One important conclusion was that the curriculum was too rigid. Thus, the year was to be divided into three terms. The first term would be an overview focused on national and international security and would be taken by all students simultaneously. They would also take military strategy and "commandership." In the second term, students would take a variety of electives. In the third, they would participate in group study of selected contemporary problems. The year would be capped by a symposium, with outside experts speaking on contemporary issues.

Second, the plan proposed that the problem of maintaining collegiality while evaluating students and the program be managed in the following way: On entry, each student would be given a baseline inventory, a self-appraisal designed to help "tailor" the year's program to the individual. The self-appraisal included measurement of attitudes, values, goals, and personality. Its results were to be given only to the individual and to a faculty "coach" or counselor—and that, only at the student's request. During the first term of study, individuals' solutions to problems would be forwarded to the faculty anonymously so that the level of the group's understanding could be assessed. Class members would then be provided with the faculty's solution to the problem, so they could (privately and individually) compare their solutions with those of the "experts." During the electives, more traditional grading would be used—except that the grades would not be recorded. During the third term's group-problem-solving curriculum, students would receive feedback in the form of anonymous peer evaluations and the equivalent of an officer-efficiency report from the team leader (a faculty member). The group solution would also receive a group evaluation. At the end of the year, a "value-ended" inventory similar to the baseline inventory would be taken by each student. Needless to say, this elaborate plan met immediate problems in application—and resistance.

It was becoming evident that collegial faculty who coordinated students' activities were no longer sufficient. Subject matter experts were needed, as, if Davis's plan were to be implemented, were skilled "personal development coaches." To increase continuity, Commandant Davis appointed a civilian, Charles M. Hersh, to the new post of director of academic affairs. Hersh held that position for fourteen years.

To advance the Army War College's goal of becoming an intellectual center, efforts were again made to ensure that the school remained under the Army staff (rather than see it moved to the Training and Doctrine Command), and the research-oriented Strategic Studies Institute (SSI), formerly the Advanced Studies Institute and before that the Advanced Studies Group, was made an integral part of the college. The SSI also began regular publication of "research memoranda."

DeWitt C. Smith, Jr., served as commandant from 1974 to1977 and again from 1978 to 1980. During the one-year interim period, one of his former deputies served as commandant. This meant that Smith had an unprecedented six-year opportunity to lead the school. He was concerned essentially with the sociology of knowledge—that is, the conditions under which learning and discovery occur. His own education at the Army War College (in 1966) had been highly structured, regulated, and formal; he did not think these conditions produced the desired end.

Smith's changes included encouraging civilian clothing for faculty and diversity in students and in their thinking.[53] He was convinced that the college's primary purpose must be the growth of the individual officer—growth not in technical understanding but in breadth and wisdom and creativity. The nation had lost a war (Vietnam), and its president (Richard Nixon) had been forced to resign. "School solutions" would not suffice. Smith wanted to ensure that the Army did not become isolated; that it would regain its confidence; and that trust between civilian leaders and military leaders would be reestablished.

When Smith arrived, Davis's new three-part program, which called for a required core, electives, and group problem-solving, was just being put into place. Unfortunately, neither the faculty nor the administration had fully bought into it. Smith preferred more flexibility. He also believed that senior officers needed a better understanding of Congress and the media. The result was another redesign of the curriculum, this time creating only two sections: a common overview and electives. (Each student was to take four of fifty-four available electives.) Writing a paper became an option, and four intensive, theoretical seminars were offered on ideology, sociology, the military and society, and political order.[54]

Data collected for the Army War College showed that fewer than half the graduates were going on to Washington, D. C., staff assignments, and that a "gap" did indeed exist in officers' preparation for command. Leavenworth's Command and Staff College instruction stopped at the level of the Army corps. The college taught strategy. Operations above the level of corps were neglected. Smith believed the Army War College had a responsibility to respond. He did so by putting some strategy, planning, and operations material into the core and by creating six elective "war-fighting" courses. War-gaming, gone for fifteen years, reemerged in a computerized format. New technology was already being used in a variety of ways in the Army, but just as university faculty have had to be pushed by their students to learn new tools, so it was found that senior officers needed to be pushed to learn and use that technology. Smith also thought that Regular Army Officers needed to know more about the reserves and brought more reserve officers to the Army War College program, including reserve officers from the Navy, Air Force, Marine Corps, and Coast Guard.[55]

The faculty's work was clearly evolving in the direction of providing expertise and teaching (as opposed to coordinating and leading discussions). It was decided that fifteen faculty could have indefinite tenure—that is, they could serve until they reached the mandatory thirty-year retirement limit; that officer specialists would be able to stay for five years; and that others would have three-year assignments.[56] Further, faculty members could be fulfilling their last assignment before retirement; they did not have to return to another Army assignment after serving at the college. Faculty development was also enhanced via two-day seminars with distinguished guest lecturers.

By 1975, the students' visit to New York was no longer confined to the United Nations; it included small-group visits to twenty-four different sites and organizations. A number of these visits were related to urban problems, but others were made to very going concerns, including Wall Street, the *New York Times,* and major corporations. In addition, the end-of-term National Security Seminar had expanded its guest list and consciously sought to bring in civilians with a variety of views. The Current Affairs Panel continued and was seen as an opportunity to stay in touch with the young and with academia. The longest outreach, though, involved the new International Fellows Program—a program not welcomed by budgeters or those who had to administer confidentiality policies. The first six International Fellows (IFs) came in the 1977–78 academic year.[57]

The Army War College may have never analyzed its Philippines experience at the beginning of the century, but an elective course on Vietnam was offered in 1975, and a contractor was hired to produce an eight-volume history under the supervision of the SSI.[58] Vietnam had left no one happy. Reflection was the order of the day. Even Congress had formed a "Military Reform Caucus."

When he became commandant in 1980, Jack Merritt ordered yet another full review of the college. The working mantra of Merritt's task force was "relevance, rigor, depth."[59] This review, and direction from new Army Chief of Staff Edward C. Meyer, who favored more contingency planning, would establish the curriculum and practices in place immediately before the period to be examined in Chapter 6 of this volume.

The new basis for organizing the curriculum came from an old friend, Clausewitz. A new translation had made his *On War* significantly more accessible. In addition, Colonel Harry Summers's well-received interpretation of the Vietnam War was based on a Clausewitzian theory of war. Students received a copy of *On War* before they arrived at the Army War College and began their course with sixteen hours of study of Clausewitz.[60]

Finally, in the early 1980s, the Military Family Program was introduced.[61] The Army Physical Fitness Research Institute was established at Carlisle, and the USAWC War Gaming Center was dedicated there.

Some argue that there have been four Army war colleges—that two were interwar institutions; the third, a Cold War school; and the fourth, a post–Cold War school, which is just emerging. The "first" War College, which was founded after the Spanish–American War and the emergence of the United States as an imperial power, graduated thirteen classes from 1903 to 1917. It borrowed from the Prussian model of master–apprentice officer training and from the Naval War College's well-developed "main problem" and war-gaming curriculum.[62] Closely linked to the War Department, the College was more of a problem solving and planning unit than an educational institution. Peers were expected to learn from each other rather than from experts. The "applicatory method" implied that there were correct answers to problems, and that those answers were provided by doctrine.[63] "Military art" was added to the curriculum within a few years, as were research assignments and the study of history. These new elements implied that there was learning to be done, not just problems to be solved by already educated officers. Although the "first" War College confined its program and planning strictly to military topics, it did not anticipate the demands that would be made on the military when the United States entered World War I.

The "second" War College operated between World War I and World War II. Its immediate postwar curriculum was based on the one big problem of mobilization.[64] Later, topics related to command, history, and research would be added to the curriculum. In 1928, though, an entirely new curriculum based on Clausewitz and divided into two sections, Preparation for War and Conduct of War, was put into place.[65] Although problem-solving and committee work remained central and learning emphasized the practical, "larger-picture" elements such as economics, politics, and international relations made an appearance in the curriculum. Also, the first plans for expeditionary forces were developed, although they did not include coalition warfare, which would be an important feature of World War II.

The Army War College was closed from 1940 to 1950. When it reopened, the Cold War had begun. Over the next forty years, the college's perspective became global. In addition, the newly reformulated college raised its intellectual aspirations. When it reopened, the plan was to make it the "apex" of Army thought. Words such as "contemplative" entered mission statements; the adjective "creative" was used to describe the kind of thinking sought; and "rigor" became a watchword. Electives also made their first appearance, creating some possibility for specialization.

Following the Vietnam War, new emphasis was given to Root's third charge: the teaching of leadership and responsible command. Perhaps most important, interaction with and the study of civilians became routine. The end-of-term National Security Seminar expanded; the Current Affairs Panel remained active; the SSI employed civilian researchers; Congress and the media became objects of study; and the New York trip expanded to include chances to get acquainted with the range of sub-cultures in urban America.

Like the country, and like warfare itself, the Army War College changed dramatically from 1903 to the mid-1980s. Some changes were predictable as the military met new challenges and accommodated to technological and political developments. Horses were replaced by tanks—and planes. Nuclear weapons entered the arsenal. Concern about the Soviet Union's expansionist intentions dominated strategy. But even greater changes were on the horizon. By 1990, the Cold War and the Soviet Union would essentially wither away, and micropro-cessing would introduce wondrous possibilities.

Commandant Richard A. Chilcoat foresaw the emergence of a "fourth" Army War College as the curriculum responded to these and other changes.[66] The changes made to the U.S. Army War College from 1985 to 1990 and in 1995–96–97 are detailed in Chapters 6–8, but it is important to remember that some issues remained unresolved, and many elements of the institution did not change. Discussion continued about the proper emphasis to give to preparation for staffing versus leading the Army, and concerns were voiced about gaps in professional military education. Further, the curriculum seemed to oscillate between emphasizing operations and the practical and strategy and critical think-ing. Complaints about the curriculum's focus were chronic, but the real problem may not have been a lack of focus so much as the changing of focus as each new chief of staff provided counsel to rapidly changing commandants and faculty. If efforts to alter and raise the level of the cur-riculum are to succeed, however, the preparation and role of the faculty will be central. But before assessing the strengths and weaknesses of the faculty, it is important to understand just who their students are. The student body, therefore, is the next object of scrutiny.

3   Army War College Students

WHO ATTENDS the U.S. Army War College? What do its students bring to the classroom? What is the composition of a typical class? What is the purpose of a full year of education for selected senior officers?

Plato's philosopher-kings completed their education at age thirty-five. They then had fifteen years of real-world experience before (at age fifty) some of them became "men of gold." U.S. Army officers, in contrast, typically finish a bachelor's degree around age twenty-one. Then, over the next twenty-some years, they first attend Officer Basic and Advanced courses; next, at intervals, they attend a variety of specialty training; and at roughly the ten-year point, some are chosen to go to a command and staff college (the middle tier of professional military education, or PME, which focuses on forging the different branches and services into an effective, operational force). In addition, officers often acquire a civilian master's degree while serving on active duty. For a select group, attendance at a war college comes at about the twentieth year of service. U.S. officers' education, then, is co-mingled with their work. And the work itself can be highly educative, because it entails a wide variety of experience and occurs in a wide variety of places.

It might be helpful to look at three career histories taken from the "Biographical Sketches" volume of the Carlisle Barracks' Class of 1997. Following this, a profile of that class as a whole will be presented, as will an account of why the students are told that they are there during their orientation.

THREE SOLDIERS' STORIES

Student A is a field artillery officer. He was born in Kansas City, Kansas, in 1954. He is a U.S. Military Academy (West Point) graduate but has not completed a master's degree. His first assignment was to Fort Sill, Oklahoma, where he served as fire director and executive officer for an artillery battery (equivalent in size to an infantry platoon). Fourteen months later, he became commander of the battery. Eighteen months later, he left Oklahoma for Korea, where he became the counterfire officer for an infantry division. After one year, he returned to the United States—specifically, to Fort Ord, California. There he again commanded a battery, this time for two years. Next he served for a year as an aide-de-camp to the commanding general of the Seventh Infantry Division at Fort Ord. The following year, he became operations officer for a battalion (still at Fort Ord). For the next three years, he served as an ROTC instructor at Bowling Green State University in Ohio. This was followed by a year's attendance at command and staff college, then by a year as operations officer for an artillery battalion in Carlstadt, Germany. After a year, he became executive officer for that battalion, and soon thereafter he became the operations officer for a division.[1] During the three years of his assignment in Germany, Student A was sent to the Persian Gulf to participate in both Desert Shield and Desert Storm. His next assignment was as a political–military officer at the State Department in Washington, D. C. After that, for the two years before going to the Army War College, he commanded an artillery battalion at Fort Bragg, North Carolina. Thus, in fewer than twenty years, this officer held twelve positions, lived in eight locations on three continents, participated in a war in southwestern Asia, taught in a university, and worked in the State Department. His is an almost classic career pattern for a successful officer in a combat branch.

Student B has a somewhat unusual career pattern. He is an air defense specialist but also has been trained as a foreign area officer (FAO). Born at West Point in 1954, he attended the University of Texas at Arlington. After graduation, he became a platoon leader in Air Defense Artillery at Fort Bliss, Texas. He next served as an assistant operations officer for a division in Korea. He returned to Fort Bliss as commander of a battery. Student B then underwent three years of training in the Russian language and in Russian area studies, which included receipt of a master's degree from Georgetown University, although the schooling was done in Garmisch, Germany, at what has become the Marshall Center. (This also certified Student B as a foreign area officer.) He then spent three years as an intelligence analyst in the Office of the Deputy Chief of Staff for Intelligence for the U.S. Army, Europe, in Heidelberg, Germany. Just as things became complex in the Soviet Union, Student B, a Russian expert, returned to the United States to attend Command and Staff College at Fort Leavenworth, Kansas. He then moved for two years to Fort Hood, Texas, as operations officer and executive officer for an Air Defense Artillery battalion. From there he went to work on an inspection team for the On-Site Inspection Agency (the site was the Soviet Union), based in Rhein Main, Germany, for two years. For the three following years, he commanded an Air Defense Artillery battalion at Fort Carson, Colorado, from which he was sent to command the Military Coordination Center for Operation Provide Comfort (to Iraqi Kurds) in Zakho, Iraq. The pattern is similar: living on four continents, lots of education, and grave and wide-ranging responsibilities. Student B is unusual, however, in having held a battalion command after committing to the long schooling of a FAO.

Student C is a Quartermaster. His business, like that of a third of the Army, is to support rather than to do combat. Born in 1950 in Enid, Oklahoma, he graduated from the University of Oklahoma with a bachelor's degree in secondary education and a master's in higher education. He did not enter the Army until he was almost twenty-four and began as a chief for the Central Post Fund at Aberdeen Proving Ground in Maryland. After a year he became executive officer for Headquarters and Headquarters Company at Aberdeen, then a company commander there, as well. After three years, he went to Kornwestheim, Germany, as a logistics officer, then moved to Darmstadt, Germany, as logistics officer for a division. His next assignment was to Butte, Montana, as a company commander for two years. From there he went to the U.S. Military Academy as a faculty member for three years and, following that, to Korea as a logistics staff officer for one year, and as chief of community management (still in Yongsan, Korea) as executive officer. He received a degree from command and staff college by correspondence while in a regular assignment. After Korea, his next (one-year) tour was as executive officer of a support and supply battalion at Fort Campbell, Kentucky. Next he became executive officer for that battalion and, after that, the director of logistics for U.S. Army Garrison. All these assignments were at Fort Campbell, Kentucky. His last assignment before going to the Army War College was as commander of a field support battalion. (He was still at Fort Campbell, although his awards show that, while there, he was assigned temporary duty in the Persian Gulf.) Student C's tours have had more geographic stability than those of many officers, but he, too, lived and worked on four continents, on the urban U.S. East Coast, and in Butte, Montana.

USAWC students have been there and done (a lot of) that.

THE GROUP PORTRAIT

Individual stories are both interesting and impressive, but what does a war-college class look like overall?[2] What composite sketch can be drawn from the 321 separate biographical entries for the USAWC class of 1997? Table 2 describes some characteristics of that class. (Note that this class is typical of a service war college.) The joint colleges would be balanced among the services.[3]

In the 321-member USAWC class (which will be treated as 320 for purposes of numerical discussion), there were 221 (read, 220) Army officers—a little more than two-thirds of the class. Less than 60 percent of the class, however, were Regular Army officers—men and (a few) women who had been on active duty for the past several decades and who expected to continue on active duty until they had completed thirty years of service.[4] Twenty Army officers were from the National Guard and had a primary affiliation with their state organizations; fourteen were Reserve Army officers with a primary civilian occupation; two were Fellows from West Point (faculty sent to the college for enrichment). Also, of the 185 Regular Army officers, a third were not in combat

TABLE 2.   Class Composition (Class of 1997)

Army	221
National Guard	20
Reserve	14
U.S. Military Academy Fellow	2
Regular Army	185
Air Force	20
Air National Guard	1
U.S. Air Force Reserve	1
Marines	10
Navy	9
Coast Guard	1
International	40
Civilians	20
Department of the Army	10
U.S. Foreign Service	4
National Security Agency	1
Defense Intelligence Agency	1
Defense Logistics Agency	1
Central Intelligence Agency	1
Federal Emergency Management Agency	1
Defense Mapping Agency	1

branches. This means that of all students at the Army War College in that (typical) year, fewer than 40 percent were "Army war fighters."

This is because there were also forty officers from the other services: twenty from the Air Force and twenty from the sea services (ten Marines, nine Naval officers, and one Coast Guard officer).[5] There were also twenty civilians, about 6 percent of the total, and one individual per seminar. (Half of the civilian students worked for the Department of the Army; six for defense-related federal agencies; and four for the State Department.) Finally, forty students, one out of every eight members of the class (and two per seminar), were from a foreign country. Thus, the USAWC was as "joint" with foreigners as the Army was joint with its sister services.[6]

The Army War College's International Fellows (IF) program began in 1977–78 with six students and has graduated more than 500 students from some ninety countries. Eighty percent of the graduates were on active duty in 1996, and twelve have led their national armies.[7] In the class of 1997, Chile, Egypt, Kenya, Nepal, Poland, Qatar, Ukraine, Taiwan, the United Kingdom, and Venezuela were among the forty represented countries (see Table 3). Yugoslavia sent an officer in 1981–82. Other former Soviet bloc officers began attending in the 1992 academic year. A Russian officer graduated with the class of 1993. The countries represented vary from year to year, although twenty-one nations have standing invitations.

Some countries pay their students' expenses; others are subsidized by foreign military sales. The IFs are fully integrated into the academic program. They do, however, receive a month-long orientation before the fall term starts. This includes programs for wives, a Washington Senator's baseball game, and a trip to Pennsylvania's Amish country, to Hershey, and to the state capitol in Harrisburg. During the year, IFs also have a ten-day field trip to as many as three countries in Latin America, as well as a trip to an Army installation in the continental United States. Each IF has an academic adviser, a military sponsor, a community civilian sponsor, and a seminar sponsor. Perhaps half have not been to the United States before, and most bring their families. (It is rumored they may bring only one wife, even if they legally have more.) In addition to networking with individuals with whom one may work in the future, benefits of the program (beyond those previously noted) include our learning about other cultures and the IFs' learning about the United

TABLE 3.   International Fellows' Origin
(Academic Year 1997)

Argentina	Italy	Qatar
Australia	Japan	Romania
Brazil	Jordan	Saudi Arabia
Canada	Kenya	Senegal
Chile[a]	Korea	Singapore
Ecuador	Kuwait	Slovakia
Egypt	Mexico	Sweden
El Salvador	Nepal	Taiwan
France	Netherlands	Thailand
Germany	Norway	Turkey
Greece	Pakistan	Ukraine
India	Philippines	United Arab Emirates
Israel	Poland	United Kingdom
		Venezuela

[a]Denotes first-year attendance.

States (our informality, directness, assurance, ethnocentrism). Possibly, another goal is to impress them: "Do not mess with this overwhelming force." The one area of difficulty involves using the IFs in the two-week strategic exercise. There, some materials are used for which they lack a security clearance, and finding the right role—one that is both meaningful and useful—is sometimes a problem.[8]

Although a majority of the U.S. military students in the USAWC class entered the military through civilian college and university ROTC programs, a significant number attended military academies as undergraduates.[9] Four each attended the Air Force and Naval academies, and five attended public academies (Virginia Military Institute and the Citadel). More than forty, though, attended West Point—roughly a fifth of the Regular Army officers. The only elite colleges represented in the class were Oberlin and Swarthmore, each of which was attended by a female State Department officer. The class had no Ivy League graduates. Eighty percent of the students already held a graduate degree on entry. Although undergraduate degrees varied from sociology to horticulture and electrical engineering, master's degrees tended to be in fields such as public administration. This is probably a function both of perceived relevance and of programs available to officers on active duty.

The average age of the U.S. military students in the class was forty-four; their average length of military service was twenty-one years (a year or two higher than in the recent past). In contrast to previous years, only 30 percent had reached the rank of full colonel or had been selected for, but not yet promoted to, colonel. Most of the lieutenant-colonels, though, would be selected for the colonel list announced just before Christmas.

Eighty-six percent of the class had held a command at the battalion level or higher. Forty percent had high-level staff experience. This represented a slight shift toward command experience and away from staff, as compared with previous classes.

As recently as five years earlier, almost 40 percent of the class had had combat experience in Vietnam, but that war has almost become history for today's students. Only five members (fewer than 2 percent) of the class of 1997 had served in Vietnam. Five percent or fewer had served in combat in Grenada, Panama, or Somalia. The principal combat experience for the class was southwestern Asia—that is, the Gulf war. Even so, only 30 percent of the class had been there. Thus, much of the class had seen no combat, and most of those who had served during a war did so in a war that was a planner's (and a war-game designer's) dream. It was a war that required a unified effort from the Army, Navy, Marines, and Air Force; it involved a host of allies; planners had all the time they needed and were given all the resources they requested; and new weapons and communications technology were tried out and worked well (although not as well as reports given to the media stated);[10] Further, there were very few casualties, and the stated goals were achieved. In short, belief in the effectiveness of planning, rationality, and dominance were strongly reinforced by the only war most of the students knew.

Although no brief or PowerPoint display says so, observation suggests that each seminar had a minimum of two ethnic-minority members—one African American and one other. (The seminar I attended was unusual in having four.) Each also had one woman as a student. However, there were only twelve Army women in the class. Only the fact that *half* the twenty civilians were women made it possible to place at least one woman in each seminar.[11] There was at least one woman from another service. Still, 40 percent of the women in the class were civilians, not military personnel.

"Old-timers" noted other things about the class. Although the bulk of the class was married and had children, there were a lot of young children, suggesting second marriages or deferred marriage or parenting.[12] Also, there were more "geographical bachelors" than in the old days.[13] The one-year move to Carlisle was apparently seen by more and more couples as too disruptive. This was especially true if one happened to have a family and home in the Washington, D.C., area, two hours away. To a subset of "geographical bachelors" known as "road runners," weekend commuting seemed reasonable.

Although much that the military does urges uniformity, there is a place for individuality. Thus, while in uniform everyone wears a name tag and a variety of insignia, badges, and ribbons that can tell the educated observer a good deal about an individual's training, experience, travels, and accomplishments. Also, soon after arriving at the Army War College, each student receives an inch-and-a-half thick volume of "Biographical Sketches" of fellow students, staff, faculty, and International (and other) Fellows.[14]

The one-page entries follow a prescribed format. At the upper right are photos of the student and his or her spouse. The only information given about the spouse is his or her name. Children's names and dates of birth are recorded.

The most prominent information displayed concerns rank and branch—with date of attaining rank—and the individual's year group (the date used for calculating years of service). These dates reveal the fast-trackers, the ones promoted early at least once, and perhaps regularly, during their career. Date and location of birth and date, major, and institution of higher education are also listed.

Most of the rest of the information provided is service-related and includes: service schools attended and date of completion (virtually all USAWC military students have attended a command and staff college); special qualifications (for example, Pilot, Ranger); battle campaigns; awards (in acronyms that are unintelligible to civilians and that, even when spelled out, would not convey the significance and respect appropriately paid); instructor experience (not common); languages spoken (not a routine skill); publications (few); and organizational affiliations (virtually all military). Entries under "fields of special interest" are largely professionally related, although a few quirky responses creep in—for instance, genealogy, real estate, vexillology (the study of flags that are different on the front and back).

There is one other class portrait of interest. Early in the year, the class takes the Myers-Briggs Type Indicator (MBTI) test as part of a unit on leadership. The intent is to enhance self-understanding, and thus to assist students in developing more effective leadership skills.[15] The MBTI is a widely used paper-and-pencil test that places individuals on four behavioral preference scales:

Extraversion–Introversion (E-I)
Sensing–Intuition (S-N)
Thinking–Feeling (T-F)
Judging–Perceiving (J-P)

The E-I scale describes what one focuses on, what gives one energy—the outer world, particularly people, or the inner world. S-N describes what one gives attention to: facts, the concrete, the practical, or theory, the abstract, the novel. T-F describes how one makes decisions: through logic and objective assessment or through empathy and the subjective. J-P describes how one relates to the world: by judging, which requires organization, planning, and predictability, or by responding, which involves flexibility, spontaneity, and openness.

These four scales yield a total of sixteen different combinations, or personality types. In discussing the results, though, it is usual to refer to single variables. One might say, for example, "He's a J. He can't stand not knowing how many miles and how much longer before we get there." One can also refer to certain commonly occurring clusters—for example, "She's an NT. She makes decisions based on theory and logic, not the human dimension." Because the MBTI is a popular, widely used management tool, it is possible to generalize about the kinds of people one can expect to find in different occupations and positions. It is also possible to analyze the way in which USAWC students differ from the general population (see Table 4).[16]

Army War College students are different from the population as a whole. They are much more likely to be introverted (I: 55 percent versus 25 percent); they are more likely to decide using logic and objective measures (T: 88 percent versus 60 percent for men and 35 percent for women); they prefer structure and organization to open-endedness (J: 78 percent versus 55 percent). But perhaps surprisingly, they are less concrete and factual than the population as a whole (S: 66 percent versus 75 percent). Still, two-thirds do fall on the "S" side of the scale (see Table 5).

Certain clusters are understood to represent certain temperaments. Thus, an SJ would be a person who prefers facts and structure to theories and open-endedness—a practical creature. An NT would be interested in the abstract but would be logical and objective—a scientist, per-

TABLE 4.   Myers-Briggs Type Indicator, Preference Comparison

	Class of 1998	General Population		
			Male	Female
E	45%	75%		
I	55%	25%		
S	66%	75%		
N	34%	25%		
T	88%		60%	35%
F	12%		40%	65%
J	78%		55%	
P	22%		45%	

Source: Calculations provided by Herbert F. Barber, Ph.D., a U.S. Army War College faculty member.

haps. Fifty-eight percent of Army War College students were SJs, as compared with 38 percent of the population as a whole. Twenty-eight percent were NTs, as compared with 12 percent of the population as a whole.

It is worth considering several (but by no means all) of the sixteen possible boxes. For instance, almost 60 percent of the class of 1997 fell into two of the sixteen boxes: ISTJ (35 percent) and ESTJ (23 percent).[17] Thus, although some were extroverts and more were introverts, these students shared an "STJ" approach to the world, one that focused on the concrete, the practical; that made decisions based on logic and objective analysis; and that was characterized by a preference for structure and organization. The only two other boxes that got even 5 percent of student responses were the other two TJ boxes: INTJ (7 percent) and ENTJ (12 percent).[18] This seems to demonstrate a strong disposition for the Army to attract and promote people who work carefully, systematically, and purposively, and who tend to be uncomfortable with the

TABLE 5.   Myers-Briggs Type Indicator, Temperament

	Class of 1998	General Population
SJ	58%	38%
NT	28%	12%
SP	8%	38%
NF	6%	12%

Source: Herbert F. Barber, Ph.D.

expression of feelings, with doubt, with the unresolved, and with surprises. As a group, then, one would not expect USAWC students to relish confronting a situation that was volatile, uncertain, complex, and ambiguous. However, as will be shown later, just that situation (given the acronym "VUCA") is what the war college and its current curriculum claim to be about.

Again, it is believed that self-knowledge improves leadership, as does understanding the varieties of human nature. Other reasons for assessing MBTI results, then, are to understand a group's tendencies—for example, a strong desire for closure—and to point out what may be missing from a particular group (such as sensitivity to the feelings of others). Thus, a leader might decide that, because the group she or he is leading is unlikely to have many, if any, FPs, she or he needs to be particularly thoughtful about what is missing from the group (such as individuals attuned to feelings and individuals who do not require decisiveness). This can be important because institutions such as Congress and the media can be very relevant to the military, but their members are likely to have quite different MBTI configurations.

It may be that the existing mix of personalities is precisely what one wants in the military. It may make it a very functional organization. Or it may be that a larger number of Ns and Fs and Ps would 1) better link the military to the citizenry it serves; and 2) increase the range of responses available among senior officers. Indeed, it may also be that, although certain responses are appropriate and serve an officer well at one level, at a higher level other attributes, such as interpersonal communication skills and flexibility, may need to be added. Senior officers have to testify before Congress, talk to reporters, and deal with foreign nationals, both military and civilian. Thus, although STJs may dominate a war-college class, NTJs or even some NTPs or NFPs may be among the class members who will win stars.[19]

WHY ARE THEY THERE?

One reason officers go to the USAWC is that, like Everest, it is there. Carlisle is the next step if one hopes to become a flag officer. Also, admission to the class is highly competitive. It's the A-list: If one gets an invitation, one goes. Specifically, only the top 4 percent of eligible officers get an invitation. Virtually all invitees attend, and virtually all attendees successfully complete the course. A second 4 percent of eligible officers are selected for the Corresponding Studies Course, which is taken over a two-year period while on active duty.[20]

Other reasons are spelled out by USAWC administrators and faculty at orientation. Arriving students may or may not be interested in explanations about why they are at Carlisle, but a formidable orientation program, with a series of briefings[21] and excursions, ensures that they have been told why the Army thinks they are there. In the orientation program, a tension becomes apparent that will characterize the year. That is the tension between education, which tries to stimulate excellent thinking without necessarily knowing what the content of that thinking will be, and training, which seeks to impart certain information or to elicit certain behavior. The USAWC insists (over and over) that it is engaged in education. The Army, however, is much more used to, and is very good at, training. A synopsis of the orientation briefing given to the class of 1997 is offered next. It sets forth the intentions of the institution. It also reveals the tension embedded in those intentions.

Imagine yourself in an entrance hall with twelve large, stained-glass windows depicting soldiery themes and with bronze busts of Carl von Clausewitz and Tasker Bliss, the USAWC's founding president. Proceed to the handsome, large auditorium known as Bliss Hall, and as "the big red bedroom."[22] There, crisply uniformed and well-groomed officers sit tall in padded red seats.[23] Red carpets cover the aisles. At stage left are a large globe and the flags of the U.S. Army, Navy, Air Force, and Marine Corps. Spanners hold the flags out so that the writing on them is displayed. At the right of the stage is the podium, with a door leading to an anteroom just behind it. There is a theater-size screen above the stage, which is actually composed of two screens with separate projector systems so that two sets of visuals can be managed at once. To the left of the globe and to the right of the podium are fourteen additional, wall-mounted flags representing the major commands. Below them are framed information papers. It is a serious, but colorful, setting. Bells have provided a three-minute, then a one-minute, warning by which time the students are seated and quiet. When the speaker enters, all rise.

The presentation begins. The opening graphic announces the motto of the college (in Latin): "Providing for the Future." It also specifies two college goals: the development of senior strategic leaders; and the acquisition of the strategic art, with emphasis on the land-power perspective.[24]

A good deal of teaching about leadership comes through the display of examples; thus, the next several slides are pictures of Carlisle graduates who went on to become strategic leaders. The prize photo shows an informal group of six, all of whom became CINCs (commanders in chief of a geographical region or of a special command). Seven portrait photos show highly successful generals, all of whom graduated in a single class: that of 1973. Four show IFs, including one from the Czech Republic, who is quoted as having learned at the USAWC the importance of "civilian supremacy over the military" and of having the skills that let one exercise "leadership of the armed forces in the democratic spirit." The presentation of role models, of heroes, of honored leaders, as people that students "can become" is a significant part of Carlisle's program. This continues throughout the year, in particular, through a series of talks by distinguished guests. It is a way of teaching that is less used in civilian institutions.

The photos of leaders are quickly followed by a photo and quotation from the Army's seniormost leader, John Shalikashvili, then Chair of the Joint Chiefs of Staff. Two points are made using quotes from Shalikashvili. The first distinguishes training ("how to do") from education ("how to think about"). The second quote emphasizes that stress and discomfort accompany growth. It is suggested, then, that one measure of success for the year will be the degree to which a student gets outside of his or her "box" and outside of his or her "comfort zone." These two themes are not unlike those found in many a civilian college orientation.[25] But can these themes have the same meaning for, and impact on, a group of mature, highly successful professionals who have spent the past twenty years within a hierarchically structured institution, and who hope to spend up to ten more years in the same institution?

Civilian college students are entering a new institution. Their instructors are grayed and presumed brilliant. The future is promising but nebulous. For most it is a time of excitement, experiment, and exploration of the unfamiliar. In contrast, USAWC students are very familiar with the military and its education system. Their instructors are known to be very much like themselves; awe is not part of the equation. And their future is relatively clear, including retirement, which will come sooner rather than later. It is gratifying to have been chosen to attend the Army War College, but for many it is a culminating more than a launching experience.

Young civilian students are urged to inquire, to think critically and creatively, and to take risks. For USAWC students, it has been more important to know than to ask. Independence and originality have not been fostered, and as the profession itself entails risk, care and safety have been continuous and central themes. Thus, the USAWC's orientation may set forth goals that sound like those of a civilian college orientation, but those goals have not been central to USAWC students' previous or anticipated future careers. And one might well ask: Just how much independent and original thinking, how much risk-taking behavior, is really desirable among those who control the nation's weaponry? Perhaps the "discomfort" some USAWC students will experience during the year comes not so much from personal or intellectual change as from the realization that the war-college year involves a transition in which some of them are being prepared to become the "them" they have long critiqued—the visible decision makers whose every word and act are carefully scrutinized.

The orientation proceeds to a rather standard history of the Army War College from its 1903 founding under the leadership of Elihu Root to the present. It sets forth the USAWC mission statement, which includes education, research, and outreach. It also displays the organization chart, which includes one center (the Strategic Leadership Center, a war-gaming facility); three institutes (Strategic Studies, Military History, and Physical Fitness Research); and four academic departments (Corresponding Studies; Command, Leadership, and Management; National Security and Strategy; and Military Strategy, Planning, and Operations) (see Figure 6).

Attention is drawn to the variety and number of other educational programs offered at Carlisle, and note is taken of the Senior Service College Fellows who are formally part of the class. These are forty Army officers who have a short preparatory course at Carlisle in the summer but spend the academic year either at a civilian educational institution, such as Harvard's Kennedy School, the University of Texas, or Ohio's Mershon Center, or at a governmental unit, such as the U.S. Institute of Peace or the Drug Enforcement Administration.[26]

The new arrivals are told that, as graduates, they "will do" ten things—far too many items to retain or bother listing, but the imperative tone is worth recording.

Enduring themes, which will be woven through the year's curriculum, are noted. They are: ethics, history, jointness,[27] and strategic vision. Strategic vision encompasses a number of things. First, for an Army

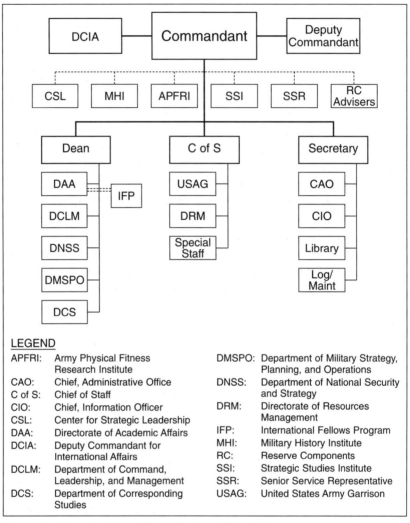

LEGEND

APFRI:	Army Physical Fitness Research Institute	DMSPO:	Department of Military Strategy, Planning, and Operations
CAO:	Chief, Administrative Office	DNSS:	Department of National Security and Strategy
C of S:	Chief of Staff		
CIO:	Chief, Information Officer	DRM:	Directorate of Resources Management
CSL:	Center for Strategic Leadership		
DAA:	Directorate of Academic Affairs	IFP:	International Fellows Program
DCIA:	Deputy Commandant for International Affairs	MHI:	Military History Institute
		RC:	Reserve Components
DCLM:	Department of Command, Leadership, and Management	SSI:	Strategic Studies Institute
		SSR:	Senior Service Representative
DCS:	Department of Corresponding Studies	USAG:	United States Army Garrison

FIGURE 6.   Organization of the U.S. Army War College.

officer, "strategic" is considered a contrast to "tactical" and "operational." It represents the broadest-scope, largest-scale, and longest-term thinking. Second, an officer with strategic responsibilities is likely to hold a position in which a new and crucial skill will be required: cooperation.[28] Third, she or he may be given an "executive" assignment—

one that requires initiative and innovation. Although cooperation, initiative, and innovation are not antithetical to what these officer students have learned and practiced before, the emphasis is different. Stress on discipline, order, and correct action is not the war-college goal.[29] Fourth, and finally, strategy is said to involve "art,"[30] because the strategist works in situations without clear-cut answers and in environments that are both complex and ambiguous. Again, training involves learning what to do. The Army has manuals (thousands and thousands of manuals, just as Wanda Gag had cats) that contain an almost limitless number of checklists designed to ensure that each individual will know just what to do in every situation.[31] (The "right" way to do things may not be practically possible for lack of time or resources, but one can at least mostly know what one "should" do.) At the war college, the third tier of PME, then, officers are asked to think beyond doctrine. They are asked to acknowledge the reality of uncertainty. They who have lived and succeeded by rules must now think of rules as man-made—as having a purpose but also as having limitations—and must understand that they may in the future find themselves in the position of having to change or even repeal rules long in place.[32]

With the USAWC's purposes firmly established, the orientation session moves on to a description of how the college seeks to achieve these purposes. Most important is the seminar and its teaching team. In 1996–97, there were twenty seminars with sixteen students each. The seminars had teaching teams composed of one faculty member from each of the three academic departments (Command, Leadership, and Management; National Security and Strategy; Military Strategy, Planning, and Operations), a historian, and *the seminar students*. Note that teaching is not considered exclusively a faculty responsibility. The USAWC seminar system considers each student a teacher. This is not unrealistic in that students are professionals who have had twenty years of military experience, and on any particular topic someone in each seminar may well know more than the individual leading the seminar that day.[33] This is especially true because each seminar is designed using a distribution principle that ensures that each seminar has someone representing the variety of experiences contained in the class. Roles reserved for the faculty, then, are those of course instructor;[34] adviser on research projects; and academic adviser. The overarching philosophy is, "We shall teach one another," "You will become your own students," and you will "learn how to teach yourselves."[35] Academic hierarchy gets short shrift.

Philosophies of education tend not to fascinate students at any level, but the Carlisle orientation spends a fair amount of time trying to engage students in understanding the learning process itself—that is, to see the differences, the deficiencies, and the value in different modes of learning. These modes are described as passive (reading, listening), active (discussing, writing), and experiential (doing). Each of the three has a role in the USAWC program. One should probably not be surprised that "passive" learning is not held in high regard. It is true that there are many lectures at the USAWC, but they are rarely given by scholars. They are given by role models. Also reading assignments feature chapters and articles more than they do books. "Active learning" at the USAWC tends to emphasize discussing more than writing. Experiential learning, however, is given a high priority. It ranges from staff rides to Civil War battlefields to extended gaming (in elegant on-site facilities).

Specific attention is given to what is called "Andragogy" (!), or adult learning, as opposed to "pedagogy" (child learning). At the USAWC, this seems to mean commitment to learning together with the faculty member serving as co-inquirer, facilitator, and resource, but not as expert. Again, the college is a place where each student is to some degree an expert, and where the faculty are near-peers. But the goal of learning from peers is not just a recognition of student talent. It is also a recognition that in a senior position, with its broad responsibilities, one cannot know all. One must learn from and rely on others, even if hierarchy sometimes seems an impediment. Officers are so accustomed to hierarchy, though, that they are specifically directed to keep it out of the USAWC seminar room.[36]

It should be noted that even when civilian graduate students are told that the seminar is a place for inquiry and discussion among peers, there is usually a pretty clear understanding as to just who is in charge, and even of just how each seminar student measures up against the others.[37]

USAWC students are further urged to inquire (not a traditional military activity) rather than advocate. They are asked to tolerate ambiguity (not comfortable to those who must issue commands). They are asked to take risks, to experiment (not likely, especially in a period of downsizing). They are instructed to have a "positive, open relationship" with their seniors and to be self-assessing, self-motivated, self-directed.

Successful leaders are sometimes alarmed to find that the peak of every institutional pyramid is a bit like Oakland: "There is no there there." They are on their own. Most institutions do not prepare their cadres for a vacuum or for lack of definition at the top. The military, however, has a great penchant for being prepared. Accordingly, at the war colleges, efforts are made to prepare a group of the services' best officers for the responsibilities of senior positions where doctrine is not always adequate to the task. This, however, can go against the military's own grain, against a culture in which clarity, definition, structure, closure, and the concrete are a way of life. One could argue, then, that when USAWC students are asked to prepare themselves for strategic leadership, they are being asked to learn a whole new array of skills.

Like those at a civilian college, USAWC students are actually in seminar (or in the second term, in an advanced course) only a few hours a day. However, each week students are issued a shirt-pocket-size "notional" schedule that fills their day from 8:30 A.M. to 4:00 P.M. Mornings are generally reserved for the core course during the first term. Lunch is an hour and a half, but the cafeteria is not crowded. Some, of course, go home for lunch, but that period is also the traditional time for the daily workout. Wednesday afternoons are reserved for the commandant and his lecture series; Monday and Friday afternoons are for special and complementary programs (mostly lectures); Tuesday and Thursday afternoons are set aside for "Directed Study." As in a regular college, there is no possibility of Army War College students doing all assigned work within the 8:30–4:00 schedule. Thus, students have to create their own study schedules by working during lunch, in the evening, or—and unlike on most campuses with which I am familiar—in the early morning. To many officers, 8:30 A.M. seems a bit late to start work.

As one civilian student who later became a faculty member (and who herself was an Army brat, once an officer's wife, and an employee of a Defense Department agency temporarily on loan to the AWC) said: "These guys are not slouches, but they have no idea at all how different they are." Being in the military, an organization called a "service"— and a service that could require sacrifice of one's life—*is* different. Indeed, there is something incongruous about the fact that in the United

States, military service is rendered to a society that is based on the belief that self-interested, individual competition is what yields all things bright and beautiful (that is, material goods, justice, and truth), or so claims the ideology of the marketplace in economics, government, and the academy. Again, servicemen and servicewomen assume the duty of defending economic competition and democracy, but neither plays much of a part in the culture they have selected for themselves. Some of us may (at least, sometimes) think we would be willing to die for something in which we passionately believe, but U.S. military personnel accept serious risk on behalf of a society whose culture is deeply contrary to the one in which they and their families dwell.

In thinking about recent and current war-college students, one should remember that a war-college class represents what sociologists call a "generation"—that is, a group that is not only of an age but that also went through the same major social and political experiences at the same age.[38] If we assume that recent USAWC classes entered the Army in the late 1970s, they represent a post-Vietnam generation. As young officers, they saw the signing of the Camp David Accords, resumption of relations with China, the seizure of U.S. hostages in Iran, and the invasion of Afghanistan by the USSR. Around their tenth year, as they began to think about staying in the military through retirement, they witnessed the Iran–Contra scandal but also the gradual thawing of relations with the USSR that began with the Geneva Summit in 1985 and was followed by the tearing down of the Berlin Wall in 1989. Soon thereafter, the Gulf war brought together an incredible coalition of military forces under U.S. direction. This, then, is a generation with limited combat experience, but one that has experienced not only success, but success based on the use of tested doctrine and plans.[39] This would seem to create confidence, but it would not seem to create enthusiasm for change.[40]

It is important to understand the generational experience, because with the military, what you have is what you will have. Although a progressive thinning of the ranks does take place as officers are or are not promoted, there is virtually no lateral entry to the military. This means that as requirements change, new skills, new experiences, and new attitudes cannot be hired in. The military must either train new folks from the entry level or retool available officers. The lack of lateral entry also increases the likelihood that senior officers will think alike. After all, they have had the same major experiences at approximately the same age; they have not had to assimilate or accommodate to new personnel with new views and experiences; and they have succeeded. What they have done (and believed) therefore must have been right.

Finally, some thought must be given to the learning environment created for these accomplished, middle-aged students. Great emphasis is given to peer learning. This accords with the early philosophy of the USAWC. In the past, military knowledge may have been largely the purview of the military itself. However, with the development of nuclear weapons, a cadre of civilian defense intellectuals was created. Civilian experts now exist. Also, at the war colleges military strategy is taught as only an element of national-security strategy. Thus, economics, diplomacy, governmental processes, regional studies, and more are now a substantial part of the curriculum. Most of the expertise available in these fields is civilian. Are officer peers likely to be able to provide that expertise? And what of advances in technology? Questions that must be addressed include: "Can peers provide the level of teaching that war-college students deserve? Are role-model lectures, seminar discussions, exercises, and gaming really the most effective route to achieving the college's stated goals?

The possibility of creating a situation in which colonels are supposed to sit in rapt attention while a nerdish, thirty-five-year-old Ph.D. drones on about airy-fairy irrelevancies appears to horrify the USAWC administrators. But is peer discussion likely to lead to critical thinking, to creative thinking, to mastery of the new? Is it likely to create "discomfort," to force individuals out of their boxes? And are these not the year's goals?

In *The Aims of Education*, Alfred North Whitehead, one of America's best-known philosophers, described learning as a three-stage process—one that can occur at any chronological age and that requires repetition each time one delves into new material. [41] He called the first stage, the one in which imagination is captured and one becomes excited, engaged, and committed, "romance." The USAWC seems quite attentive to this stage. He called the second stage "precision." In this stage, one digs deeply, systematically, meticulously, and individually. Lectures by experts and critical reading contribute, but this is a tedious and solitary stage that masochists may relish, but most folks need the adrenaline created by the romance stage to carry them through to completion.

Only in the third stage, "generalization," does one have the possibility of being "creative," of producing a new perspective or conceptualization. Unfortunately, Whitehead noted, some confuse the startles, the imaginative responses of the first stage, with those of the third. The third, he emphasized, can occur only after the second. It sometimes seems that the USAWC is reluctant to expect too much "stage two" of its students. As a result, it settles for something less than stage three.[42]

There are scholars who study the sociology of knowledge. They try to analyze what environments are most conducive to the advancement of knowledge. There is, of course, no perfect agreement among them about either the nature of that environment or the most effective pedagogy, but the highest forms of knowledge do seem inevitably to require specialization and the capacity to deal with the abstract. Perhaps military students and faculty who will return to their profession after a short time at a war college should not be expected to aspire to the standards of the academy. But shouldn't expertise and the abstract, as well as "discomfort," be part of their USAWC experience? And can that experience be provided by faculty peers? Specifically, can the current USAWC faculty stretch its students? The next chapter will consider the faculty: its skills, its tasks, its expectations—and the expectations others have of it.

4   Army War College Faculty

IT'S HARD TO TELL the faculty from the students at a war college. Faculty may be older, but three years in one's fourth decade is not always self-evident. Still, although the faculty, which will be profiled in this chapter, does differ from the student body, it differs far more from a civilian college faculty—particularly in degrees earned. The content and style of civilian college and USAWC faculty work is also quite different. Finally, at the Army War College, great emphasis is given to evaluation. Most civilian schools do conduct teaching evaluations, but war college evaluations are much more extensive.

FACULTY PROFILE

On days that uniforms are being worn it is hard to tell whether a particular individual is a student or a faculty member. Collectively, however, the faculty would be more civilian,[1] and most of the military faculty would be "bird," or full, colonels as opposed to lieutenant-colonels. Although the Air Force and sea services would be represented, a higher percentage of the military faculty than military students would come from the Army. Further, although more than 10 percent of the military students are International Fellows, one would not expect to see a foreign uniform in a faculty group portrait.

It is easier to tell the USAWC faculty from the faculty of a civilian graduate-degree-granting institution. Civilian schools, of course, have almost all civilian faculty. More important, there is a great difference in the preparation, or the schooling, of the two faculties. At civilian schools that grant graduate degrees, almost all faculty hold Ph.D.s (with the exception of the arts, such as music, and some vocational faculties, such as nursing). At the Army War College in 1996, only thirty-one of the 133 faculty—fewer than one-quarter—were listed as Ph.D.s.[2] Several of those were visitors. Also, the Ph.D. faculty were not distributed evenly among the departments. In fact, many listed as faculty were not in teaching departments at all. They were located in other USAWC units.

The current college organization includes four teaching departments: Command, Leadership, and Management (DCLM); National Security and Strategy (DNSS); Military Strategy, Planning, and Operations (DMSPO); and Department of Corresponding Studies (DCS). In 1996, all but National Security and Strategy were chaired by active-duty officers with master's degrees.[3] Among the twenty-some faculty in Command, Leadership, and Management there were only four Ph.D.s: One was a military chaplain, and three were civilians, two of them retired military. The smaller Corresponding Studies Department had one Ph.D. (and one faculty member with only a bachelor's). Military Strategy, Planning, and Operations had no Ph.D. faculty. National Security and Strategy, the largest faculty (with more than twenty members), however, was roughly 50 percent military and 50 percent civilian, and 50 percent Ph.D.s and 50 percent master's degrees. (Only one of the Ph.D.s was held by an active-duty officer. There was also one bachelor's degree and one JD.) Only one teaching department, then—DNSS—even faintly resembled what one might find in a civilian faculty. Further, the teaching departments collectively accounted for only about a third of USAWC Ph.D.s. Where were the others?

Many were lodged in the Strategic Studies Institute, a "supporting institution" that concentrates on research. Its faculty have offices in the same building as the teaching departments and cooperate with that faculty. For example, SSI analysts might supervise one or more student research projects, or they might offer an elective course in term two or three. Although the SSI is typically chaired by a colonel with a master's degree (perhaps surprising, in 1996 that degree was from Berkeley), many of its approximately fifteen members are Ph.D.s, and most of them are civilians with Ph.D.s from strong programs such as Johns Hopkins, Duke, Ohio, Chicago, and George Washington. The SSI, though, is not an ethereal center for cerebration. Founded in 1947 by Dwight D. Eisenhower to help the Army think through what the atomic age meant for war fighting, the SSI is an agent for the Army's Deputy Chief of Staff for Operations and Plans. As such, it is asked for quick (and some longer) responses to issues confronting the Pentagon; it also regularly prepares and publishes monographs on a range of strategic issues, and it sponsors or co-sponsors conferences with academic institutions and industries. Analysts are expected to publish (in 1996, three studies per individual per year). Although the researchers may propose their own topics, scholars in civilian institutions are much better positioned both to choose their own topics and to undertake long-term projects.[4]

Two of the remaining Ph.D.s were located at the USAWC's small Army Physical Fitness Research Institute; another was held by the Reserve Officer adviser; and two were found at the Center for Strategic Leadership, a high-technology laboratory that conducts war games, simulations, teleconferences, and more for the Army as a whole. In 1996, neither its director, nor the USAWC's academic dean, nor the USAWC commandant held a Ph.D.[5]

The academic program, which expects soon to be offering master's degrees accredited by the Middle States Association of Colleges and Schools, is run for students who mostly already have master's degrees and by faculty who themselves mostly have only master's degrees. Further, except in the Department of National Security and Strategy, most of the teaching faculty are active-duty officers. Although they may bring wide-ranging experience to the seminar, and although some of them have been engaged in training, few have had any previous experience in education, nor have their careers provided much time for exploration or contemplation.[6] They have been busy. Further, even faculty who have master's degrees may or may not hold their degrees in subjects relevant to their teaching assignments.[7] Finally, an individual's assignment as a faculty member is likely to last for three or fewer years.[8] In short, USAWC faculty and students are near-peers—not just in age and as fellow officers, but also in the level of their education and even in the amount of time spent at the war college.

In contrast, faculty in civilian graduate-degree-granting schools are likely to have had years of preparation for their first full-time position. (Six years of schooling after the bachelor's degree would not be at all unusual for a social scientist.) As graduate students they probably taught undergraduates under the supervision of a faculty member, and because of the competitiveness of the academic job market, even new scholars are likely to have publications to their credit. For them, securing a teaching position is not a matter of receiving an assignment; it is a matter of competing in a national pool against all other new graduates in their specialty. Typically, the number of applications for any particular position begins at more than one hundred.

CONTENT AND CULTURE OF FACULTY WORK

For most faculty at civilian schools, being a faculty member *is* one's career; it is not a three-year (or shorter) interlude. Consideration for tenure[9] comes only after six years of essentially probationary service. It is awarded only if recommendations secured from peers throughout the country concur that one's work is nationally competitive.[10] Like the military officer, one does not become a civilian academic to maximize income. Unlike the military, though, there are only two professorial ranks above the entry rank of assistant professor. One can easily top out at (full) professor by age forty. One's salary can top out, too. Even though a rank once achieved is maintained, raises are linked to continuing performance—that is, to merit.[11] Merit usually involves three factors—teaching, service, and publication—and the area in which a faculty member is most likely to prove deficient is publishing. There are plenty of service jobs to do, and classroom pressures tend to keep teaching up to a certain standard. But publishing is work one does all alone and with few deadlines. It is the easiest thing to let slide.

USAWC active-duty faculty are not expected to do research; nor are they richly rewarded if they do. The civilian teaching faculty, particularly those who identify with civilian faculty at civilian schools, may have research aspirations. As will be shown later, however, the other duties expected of them make substantial research difficult.

Civilian faculty in civilian schools are almost certainly among the most individualistic, self-defining, self-scheduling, unsupervised drawers of good salary known to our economy. Peers do review one's research, and students do provide teaching evaluations, but the content and conduct of one's work is very much left to the instructor. For example, at a large university several "Introduction to American Government" courses may be offered each semester. Over a several-year period, five or six different individuals may teach that course. It is almost certain that each syllabus will be different, as will be the books assigned by the instructors.[12]

Civilian faculty who teach in an elite graduate program may teach only one or two courses per term. Scheduled "contact hours," including office hours, may come to fewer than ten a week. Even though faculty routinely report working fifty or more hours a week, that work is often done at home or in the library. Indeed, civilian faculty may come to campus only one or two, possibly three, but not four or five days a week. (Scientists who work in their university laboratories are likely to be on campus all day, five days a week, but they may travel extensively—even while classes are in progress.)

In contrast, USAWC faculty are on campus much of the day, every day (and early in the day).[13] Many of the military faculty live on campus—in military housing. Faculty have large (but usually shared) offices, with computers, printers, coffee, secretarial support, and readily available colleagues. Their formal teaching hours may not be onerous,[14] but Army War College faculty have many collateral or "additional" duties that add up to a large number of contact hours. For example, a DNSS faculty member typically teaches the department's core course over a seven-week period for three hours a day three times a week. (More about the core curriculum later.) DNSS faculty also have full-day responsibilities during the class trip to New York City; during Media Day; and during two exercises, one on the interagency process and one on national military strategy. A DNSS faculty member would also typically offer several electives (Advanced Courses) in the winter and spring. In addition, she or he would participate in a two-week (all-day) Strategic Crisis Exercise, in "briefbacks" for Regional Strategic Appraisals (reports back to one's seminar on the region one studied), and, at the end of the year, the week-long National Security Seminar. In addition, faculty typically have five advisees whom they must counsel; further, each student must read and report to his or her adviser on three books he or she has read independently. A faculty member may also be asked to supervise student Strategy Research Projects (a required research paper—and something that many students have never before had to write).[15] Faculty may also be asked to serve on departmental and interdepartmental committees, to review draft versions of official manuals (the USAWC reviews all Army manuals—up to 100 a year), and to teach in one of the two-week in-residence courses given to Corresponding Studies students during June and July when the college is not in session. Faculty are expected to attend a large number of guest lectures and may be asked to serve as escorts for distinguished visitors.[16] In addition to required duties, there are "expected" events, many of which are social activities, including four formal balls. There are also seminar intramurals, Jim Thorpe Day to support, IFs and new faculty to sponsor, and Military History Institute lectures to attend. USAWC faculty give a lot of time. They have a lot of contact.

And what is their reward? USAWC faculty have good students, interesting colleagues,[17] an extensive library, travel money, no field duty, and no deployments—but very little time. Their most measurable reward may be salary, and there a discrepancy is evident. Military faculty are paid according to their rank. Military USAWC faculty were making base salaries of $50,000 to more than $90,000 in 1996.[18] Most, though, fell in the range of $60,000 to $80,000. In addition, military faculty received housing supplements, health care, and commissary and post-exchange benefits. Civilian faculty salaries ranged from some $40,000 to one of more than $90,000. (The military also had only one of more than $90,000.) Most civilian faculty, though, fell in the range of $50,000 to $70,000—$10,000 less than their uniformed colleagues. And, of course, the civilians had no supplements.[19] This significant discrepancy in pay, with the more educated civilians making noticeably less than their military peers, creates a tension that is not easy to resolve. It is aggravated when budget constraints create rules such as the one that says civilians can be given salary increases only at the time their contracts are renewed (typically every three years). It seems almost certain that USAWC salaries do not act as a recruiting incentive for the best civilian scholars—not when brand new Ph.D.s can command salaries of $45,000 or more in their first full-time position. It is true that academic jobs are currently in short supply and that a renewable-contract war-college job might seem better than no job, or a part-time job, or a one-year job. However, most young Ph.D.s would almost certainly choose a tenure-track position in a civilian college or university over a contract job at a war college, and given the high demands on USAWC faculty members' time, which makes it hard to compete in research, even a temporary war-college appointment would probably be unattractive to people who hoped eventually to return to a civilian campus.[20]

Given the demands on time, the lack of academic expertise among the military faculty, the discontinuity of faculty service, and a limited ability to compete against civilian institutions for top scholars, how does the USAWC manage to offer a sound program? One important way is through collective preparation and implementation. In this, the style of USAWC work could hardly be more different from that at a civilian school.

At a civilian school, it would be quite possible for a new faculty member to receive little formal orientation. Department colleagues might take her or him to the faculty center for lunch; the business office might provide information on benefits, parking fees, and how to get travel reimbursements. The library might offer a tour, and the dean, a coffee hour or reception, but these would not be required events, and little would be said about teaching philosophy or about what precisely was expected of new faculty members either in the classroom or in their research. Typically, a faculty member's syllabi would not receive prior review, nor would anyone screen the books ordered for student purchase.

In contrast, in 1997 new USAWC faculty received a (measured) two-inch-thick orientation notebook with tabs running from "A" to "FF." The book included a Staff and Faculty Manual and a Resident Student Manual. It included a table of contents of three recommended books on teaching methods (available in the library), a discussion of the Socratic method,[21] and a manual prepared at the Army War College in 1994 on "Seminar Facilitation Techniques." The latter included both tips from (named) "expert faculty" and responses to a questionnaire by some thirty (unnamed) faculty. Examples of questions asked were: "What do you do if there is a student in your seminar that you just cannot get along with?" "If it is difficult to determine what an International Fellow is saying, what do you do?" and "How would you handle a student who was insensitive to others in the seminar?" Also included in the notebook was a compilation of faculty instructor comments about techniques and challenges for each of the core courses for the previous *seven* years. This represents a serious passing on of collective experience, of collective wisdom. Not only does it provide access to the experience of others, it also gives new faculty an opportunity to talk with one another about what can be gained from their predecessors' experience.

The handbook includes student evaluations of each core course for six previous years. There are also evaluations of the curriculum as a whole. These are provided from a variety of perspectives including the faculty, students, the Academic Board,[22] graduates, and general officers.[23] The military is used to preparing "after action" reports and to holding "lessons learned" conferences. Such feedback can become ritualized, can obscure rather than clarify, may not get released, and, even if valuable and insightful, may go unread. Still, there is nothing approaching these feedback efforts in civilian academic institutions.

Our culture generally credits intellectual work to an individual. (See Nobel and other prizes and the outlandish salaries commanded by academic superstars.) However, although civilian universities may follow a John Stuart Mill model in seeking to foster individual genius and to prevent its stifling by convention or the likes of Mrs. Gundry, the Army War College works quite differently. Even if the brilliant skeptic David Hume is not self-consciously its model, he might be called on to lend legitimacy to its approach—an approach that does not depend on the nurturing of individual genius or expertise. Hume basically said that, because we cannot know for sure, our actions must be based on probabilities. Thus, although one cannot stand in a room and say with certainty that there are two solid walls, one with windows and one with a door, when it is time leave, one will first try what appears to be a door. For, Hume said, when a decision must be made, one is wise to follow society's collective wisdom—wisdom gathered from the experience of many people and over much time. The Army War College faculty operates very much on the collective-wisdom model—a model that, incidentally, is conserving and conservative.

In support of the two-inch-thick orientation notebook, new faculty are also given a *five-day* orientation—one that they attend. Faculty refer to students as "fire-hosed" with information in the opening weeks, but new faculty, too, are "fire-hosed." When one is new—and not just to the institution (the Army War College) and to the task (educator), but also to the subject matter one must teach—great effort is required just to keep from disgracing oneself. The question of doing critical or creative thinking (what the faculty is supposed to be drawing out of their students) is not likely to arise.[24]

Once oriented, war-college faculty continue to work collectively and in a social rather than an isolated setting. As noted earlier, the three subject-matter departments are each responsible for staffing a core course given separately but simultaneously to twenty different seminar groups. Each department member teaches the department's core course to one of those seminars.

One person, the course director, is ultimately responsible for the overall course content and for preparing the course directive provided to each student.[25] The director also conducts preparation sessions for seminar faculty; weekly in-progress reviews, which help to ensure that seminars are in sync; and an off-site, post-course critique. Again, these are not just good things that one *might* do. They *are* done, and faculty do attend.

In addition, many faculty are made responsible for the preparation of one particular lesson. This responsibility includes defining the objectives of the lesson and the main topics to be covered, specifying reading assignments, listing supplemental reading materials, and preparing slides, overheads, or other teaching materials. The faculty member responsible for a lesson must insure its continuity with the preceding and following lessons, and, most important, make it possible for his or her fellow faculty member who must teach the lesson to be effective—even if he or she has no previous knowledge of or experience with the topic.[26] This is accomplished by preparing instructors' notes and by briefing instructors (collectively) before they teach the lesson. Following this model, twenty mostly nonexperts can teach and contribute to the development of a course.

It is clear that the faculty are well trained. They can transmit course materials to their students. But are they educators? Can they induce critical thinking? Can they lead students through Whitehead's stage of precision to creative thinking? Do they know the literature on which the materials they are transmitting have been built? Can they identify unspoken assumptions? Can they trace a series of logical deductions and detect inconsistencies? Do they know the intellectual debates in which the materials feature? Do they know what is not known?[27]

One might think of the faculty's course preparation and teaching as a variation of the "committee system" at work (as discussed in Chapter 2). It is also similar to the way teaching assistants (graduate students) participate in the teaching of an undergraduate course under the direction of a faculty member, a difference being that in a civilian institution, several lectures a week are typically given to the students en masse by the faculty instructor. The teaching assistants may give one or two lectures over a semester, but their primary duties are to grade students' work and to lead small discussion groups, where students have the opportunity to ask questions and participate in discussion.[28]

During the second half of the year, faculty teach electives. A large array is offered. Some of these courses, such as "Advanced War Fighting," are offered in sections, and some are team-taught. However, in many of them the faculty instructor does have the kind of individual responsibility one would find in a civilian institution. A problem is that faculty members sometimes find themselves assigned to teach course they know little about. In a large civilian school, one would ordinarily teach upper-division and graduate students only in one's area of specialization.

The Army War College is not unaware of the faculty's collective lack of expertise, and it has instituted several corrective practices. First, it has created a Military Faculty Tenure Program under which a colonel already at the college who is scheduled for a new assignment can instead be given a form of tenure. That is, the faculty member can remain at Carlisle until mandatory retirement, subject to satisfactory annual reviews.[29] However, policy permits the tenuring of no more than 10 percent of the military faculty, and the process is competitive. When a slot is available, formal nominations are made to the Academic Board, which selects from the nominees by secret, rank-ordered voting. The board's recommendation about each candidate is then forwarded to the commandant, who awards the tenure.

There is more stability among the civilian faculty. Civilian faculty were once civil-service employees; since 1991, however, their status has been defined under Title 10 of the U.S. Code. Thus, they are referred to as "Title 10 Faculty." At the USAWC, five Title 10 slots are allocated to the DNSS, two to Corresponding Studies, and one to the other two departments. In addition, two are located in the Directorate of Academic Affairs, three in the Center for Strategic Leadership, and nine in the Strategic Studies Institute.[30] Candidates for these positions go through a formal and rather standard recruitment process. The first year is a probationary year, but after that, employment is controlled by one- to five-year (but usually three-year) renewable contracts. Eligibility for "appropriate" security clearances is a condition of employment. Also, as government employees who enjoy a position of "public trust," Title 10 faculty are expected to have "a sense of duty, to offer selfless service, to demonstrate integrity and to place the interest of public service before one's private or personal interest."[31] Ranks are instructor (for those lacking the Ph.D.), assistant professor, associate professor, and professor, and when selected by the commandant for an administrative position, supervisory professor (department chair), dean, or academic dean.

The intent of the Title 10 legislation was to bring more civilian expertise to the war colleges, but it is not clear that Title 10 civilians accomplish the purpose of bringing outside, fresh and expert thinking to the faculty, for in fact many civilian faculty are enjoying second careers. Their first career was military. They are civilian only by dint of retirement. According to one document, seventeen of thirty-five—of nearly half–of the civilian faculty listed were identified as retired military.[32] Even if these data are not fully representative and, say, only a third of civilian faculty are retired military, one wonders whether their expertise is special or whether they were just best positioned to succeed in the recruitment process.[33] It is true that in some areas—for example, Military Strategy Planning and Operations—one would not expect to find much expertise among civilians, but that department's faculty is almost entirely active-duty. Thus, civilian faculty who are retired from the military are not concentrated in areas where civilians lack expertise. Indeed, four of the nine Title 10 faculty in the SSI are retired military. Filling Title 10 slots with retirees also aggravates any effort to increase the number of minorities and women among the faculty. Just as the problem of finding one woman for each student seminar was solved by overloading civilian students with women, so civilian appointments of women and minorities could be a way to respond to a faculty-recruitment problem that is difficult to manage in a system with little lateral entry.[34]

EXPECTATIONS AND EVALUATION

USAWC faculty and students have handbooks that make expectations clear. The usual way to evaluate students, however, is missing. USAWC students do not take exams; they do not receive grades; there are no class rankings; and there are no "honor" graduates.[35] The USAWC considers this important to its desire to de-emphasize competition. It perceives its students as competitive by nature and believes that that competitiveness is reinforced by both the Army's up-or-out promotion system and downsizing. (Both factors, some believe, have contributed to an unfortunate "zero-defect" mentality.) The college wants students to remember that risks will sometimes have to be taken and errors made—that growth, not specific achievement, is the purpose of the USAWC year. Thus, to encourage growth, the school has resisted strong pressure to put a grading system in place.[36]

The military is a very hierarchical organization. While enlisted personnel may have numerous peers, buddies, officers are more often in a position that calls for them to give and take orders. They do not work among numerous peers as often. The Army War College, however, places them in a setting of equals that is intended to foster the development of skills that relate to cooperation, consensus-building, and negotiation. All these are seen as important skills required in the students' future assignments—assignments that will include working with the other services, with civilians, and even with foreigners. Again, grading is seen as a detriment to the learning of cooperation, consensus-building, and negotiation.

Although there is no grading, student assessment is done. However, it is supposed to be conducted "in the spirit of mentoring."[37] Again, the goal for the year is not the transfer of specific information that might best be advanced by rewarding those who transfer the most. The goal is the development of skills, the expansion of perspective, increased comfort with not finding "the" answer. Still, each officer does need an Officer Efficiency Report (OER) in his or her file at the end of the year, and each officer knows that that report will be prepared by his or her faculty adviser, or mentor.

The faculty adviser bases the OER on a student's accomplishment of goals set in the individual learning plan designed separately with each advisee at the beginning of the academic year, and on Academic Feeder Reports (AFRs). These are prepared by course instructors for each student at the completion of each course. The summary evaluations given in AFRs are E (exceeds expectations), M (meets expectations), NI (needs improvement), or F (fails to meet expectations).[38] There is no curve. Everyone could theoretically "exceed." But everyone must "meet" and keep trying until he or she does. The course instructor's assessment takes into account four things: the student's preparation, participation, and performance on oral assignments, and performance on written assignments. Thus, a year-end overall judgment, created collectively, is the Army's solution to evaluating without stimulating competition.

What is most unusual is the evaluation of the curriculum. It is extensive and continuous, but not all of the evaluators are content experts. Not all know what could have been included, what was omitted, what the most recent literature says.[39]

As soon as a core course has been completed, students provide evaluations consisting of both structured responses and unstructured comments.[40] The twenty-some faculty who taught the course attend an off-site retreat to review the course lesson by lesson. In the spring, when formal approval for the following year's courses is sought from the Aca-

demic Board,[41] part of the discussion involves the previous year's critiques. Again, the collective decision-making does a good job of elimi-
nating the quirky, but it is less clear that it is a good mechanism for
extracting the newest, most insightful, or path-breaking.

Even more unusual are the surveys taken of graduates (alumni) to
determine the degree to which they believe the Army War College curriculum prepared them for their post-college assignments, and the survey of general officers (generals) taken to see how well they (the employers, if you will) think students have been prepared for their future work.
Because USAWC alumni are few in number—and generals are even
fewer—and because military personnel can be easily tracked, at least
until retirement, the Army War College can conduct such surveys with
some ease. Civilian colleges and universities talk about doing such surveys far more than they actually do them.[42]

In a survey prepared in 1992,[43] graduates from 1983 to 1991 (queried
in a combined survey) gave the Army War College an overall score of
almost 4 on a five-point scale for meeting its stated objectives.[44] Scores
below 3.5 were for physical fitness;[45] for preparation for serving in a
combined force or in coalition forces; and for writing theater campaigns
for unified, joint, combined, or coalition forces.[46] Scores higher than 4
were given for preparation for: setting an ethical climate; service in
positions of broad scope and responsibility; thinking strategically;
understanding the role of the military in a democratic society; and
making better decisions and giving better advice. Note that these are,
in fact, very much what the USAWC was trying to accomplish—the
widening of the purview of the professional officer. None falls into the
realm of training topics.

Scores for particular curriculum topics were lower. The only scores
higher than 4 were given for ethics and values and for communication
skills. Scores lower than 3 were given for strategic nuclear concepts, JSPS
(Joint Strategic Planning System), JOPES (Joint Operations Planning and
Execution System), unified theater planning, and security assistance. In
a somewhat harsh response, the first three of these topics (strategic
nuclear concepts, JSPS, and JOPES) were listed by 15 percent or more of
the graduates as "not at all useful." Still, overall, 87 percent of the respondents believed the right topics had been covered, and 90 percent believed
that the generalist curriculum, as opposed to a specialist curriculum,
was the right one. More than 70 percent found the work academically
challenging; 97 percent said it was worthwhile.[47]

The evaluations from year to year are similar. Certain areas for improvement emerge, but scores rarely fall below 3 and infrequently top 4. This is similar to teacher evaluations at a civilian college, where the superstar and the lemon are identifiable, but most faculty are rated good or very good and learn about one or two things they might amend.

A general officers' survey (only some of whom would have been USAWC alumni) asked for opinions about whether the Army War College was meeting its stated educational objectives; what the focus of the curriculum should be; the adequacy of the curriculum compared with sister war colleges; and how officers should be prepared for the next five to fifteen years.[48] The college was preparing for change. Its own estimate was that planning and implementing a new curriculum is a two-year process.[49] (Few civilian institutions could manage that speed. Although individual courses can be quickly modified or new ones designed, changing a whole curriculum, even in civilian schools, requires extended consultation and consensus-building, tasks slow to advance in individualistic institutions.)

The generals thought the college met its objectives, rating this at 4 on the five-point scale. The lowest scores (around 3.5) were for training to be innovative and initiating, and for service in joint (U.S. military) forces and in coalition (allied) forces. The highest score (4.3) went to teaching the role of the military in a democracy.

There was strong support for a "generalist" rather than a "specialist" curriculum and for the understanding and evaluation of the Army War College experience as a whole rather than as merely academic training.

Sixty percent of the generals who responded had themselves attended the Army War College. Twelve percent had attended the National War College, and a similar number had attended the Industrial War College. Almost 9 percent had attended the Naval War College, and close to 3 percent had attended the Air War College. Three percent were Senior Service College fellows; two had attended foreign war colleges; and only one attended no war college at all. Thus, collectively, there was experience with the variety of war colleges, but each respondent had of course attended only one school and was offering only an opinion. Thus, what is produced is a reputational response, not one based on weighing comparable data. In response to the statement "USAWC graduates are better prepared than other war college graduates," 20 percent agreed, 20 percent disagreed, and 60 percent were neutral. More than 70 percent believed that there was no difference among the colleges as far as career enhancement, although 11 percent and 14 percent, respectively, thought there was an advantage to attending the Army War College or the National War College. When asked whether they would recommend the Army War College *over* other colleges, about 60 percent agreed (approximately the same percentage, but not necessarily the same 60 percent who had attended the college); 20 percent were neutral; and 20 percent disagreed.

Thinking ahead is always difficult. At best, most of us extrapolate. General officers' predictions of the senior-leader environment in 2000 varied widely. There was some agreement that the Army would be smaller; that more of it would based in the United States rather than abroad (forward deployment is difficult when you do not know what is "forward"—that is, who or what poses the threat); and that it would be involved in more joint operations.[50] Skills they thought new officers would need included oral and verbal communication, strategic thinking (including a grasp of the world as others see it), and technological competence. Some suggestions for the curriculum included travel outside the United States and to joint commands, and speakers with "contrary opinions."[51]

The Army War College has a huge faculty. If all those described as faculty are counted, the student-to-faculty ratio is 2.4-to-1. If one counts only the faculty assigned to teach the core curriculum (four faculty for each of twenty seminars of sixteen students), the ratio is still 4-to-1.

Civilian schools with similar ratios tend to be institutions such as the California Institute of Technology, where large amounts of faculty time are devoted to research. At the Army War College, however, the large faculty is used for intensive teaching. Although it might be possible, for instance, to eliminate the historian from each seminar faculty group,[52] the ratio of 5.3-to-1 would still be remarkably low. Indeed, changing the ratio dramatically would require a radical change in the system. Two things would be involved.

One would be the use of large lectures and correlatively fewer seminar hours. At present, there are many all-class lectures, but almost all of them are by visitors, and most of those visitors have been invited because of the positions they hold, not because they are academic experts. Second, students would have to spend more time in individual study and research. This would introduce more variability into a system intended to provide a common experience for the first half of the year. Also, if more time were spent in solitary work, a system of accountability would be needed. Typically, this has involved grading, but the Army War College is as wedded to its policy of no grades as it is to its seminar system.

It is true that the Army War College is serious about its teaching.[53] Its efforts to prepare faculty to teach are remarkable.[54] The planning for every element of every class and the course directives given to each student would shame most seasoned faculty members at civilian schools. In contrast, a scholar at a civilian school puts more time into the material and less into presentation. Civilian-graduate-school faculty prepare their subject matter for years. Often they are engaged in related scholarly research. Many participate in an "invisible college" of fellow experts at other institutions who read and critique one another's work. Their subject matter can involve a lifetime of commitment. For many, knowing more about a topic than anyone else is a sufficient and fulfilling goal.

Although they are well trained to teach, USAWC military faculty (two-thirds of the total faculty and a larger percentage of the teaching faculty) have not been deeply immersed in their subject matter. Sometimes they find themselves teaching lessons—for example, on the federal budget process—whose content they have never considered, except for one day when they were Army War College students. What are the consequences of having so many faculty members who have vast experience but who are neither experienced as educators nor academically expert?[55] These faculty not only lead seminars; they also critique students' independent reading and supervise research projects, guided principally by the crash training they receive at the USAWC orientation and by peer advice and support.[56]

In fact, much of the USAWC faculty who hold the rank of colonel and receive excellent salaries actually function like civilian school graduate assistants in that they teach material selected by others. Teaching assistants, however, teach only undergraduates and are paid a pittance. At the USAWC, the department chairs and the dean, those in charge of the teaching and curriculum, are often active-duty colonels who hold only master's degrees. To the degree subject-matter expertise exists, it is concentrated in the civilian faculty and, in reality, in one research institute and one of four departments.

In theory, at least, recruitment for military faculty is selective and competitive.[57] Some students stay to teach immediately after attending the Army War College. It is preferred, though, that military graduates complete another, "real military" assignment before joining the faculty. Before downsizing, graduating students typically could expect five to seven more years of service and two to five assignments before retirement.[58] With downsizing, and with USAWC appointments set at three years, a faculty position is increasingly becoming a pre-retirement billet. There is some concern that this is not the message the Army should be conveying.[59]

The 25 percent of the USAWC faculty with Ph.D.s are concentrated in the third of the faculty that is civilian, but even those faculty members should not be thought of as practicing their trade as it is practiced at civilian schools. First, many of them are located in the SSI or in other non-teaching units, giving them no responsibility for the curriculum, although they are a potential resource for those who are responsible. Second, their bosses are active-duty officers with master's degrees. Third, as discussed earlier, the work they do is different from that done in civilian schools. Fourth, half of them are "military" in that they are retired officers. Fifth, the insecurity (relative to civilian academic appointments) of their typical three-year contracts means they are not likely to try to assert expertise in the face of a superior's contrary view or a contrary consensus.[60]

Further, there is a balance that has to be worked out between the authority of the military in a military institution and civilians with expertise, between those trained to work collectively, to find closure, and, when necessary, to submit to the judgment of others,[61] and those who are trained to seek unique, "pretty proofs," to continue inquiry indefinitely, and to submit one's judgment only to the tests of logic and evidence.[62]

Evaluation plays an important part in curriculum development, but one gets the feeling that a reason for so much consultation is that no one person or group is accorded deference as an academic or subject-matter expert. Dependence on so much feedback also seems to leave little room for the unorthodox or the experimental. Still, when queried, the alumni and general officers report satisfaction with the "war-college year." In the next chapter, that year—one that involves a comprehensive, a total, experience—will be described.

5   The Carlisle Experience

SOCIOLOGISTS CALL the military a "total" institution. This refers to an institution that not only puts great demands on an individual's time, but, more important, affects most aspects of an individual's life. Some military assignments are more total than others. Commanding a brigade in Korea is different from a stateside assignment managing contracts. At first glance the Carlisle, or the Army War College, experience seems to be among the "more total" assignments—very military. The town, the post, and the year's cycle of activities make up an all-encompassing phenomenon that includes such things as participation in intramural softball, volunteering time and cookies for community events, and even (as directed by the commandant) spending more time with one's family. Administrators call the Carlisle experience "holistic," and students do report feeling immersed. At the same time, though, there is a significant effort *not* to control all of the student's time and all aspects of his or her life. A variety of elective and optional programs is available, and individual growth and reflection are encouraged—very academic. Let us explore the Carlisle environment: the town, the post, and the cycle of annual activities. Let us consider the aspects of the year that reflect the military culture and those that exhibit academic culture.

THE TOWN

Carlisle, Pennsylvania, is a town of about 18,000 bisected by LeTort Creek, which yields fine fishing and harbors intimidating (Canadian) geese.[1] Within an hour's drive are Harrisburg, the state capitol; Hershey, where the street lamps are shaped like candy kisses; Three Mile Island, the site of a near-nuclear disaster; Gettysburg, the site of a Civil War battle and of Lincoln's famed address;[2] and Lancaster, focal point of a thriving Amish community that forbids cars but permits in-line skates and attracts busloads of tourists eager to see quaint buggies, patchwork quilts, and the oddly named town of Intercourse. Two hours on the freeway takes one to Philadelphia; to Baltimore ("Balmore"); to Washington, D.C.; and to Penn State University at College Park. Carlisle is small-town living, but there are attractions within a short radius, and there is ready access to three major cities—and several outlet malls.

The rolling landscape supports prosperous farms.[3] Mountains and rusticity begin just north of town.[4] Indeed, "from (or on) the other side of the mountain" is a phrase used to refer to crude, unsophisticated, or bigoted behavior.

Carlisle is both a historic and a relatively sophisticated town. It is colonial—that is, it was founded before the Revolutionary War. Its oldest existing public building, the First Presbyterian Church, was built in 1754 and sits solidly at the main intersection of Hanover and High, across from the Episcopalian church and across from the old Cumberland County court house, which even today displays damage from the Civil War. The new county court house occupies the fourth corner. The fact that two sides of the main intersection are occupied by churches suggests (rightly) that churches are important in Carlisle. In 1996, there were fifty-eight listings under "churches" in the yellow pages; thirty of these were within the city limits. Also, a lively and lengthy revival is held at the county fairgrounds each fall.

The town was modeled after Carlisle, England, and one civic building is a replica of the English Carlisle's castle.[5] John Dickinson, a signer of the Declaration of Independence, founded a liberal-arts college in Carlisle in 1783, and Dickinson Law School (now part of Penn State) is located there, as well. The town cemetery features a larger-than-life monument to Molly Pitcher, who fought at the Revolutionary War's Battle of Monmouth, in New Jersey, after her artilleryman husband fell in battle. The nearby Molly Pitcher Hotel, which once catered to military families, now serves mostly welfare clients.

The town supports (and is supported by) the trucking industry;[6] it possesses a large blue-collar population and a number of well-tended trailer parks. But Carlisle is also the county seat, and the presence of a county court house means there is a community of lawyers.[7] Carlisle has a hospital, too, which provides employment for a variety of medical professionals, and several attractive retirement communities with affluent and educated consumers.[8]

Carlisle supports several gourmet restaurants and one that features California cuisine, as well as numerous 1950s family-style restaurants with chirpy waitresses, huge portions of food, and no meals served without dessert. Carlisle was not a Quaker settlement.[9] As the entrance to the Cumberland Valley, however, it appealed to those going west, large numbers of whom initially were Scotch Presbyterians, and later German Lutherans. (As late as the mid-nineteenth century, Carlisle Lutherans split into two congregations, disagreeing over the issue of whether church services should be conducted in German or in English.)

There is a roller-skating rink, a tattoo parlor, a bowling alley, a struggling coffeehouse, and many flourishing bars. In summer and fall, there is an outdoor farmer's market with Amish pumpkin bread. And there is always some participatory event—a three-man basketball tournament, a flea market, a gathering of Corvette owners, the Octuba Fest featuring craft booths and a series of tuba concerts, a college or high-school sports event, an amateur art show. Participation is an especially attractive characteristic of Carlisle—one is invited to be a part of things, and one does not have to be expert to join in. Amateurism is just fine. Thus, the street islands bloom with flowers planted by the ladies of the local garden club; their homey displays do not bear the imprint of either the landscape architect or the city employee. Church murals are painted by congregants, not professionals. And the local crafts in dolls, woodcarving, basketry, and wreath-making are done well and seemingly by everyone.

There are enough African Americans in town to make Martin Luther King's birthday a high-school holiday.[10] There is money, and there are estates outside of town. The *New York Times* is available, and there is a local daily, as well. Carlisle has a number of men's clubs, including Moose and the White Circle. There are also some drugs, some street people, and a murder or even two. In short, Carlisle is an attractive and complete small town. It is more sophisticated than many towns its size, but it is not dominated either by the Dickinson College students or by the Army War College students and their families. It is easy to slip into the town's routine. On your second visit to a local restaurant, the waitress is likely to say (correctly), "You're milk, aren't you?" One feels welcome. Even the houses typically have (electric) candles in the windows, carrying on a tradition of welcoming the traveler.

The town and the post are comfortable with each other.[11] There is one way, though, in which their landscapes differ. By 7 A.M., the local chain grocery is serving donuts fresh from boiling oil, and they are selling rapidly to folks on their way to work. Other local delectables include french-fried sweet potatoes and platters of regular french fries smothered in white gravy. Physical fitness is not an obvious priority among the towns-people. There are a lot of heavy (and tattooed) people, male and female, young and old, in Carlisle. On post, the population is fit—aggressively fit (and not visibly tattooed).[12] One simply cannot help noticing that the Army's unforgiving uniform shirts rarely reveal even an embryonic paunch.

THE POST

Carlisle Barracks, also bisected by LeTort Creek, has an interesting his-tory. It is the second-oldest active military post in the country.[13] It first became a military encampment in 1757 when British and American troops were sent to combat trouble being made by French-supported Indians. Skirmishes evolved into (Chief) Pontiac's (losing) War. With peace, the encampment fell into disuse in 1765, but an arms industry had been established there, and in 1776 the Continental Congress estab-lished an ordnance center at what was then being called "Washington-burg." A seemingly indestructible gunpowder magazine erected then serves as a museum today. In 1794, Carlisle was the site of a mobiliza-tion of federalized troops given the assignment of putting down the Whiskey Rebellion among western farmers.[14] President George Wash-ington himself led 14,000 troops as far west as Fort Cumberland before returning to his presidential duties.[15]

From 1838 to 1861, Carlisle served as the site of a Cavalry School; it especially trained troops to be sent west for the purpose of fighting Indians. During the Civil War, it was briefly occupied by Confederate troops, then fired (burned) by the Confederates before they went south to the Battle of Gettysburg. After the Civil War, the post was returned to training, but the War Department soon decided to move training to St. Louis, closer to the action—that is, the subduing of Indian tribes.

And then—irony.[16] The Indian fighter Lieutenant Richard Henry Pratt (who eventually would become a brigadier general) transported a group of "troublesome" Indian prisoners to St. Augustine, Florida, then helped them find work there. He later made it possible for some of them to attend Hampton Institute, which had been established to provide an education to newly freed slaves.[17] Next he persuaded the Secretaries of War and of the Interior and the Commissioner of Indian Affairs of the value of residential education for young Indians. Pratt was given permission to establish the Indian Industrial School and was given Carlisle Barracks as the site.[18]

The school opened in 1879, and Pratt soon had almost 150 students. The school, which would grow in size to more than 1,000, preached (literally) self-respect, self-reliance, and personal responsibility. Its motto was "God helps those who help themselves." Pratt insisted on the use of the English language both because the children were being trained to live in the white man's world and because they spoke as many as seventy different tribal languages. The education was vocational and moral and was for both girls and boys. Discipline was strict, and students wore uniforms. At Carlisle today, photos are displayed of newly arrived Indian children in their tribal dress—and of the same children in white men's dress and with neatly trimmed hair four months later. There is also an Indian cemetery by the back gate for those who died while in residence.

Sports, particularly football, were an important part of the curriculum, and Coach "Pop" Warner and player Jim Thorpe became celebrities as Carlisle Indian School beat the likes of Yale, Harvard, and Syracuse. Jim Thorpe's 1912 Olympic victories are honored by a statue at Carlisle's main intersection, and another Carlisle Indian School athlete, a long-distance runner named Louis Tewamina, won Olympic medals in both 1908 and 1912.

Pratt's twenty-five year mission as head of the school was to "civilize" (assimilate) his charges; that effort was not without critics.[19] With his retirement, school discipline relaxed, more attention was given to native arts and crafts, and evening lectures on morality were discontinued. The new leadership lacked Pratt's fervor and his certainty about what was "good for" the students. When the Army reclaimed the post for use during World War I, the school was closed permanently.

For two years after World War I, the post served as a rehabilitation hospital for returning U.S. soldiers. It then became the Medical Field Service School, providing a five-month basic course for Regular Army medical officers and a six-week course for National Guard and Reserve (medical) Officers. This was also the site of medical training for non-commissioned officers (NCOs). In the six years following World War II, six different Army schools occupied the site. In 1951, the Army War College arrived—and stayed.[20]

Like other Army posts, Carlisle Barracks provides. It provides a credit union, a post office, a Post Exchange, a commissary, a medical and dental facility, a guest house, a veterinarian, a barber shop serving men and women, an auto-repair center, a stable, a golf course, a bowling alley, two fitness centers, a track, soccer fields, tennis courts, a movie theater, a chapel, a child-development center, a thrift shop, a craft shop with lessons, a travel agency, outfitters (a rental shop for every possible outdoor activity), and 321 housing units.[21] During the Carlisle year, one could actually be so un-American as to go without a car. All of life's necessities, and many of its pleasures, are easily accessible by shank's mare—even if one lived off-post, a bicycle would do.

On any post, order is the order of the day.[22] Rules permeate. For example, Regulation 210-4 governing post housing is a half-inch thick. Gruesomely detailed directions, down to the level of cleaning screen doors and maintaining fire alarms, are provided. Eligibility for housing is specified by rank, by time in service, and by marital status, number of children, and assignment. There are two housing units for general officers, thirty-two for colonels, 182 for students and for majors, twelve for company-grade and warrant officers, twenty-one for senior NCOs, and seventy-two for junior NCOs. Some of the housing is "designated"—for example, that for the commandant, the dean, and the sergeant-major. Others are allotted by priority—for example, to the class president and to the commandant's aide-de-camp. Each year, a varying percentage of housing is reserved for student, as opposed to "permanent party" (faculty, staff, and others), officers, but close to half the student military families live on-post, most of them in College Arms (better known as "Smurf Village"), a set of split-level, white frame houses with outdoor storage sheds but no garages.[23] Permanent party officers often have handsome red-brick semi-detached homes. The commandant presides from a stone mansion, which was originally a private home but is now a part of the post. Homes have the names of occupants in plain view. Also, most of the post buildings have plaques that explain their names.

Again, there are a lot of rules for those who live on-post. For example, one memo makes clear the expectations for the annual "spring clean-up." It specifies fertilizing and seeding bare spots in the lawn, trimming hedges, and returning snow shovels.

Other rules apply to all members of the community. For example, at the post movie theater, one stands up when the National Anthem is played before the show. Coffee is available to take to seminar rooms, but cups may be moved through the hallways only with secure lids. All smoking is done outdoors, even in the dead of winter. A memo even details five levels of dress prescribed for social functions and notes that "social" (in contrast to working) name tags should be worn at events that call for civilian clothing.[24]

One well-practiced routine concerns Bliss Hall lectures by visitors. Ten minutes before a lecture is to begin, a warning bell is sounded in Root Hall.[25] Two minutes before the lecture, a second bell sounds; students should be in their seats. At thirty seconds, lights flash and students stand to honor the entrance of the speaker. Each student has an assigned seat, and roll is taken by the student seminar leader. Lectures are not for attribution but are followed by a question-and-answer period that, like the talk, is off the record. Questions are expected to be "respectful," and a sufficient supply of such questions is ensured in advance.

Another routine—one that requires an occasional reminding memo—involves appropriate behavior related to "Retreat." This ceremony is performed daily. It includes the playing of "Retreat," the firing of a ceremonial cannon, and the playing of "To the Colors." When Retreat begins, everyone within earshot must stop, face the music, and stand at attention. After the cannon is fired, one places one's hand over one's heart for the playing of "To the Colors." Participation in the ceremony is expected of anyone on-post who one can hear the music, which is everywhere—on the golf course, on the track, in the parking lot.[26] If one is in a car, one must stop and get out.

Attention to safety is another characteristic of post life.[27] Drivers may not exceed 15 miles per hour on-post; even adult bicyclists must wear helmets; softball is made safer by having two home plates and forbidding sliding;[28] no one swims or wades in the creek. The commandant's annual safety message is a routinely scheduled event.

Everywhere one finds the marks of past events and of those who went before.[29] At the main entrance to Root Hall is founder Elihu Root's sword, a piece of the Berlin Wall, pictures of the Army chain of command, and the service flags. On the first floor are displays of chiefs of staff, of previous commandants, and of previous deputy commandants. There are class photos from 1921 to the present and staff and faculty photos from 1950 forward. Distinguished fellows and academic-chair holders hang for all to see. Even department chairs' photos are on display. One colorful area presents the flags of the International Fellows' countries, displays gifts from the IFs, and records the members of each class on a plaque. In the coffee shop, graduates are listed by their branch of service—or, if the graduate's service is the Army, by branch within that service.[30] One niche honors the Buffalo soldiers, African Americans who fought for the Army in the West after the Civil War. There are particularly fine oil paintings on Civil War themes.[31] The second and third floors contain a study room and a seminar room for each seminar group.[32] Each of the rooms is named for a military leader, and a brief bio of the leader is placed by the door.

Communications are continuous. In recent years, e-mail has assumed the same importance at Carlisle that it has at many other institutions, but the printed word (read and unread) continues. The *Carlisle Barracks Banner* is published once a month for the garrison; the Community Center puts out a monthly "Good Times Guide"; there is also a monthly "Civilian Personnel Bulletin"[33] and a weekly "Historic Carlisle Barracks, Pennsylvania Bulletin," which contains official notifications, job opportunities, unofficial items, found property, for-sale listings, wanted items, and special notices.[34] Because there is so much "expected" behavior, military personnel—especially those living on-post—probably have to glance at the weekly Bulletin, at the least.[35]

For the student, however, the most essential communication is the three-and-a-half-by-four-inch "Weekly Schedule," which is placed in each student's mailbox each week and fits neatly into any shirt pocket. This provides details about all official events: time, place, dress requirements and options, whether attendance is required or voluntary, and whether guests may attend. Topics to be discussed at each seminar meeting are listed; Bliss Hall lectures and speakers are announced; noontime lecture topics and speakers are listed; and "complementary" programs (usually in the afternoon) are listed. This is the students' bible. Carefully filed, it becomes a nearly complete record of the year's events.

As described earlier, the War College experience seems enveloping and military. But perhaps the policy on student dress best illustrates that the experience is neither fully "military" nor fully "academic." Except during visits from very senior officers and civilians, civilian dress is authorized for students and faculty. Nevertheless, large numbers of students wear their uniforms. One reason is that, at the USAWC, civilian dress does not mean "student" dress; it means "business attire"—that is, jackets and ties for men. It is hot when students arrive in Carlisle in August. An officer in uniform can wear short sleeves and go tieless. As a result, many students wear uniforms even when they are not required as a matter of comfort.[36] However, on rainy days, civilian clothes appear. Why? Because Army men in uniform may not use umbrellas. In civilian clothes, they may.[37] Pragmatism, then, seems to govern students' behavior. Policy does give students an option—business attire—but it does not give them free rein to exercise their individual taste and judgment.[38]

Life on- (and off-) post involves many rules and expectations. Most are familiar to officer students, but civilian and foreign students are sometimes bewildered, bemused, or irritated. Military students have had twenty years of experience with military obligations, and the efficiency and predictability involved can provide comfort. But the year's cycle at Carlisle is new to the students (and to first-year faculty and staff); that cycle reflects more continuity than it does change, however. Looking back over ten years, one can see that, although adjustments have been made, the template for the year is relatively unaltered.

THE YEAR'S CYCLE[39]

August

"In-processing" is a little like freshman orientation, except that most Carlisle students bring families and their household goods. They are not setting up a dorm room with posters, a CD player, and a computer. They are setting up homes. Incoming staff and faculty have a sponsor who has recently gone through the in-processing procedure to help ease the pain, but most military personnel and their families are seasoned movers who quickly complete in-processing's numerous required steps, such as obtaining identifying stickers for their cars.[40]

There is something of the freshman orientation thrill of an opening day. After all, considerable competition was involved in obtaining the assignment to Carlisle. But college freshmen are embarking on the adult adventure: They have sixty years of unknowns ahead of them and good reason to be optimistic about their futures, even if the content of those futures is hazy. In contrast, most Army War College students have, at most, a promotion to colonel or captain ahead of them and the prospect of a limited number of rather predictable future assignments before they will become "U.S. Army [or Navy, or Air Force or Marines] ret."

The first day's orientation includes presentations by the commandant, the garrison commander, the Physical Research Institute, and the Family Program; a review of the curriculum; remarks by the appointed class president; and, at the end of the day, the first meeting of the seminars.[41]

The next day includes briefings, a tour, an assessment of communication skills, and a battery of psychological tests, including the Myers-Briggs Type Indicator. By the third day, seminars are meeting at their regular time, 8:30–11:30 on Monday, Wednesday, and Friday,[42] and they are discussing the results of the tests given the day before (which have already been processed and distributed to the seminar's faculty leader). The thrust of the lesson is how individual preferences and characteristics affect group dynamics, and therefore team-building, in theory and in practice. Also, at 6:45 a.m., some seminars have had blood drawn in preparation for the very thorough individual physical assessment each student receives. In addition to blood tests, there are body composition and waist-to-hip ratio measurements. There is strength and flexibility testing; there is an evaluation of aerobic endurance; and there is an assessment of stress management. (Those who fit what is called the Type A profile, which involves a heightened adrenaline response, are recommended for a special program to convert them to Type B.) Each individual graduates from testing with a personalized set of recommendations designed to improve his or her "wellness." The program can be followed individually, or one can elect to join any of a series of classes, which are provided throughout the year.

By the second Monday, one week later, the chief of staff of the Army has addressed the class, and a formal review and commandant's reception has been held. Welcoming events have also been held by the Officers' Wives Club,[43] the Community Support Center, the Chapel, and

Youth Services. The Military Family Program has given its first presentation and will continue to do so on Tuesday evenings.[44] Required orientation sessions are completed with briefings at Collins Hall for groups of four seminars at a time. Complementary sessions on sports injuries, on a variety of computer software programs, and on e-mail, and an introduction to the "Cooperative Degree Program," which permits students to get a master's degree from nearby Shippenberg College while attending the Army War College, have also been presented.

Week four brings individual meetings with a faculty adviser to agree on an individual learning plan for the year. There is also an introduction to the Strategy Research Project (SRP), a written assignment required of each student; this is offered by the editor of the Army's academic journal, *Parameters*, which is published at Carlisle.[45] Voluntary noon lectures have also begun. Little time has been wasted. Students plunge rather than ease into their work.

September

School routine has been established, but social events continue—for instance, the president of Dickinson College hosts the International Fellows, and the Air Force celebrates its birthday with cake for all and a Stealth flyover. The staff ride to Gettysburg is urged, but not required, and families are invited. The Navy, Coast Guard, and Air Force students sponsor the Air/Shipwreck Ball, a rather rowdy event with a parade and floats built by each seminar, followed by dinner and dancing at the Community Center.[46]

October

International Fellows make a two-day trip to Washington, D.C., and preparations are made for the New York City trip for the whole class *and* their spouses. The group leaves on a Sunday morning and does not return until late Wednesday afternoon. The focus is the United Nations, but the group (divided so that one member from each seminar is in each of twenty groups) visits a wide variety of institutions, from the *New York Times* and the Stock Exchange to a prison and a public school. This is part of the broadening of the vision of the men and women who will be senior officers. Most were not raised in urban areas.[47] In fact, in my seminar a third had never been to New York City, and another third had been in the airport or paid only a brief visit. They were not afraid, but there was something akin to apprehension about the trip, perhaps because their wives would be on their own for much of the trip, and they, too, lacked New York and other big city experience.[48] Media Day involving a Bliss Hall lecture and discussions with a member of the media—one per seminar—is also an October event. The IFs' ten-day trip to Latin America comes at the end of the month.[49]

November

November brings the first exercise: a two-day event that tests learning about the interagency process. There is also a staff ride, a celebration of the founding of the USAWC, and a very formal Marine Corps Ball held off-site in a motel ballroom.

December

The end of the year sees another staff ride; completion of the core curriculum, except for two post-Christmas exercises; the traditional Senior Citizens' Holiday Tea;[50] too many festivities (including a musicale and the Community Center's "premier" event, the New Year's Eve party); and a two-week recess.

January

The new year begins with good resolutions and a three-day campaign-planning exercise; the latter is quickly followed by a three-day "Military Operations Other Than War" exercise. When the new term begins, the seminars become inactive, but their identity remains intact. Seminars may meet occasionally to discuss a Bliss Hall lecture or for social events, but classes are no longer seminar-based. Students are now engaged in their electives, the Advanced Courses. The preparation of Regional Strategic Appraisals also begins. During this process, students meet with others studying the same region rather than in their seminars. Briefbacks (to the seminar groups) on the conclusions of the Regional Appraisals will be done in February.

February

February is short and cold. Even so, staff rides continue. Students begin to focus on what are essentially term papers, their SRPs. Regularly planned events for late winter are the Officers' Wives Club Auction, the West Point Founder's Dinner, and the Class Leadership Social.

March

Faculty advisers meet with advisees to assess progress on their individual learning plans and to chart out the work to be completed by the year's end. The mother of all strategic exercises, the two-week Strategic Crisis Exercise, is held. Everyone participates.

April

Spring recess brings the first term of electives to an end. When classes resume, people not only begin new electives, they almost certainly start to think about their next assignment (and move). Still, a major chunk of academic work remains, as does another week-long field trip in North America and a two-day trip to West Point for the IFs. There is also a major sports event in April—Jim Thorpe Day. This features vigorous competition and "old guys puking." The teams are fielded by the different war colleges, and sponsorship is rotated among them.

May

A three-day Washington, D.C., field trip begins the month of May. It is also the time scheduled for the Army's ball. The National Security Seminar, with some two hundred visitors, ends the semester, but preparation for it is another source of competition for time—along with the completion of academic work (in particular, the SRP), faculty adviser conferences, and preparations for moving and new assignments. Still, there is enough time for a set of celebrations. These include an all-class picnic and a reception which precedes *the* day.

June

Graduation.

ELECTIVES AND OPTIONS

The USAWC now offers students a good deal of choice.[51] In the early years, the Carlisle curriculum was prescribed. Now it is roughly 50 percent prescribed; the other 50 percent is made up of elected courses; SRPs, with a choice of kind of project and of topic; and Regional Strategic Appraisals, in which students choose the region they want to study.[52] This amount of choice is not so different from what one would find in a civilian master's degree program, except that many of the civilian programs cannot be completed in ten months. Many are designed for a full year's work, and the most prestigious are often two years in duration.

The War College also provides an extraordinary number of optional programs. There are intellectual programs such as the Army History Institute lecture series, the noon lecture and discussion programs, and the staff rides. There are a variety of self-improvement courses, such as those on computer skills. A variety of service opportunities, such as leading a Scout troop, are strongly encouraged. Then there are the ice-cream socials; the golf and tennis tournaments; the luncheons with guest speakers, including those for Federally Employed Women and for Hispanic American Heritage Awareness; and the speeches to be given for the Speakers Panel. Then there are the recreational classes—dozens and dozens of them. There is Fat Busters;[53] there is an array of crafts classes in a magnificently equipped shop; and there are even dance classes.[54]

It is hard to judge whether these options represent opportunities for the "growth" so emphasized in USAWC orientation programs or are better described as distractions, as ways to keep very busy with worthwhile activities, but not activities that would challenge, contradict assumptions, or stimulate critical or creative thinking.[55]

The War College is wrapped in history; it is well provisioned; its ethos emphasizes service, country, community, family, fitness, and participation. That ethos is subscribed to by both faculty and students and possesses a reality. In a significant sense, military personnel are idealists, but they are realists, too. Thus, the ethos is not always taken literally, and even if assumptions and values are not challenged, they are not necessarily accepted by each individual in full. The civilian academic ethos emphasizes intellectual mastery and discovery. It features freedom, individualism, competition, specialization, even eccentricity. Critical and creative thought is highly valued, but, admittedly, commitment to this ethos is probably stronger among faculty than among students,[56] and probably stronger among liberals arts faculty than among professional school faculty.[57]

The skilled faculty member provides just the right amount of information, of freedom, and of criticism to stimulate the individual student's best efforts. Army War College faculty are thinking about how to provide the right amount and kind of stimulation when they refer to students as being in one of four zones: the "yawn" zone, the "comfort" zone, the "challenge" zone, and the "panic" zone. Ideally, all students would be working in zone three all the time. Electives and optional programs, plus the individual learning plan established by and for each student, are intended to differentiate the year's experience so that different challenges are presented to different students.

What one does not see in the seamless small town, post, year's cycle experience, however, is controversy, contradiction, novelty, provocation, or obdurate opposition. These are all found on civilian campuses and may be essential ingredients of academic freedom and the advancement of knowledge.[58]

Perhaps the military impulse to the uniform is best observed in the control exercised to keep seminars on the same track at the same time during the first half-year. There are no experiments with material or process in the core curriculum.[59] In a civilian university, students can have quite different experiences in a course with the same title; they can also observe faculty disagreeing with and even contradicting one another.

Another difference lies in the fact that student leaders both for the class and for each seminar are referred to as presidents and as chairs but are not elected. Leadership, as befits a military but not a civilian institution, is appointed. Also, considerable amounts of seminar time are devoted to organizational matters, including the organization of social events. Thus, the nine hours a week in seminar are by no means the equivalent of three graduate seminars in a civilian institution. Also, there is always an element of control in the seminar environment, whether it is intentional or unintentional.[60] Titling the syllabus "Course Directive" and describing objectives for each assignment and seminar comes more from the "training" tradition than it does from that of "education."

In a civilian academic setting, no one would be concerned with scheduling students' time. At the Army War College, though, the "Weekly Schedule" accounts for most hours of most weekdays. Seminars meet Monday, Wednesday, and Friday morning. Tuesday and Thursday mornings are for speakers. Monday and Wednesday afternoons are for required complementary programs, Tuesday and Thursday afternoons are course director's time, and Friday afternoon is "not time off." Even time for individual study is scheduled, for it seems to be important to be able to demonstrate that a student's time is being put to profitable use. Efforts are also made to avoid boredom among students, efforts that would not be a part of the civilian graduate experience. Thus, things tend to happen in snippets,[61] and variations even in location are encouraged. For example, seminars may go out to breakfast together, perhaps to Dickinson College, then hold the morning's seminar there. (An off-campus meeting also involves permission for students to dress informally, meaning no ties.) In the seminar, a variety of techniques are used—slides, discussion, student presentations, guest speakers. A civilian seminar would rely more heavily on faculty expertise and student discussion based on considerable preparation.

But perhaps the greatest difference between the USAWC and a civilian school is what creates tension among students. In a civilian school, the greatest tension generator is certainly grades. The USAWC, though, has taken care to deemphasize the evaluation process. At the Army War College, the greatest tension comes from two sets of decisions, both of which are made outside the college.

The first involves the release of the "Colonel's list." This is the Pentagon's list of those who will be promoted from lieutenant-colonel to colonel. In 1995–96, half the military students were on the list or had hoped to be there. Promotion calls for celebration, and because so many Army War College students were promoted, a number of parties ensued. Tension comes because some students selected for the Army War College, who have appropriately high expectations, will *not* be selected.[62] There is acute sensitivity to the possibility that oneself or a fellow seminar member will experience this disappointment. Thus, the commandant's staff notifies non-selectees ahead of time by telephone and treats the information as a private matter. How and when to share information about non-selection is left to the individual.

The second anxious period involves the period before the posting of students' next assignments. Those who aspire to stars hope for a brigade command. (Not receiving one is not so devastating as not being promoted to colonel.) Lots of students do not receive such a command. Also, through consultation with assignment officers,[63] one may have a pretty good idea ahead of time as to what one's future holds. Also, there is time to develop a rationalization, an explanation of why one is well satisfied with what one gets.

Finally, the holistic Carlisle experience persists in treating students as family members, even though many are single, divorced, or temporarily away from their families. At civilian schools, students are perceived as individuals, and students' spouses certainly are not treated as participants in a two-person career. Indeed, if married, those students are likely to be in two-career families, which creates different complexities. The fact is that the military, too, now includes many two-career families—and many two-military-career families, as well. It has begun to make appropriate adjustments. Still, those adjustments become more difficult as spouses advance in rank and accomplishment.[64]

The Carlisle experience is enveloping. It is like no other Army assignment, but it is also different from a civilian graduate-school experience.

The Hessian Powder Magazine was built by Hessian POWs in 1777. It now houses a display of Carlisle Barracks history. All photographs herein courtesy of the U.S. Army War College.

Quarters Three was the headquarters for the Carlisle Indian Industrial School and now serves as family quarters for the Army War College.

Several dozen of the thousands of Indian children who attended the
Industrial School died there and were buried in a small cemetery.

Root Hall is the Army War College academic building housing offices, seminar rooms, and a library.

Seminar discussions are the heart of the curriculum. Each seminar includes a representative mix of all services, active and reserve components, civilians and International Fellows.

The Army War College hosts about 500 guests from area nursing homes during the annual Senior Citizens Holiday Parties.

Jim Thorpe Day pits the senior service colleges against each other in sports competition, in memory of U.S. Olympic athlete and Carlisle Indian School alumnus Jim Thorpe. Here, Army soccer players vie with Navy students.

Proud graduates include students from each of the U.S. military services, International Fellows, and civilians.

The Hall of Flags reflects the international character of the student body and connects the academic building, Root Hall, to Bliss Auditorium.

Stained glass windows in the Bliss foyer reflect military traditions and history. This states the Army War College mission—"Not to promote war but to preserve peace."

6 The Cold War Curriculum at the Army War College

IN CONSIDERING the curriculum, it is helpful to recall the political and military events that were part of the faculty's and the students' experience.[1] The principal focus of the chapter, though, will be the core curriculum offered to the class of 1984–1985—that is, the material studied by all members of the class. Other elements to be considered include the roster of invited guest lecturers and the content of the exercises, the elective courses, and the student research papers.

BACKGROUND FOR THE CLASS OF 1985

It is easy to forget that the U.S. military has not only been a "standing" military since World War II, it has been active during the past fifty years. Although 1945 brought an end to World War II and many troops did come home, President Harry S. Truman kept the military busy. The Truman Doctrine (1947) committed us to assisting countries threatened by communist takeover (most specifically, Turkey and Greece); in 1948, Truman ordered the Berlin airlift to break a Russian blockade of West Berlin; in 1949, he helped to establish the North Atlantic Treaty Organization (NATO) based on the principle that an attack against one would be an attack against all. China became a communist state in 1949, and in 1950 Truman won United Nations' approval for a "police action" led by the United States to rid South Korea of invaders from North Korea. The Korean "non-war" continued until mid-1953, with more than 30,000 U.S. casualties.[2] Truman's firing of his commander in Korea, General Douglas MacArthur, established that he, Truman, was the commander-in-chief and that the ends pursued in a war could appropriately be limited. Thus it was (re)established that war was an instrument of policy, that it was not an all-out fight caused by the failure of policy. Truman also sent the first military advisers to South Vietnam and authorized the first explosion of a hydrogen device. In sum, under Truman, the United States went almost directly from a hot war to a cold war, without passing peace.[3]

The Cold War continued under the next president, former General Dwight D. Eisenhower, and our global commitment became even more evident. We did not attempt to "roll back" communism when anti-government riots occurred in East Berlin, in Poland, and in Hungary. However, we did support a coup in Iran; we did join the Southeast Asia Treaty Organization (SEATO), which extended U.S. defense commitments to Australia, New Zealand, the Philippines, Pakistan, and Thailand; and we did send 5,000 troops to Lebanon to protect a threatened government there. The first nuclear submarine was launched; so was the first U.S. satellite.

President John F. Kennedy's two-year presidency included the aborted invasion of Cuba's Bay of Pigs and the Cuban Missile Crisis. Kennedy also ratcheted up defense spending and the U.S. role in Vietnam (by saying that U.S. troops would fire if fired upon and by committing 15,000 troops there).

President Lyndon B. Johnson may have preferred to focus on civil rights and his "war on poverty," but he had to face the fact that the United States was now fighting a war in Vietnam.[4] He sent military planes to Laos and obtained authorization for presidential action in Vietnam through the Tonkin Gulf Resolution. Vietnam became another "non-war," but this time it was a U.S., not a UN, war.[5] Bombing of North Vietnam and firing into Cambodia was begun. By the end of 1967, almost half a million U.S. troops were in South Vietnam, with others offshore and in Thailand. In addition, some 14,000 U.S. troops were sent to the Dominican Republic. In the United States, unrest, including urban riots, became frequent. The "New Left," ecology, and feminist movements emerged; hippies and religious cults appeared; rock music prevailed; and the antiwar movement became ever larger and more active, deeply distressing many in the military, which saw the movement as undermining their efforts and sacrifices and directed at them.

Antiwar protests brought hundreds of thousands of people to Washington, D.C.; news of the My Lai massacre by U.S. troops became public; and Vietnam peace talks began under President Richard M. Nixon.[6] Two different things occurred simultaneously under Nixon: First, there were incursions into Cambodia, renewed bombing of North Vietnam, and the placement of mines in North Vietnamese harbors. At the same time, however, U.S. troops were being brought home.[7] By the end of 1971, the number of U.S. troops in Vietnam had been reduced to 140,000. The last troops returned in 1973, after the signing of peace accords in Paris.[8] An important aftermath to Vietnam was the passage of the War Powers Act, designed to prevent presidents from committing troops to conflicts abroad without approval from Congress.[9]

The military was less favored during the presidency of the Annapolis graduate Jimmy Carter, and things were relatively quiet until the last year of Carter's presidency, when sixty-three Americans were taken hostage at the U.S. Embassy in Tehran. About the same time, the Soviet Union invaded Afghanistan.

Immediately after the inauguration of President Ronald Reagan in 1981, the hostages in Iran were released, but Reagan's strong support of the military and the Defense Department led to more spending and more activity. In 1983, 241 U.S. Marines and sailor peacekeepers were killed in a bombing in Lebanon. Only two days later, the United States (with some allies) invaded Grenada.[10] In the fall of 1984, the class of 1985 began its year at Carlisle Barracks. Shortly afterward, Reagan was re-elected in a landslide.

In sum, the class of 1985 (participants in what has been called the "third" War College) had as its background a military dealing with a nuclear world and, in particular, with a nuclear-armed major antagonist, the Soviet Union. That military had also recently fought two "nonwars" in Asia. In one, Korea, the United States settled for limited objectives after publicly firing its military commander. The second, Vietnam, was seen simply as a defeat. The new War Powers Act made future presidential commitment of troops without congressional authorization less likely, but the global reach of U.S. policy and commitments remained unchanged. The vulnerability incurred by that reach was exemplified by the taking of U.S. hostages in Iran and the barracks bombing in Lebanon. Nevertheless, ten years after the United States' departure from Vietnam, the military—and the Army, in particular— was "back" from its postwar Vietnam doldrums. A feeling of confidence had been restored. There was even a sense of wanting to prove commitment and efficacy. One faculty member remembered T-shirts he wore at the time: "I'd Rather Be Killing Communists," and "Go Ahead, Gorbachev . . . Make My Day!" The year 1985 was a period of strategic clarity and high morale.

THE CORE CURRICULUM

A preview of the curriculum is provided by a look at "the issue," the collection of materials given to each entering student.[11] The first notable thing is that merely collecting one's issue involved a significant test of one's physical fitness: Each student was given fifty-four items. Roughly half of these were official service reports, Army pamphlets and regulations, and Army Field Manuals (eleven of them). A few were reference works, including the *Air Force Almanac*, the *Guide to Current American Government*, and the *U.S. Army Budget*. But many substantial volumes were also included. Among the better-known authors of distributed works were Bernard Brodie, Dean Rusk, Carl von Clausewitz, Samuel Huntington, John Keegan, Henry Kissinger, Lawrence Korb, Walter Millis, Russell Weigley, and Harry Summers.[12] No volumes on the history or foreign policy of the Soviet Union were included.

The prospect of being asked simply to master their "issue" must have sobered new students; in addition, however, each seminar room included thirty more volumes. Many of these were reference books—for example, *Webster's New Geographical Dictionary*—but half a dozen considered the armed forces and security strategy of the Soviet Union. The largest group of seminar-room volumes focused on organizational behavior, management, and decision-making.

The twenty-five-page "Curriculum Pamphlet" is a syllabus, the map that helps students navigate the year. Three purposes were listed in the "Curriculum Pamphlet" for the class of 1985: 1) acquiring skill in the art and science of land warfare;[13] 2) (reinforcing) strong personal and professional values; and 3) developing sensitivity to the political, economic and "societal" factors that influence the nation's security and well-being.[14]

Students were told that, over the course of the year, they were to expand their vision so that they would be prepared to consider the full spectrum of national power; the theory of war as a political, social, and moral phenomenon; and the relationship between military force and national political aims.[15] Students were also told that, in the future, they would be initiators rather than just implementers of policy, and that they would have to perform well not just within the framework of certainty provided by Army regulations and field manuals, but in a new environment characterized by complexity and, more important, by ambiguity.[16] This was all to occur at the same time that the students were to acquire the skills to manage large combat formations (at the corps level and higher).

In 1984–85, the "Common Overview," the core curriculum, made up thirty-three of the forty-four weeks of the schoolyear. The last week was devoted to the National Security Seminar. Thus, only during the ten weeks from the end of March to the end of May did students pursue electives. Most of the year's work was clearly defined and done by all. The course of study may have been complex (see the curriculum's conceptual organization later), but it was hardly ambiguous.[17]

Organizationally, the core was divided into ten courses. These proceeded through four "phases" and focused on eight themes. Examining this curriculum in detail will provide a basis for comparison with the curricula of 1990 and 1995–96–97.

Let us look first at the phases. Phase one was described as one of achieving knowledge of self. This corresponded directly to Course 1, "The Requirements of the Professional Leader." Phase two involved the acquisition of concepts, theories, and approaches to the art and science of war and the military profession. Its intent was to assist critical thinking by raising the level of abstraction. This was the explicit purpose of Course 2, "Politics, War, and Strategy." Course 3 through Course 6 dealt with abstractions and participated in phase three, the study of the concrete through history and case studies. Phase four was one of applications. This involved exercises, writing, simulations, and other forms of learning-by-doing. Applications were part of all the courses from Course 4 through Course 10.

Eight themes were woven through the ten courses. The first was planning—strategic planning, joint planning, resource planning, mobilization planning, contingency planning, and the Planning, Programming, and Budgeting System (PPBS). The second theme, ethics, considered the ethics required of a senior professional and moral questions involved in the formulation of national-security policy. Theme three was Soviet studies, which was covered in five of the ten courses and often considered in parallel with U.S. institutions to encourage comparison.[18] The other five themes were personal and family health and fitness, total Army,[19] history, echelons above corps, and the future.

1985 COURSE DIRECTIVES

Each course was accompanied by a directive, a super-syllabus.[20] The first week of the first course, "Requirements of the Professional Leader," involved individual assessment using the Myers-Briggs Type Indicator, a health self-appraisal, the Fundamental Interpersonal Relations Orientation–Behavior (FIRO-B) assessment, the Sperry Listening Profile, a Stress Type Assessment,[21] a Terminal and Instrumental Values and a Conflict Handling Styles Survey, and other measuring instruments. Individual assessments were confidential, although they were aggregated so a group profile could be constructed and discussed.[22] The purpose of all this was to increase self-awareness and awareness of the differences in others, and thereby, hopefully, to enhance communication and group cooperation.

The next two weeks were devoted to senior command, leadership, and management; ethics and professionalism; and the human dimension of combat.[23] In addition to the seminars, there were three lectures during seminar time and three complementary lectures, one on professionalism, one on leadership and management, and one on professional values. These were given by three generals (two retired and one active-duty).

One session or lesson was specifically devoted to a formal consideration of ethics. This included an introduction to moral philosophy; an examination of how classical views relate to professional military values; and consideration of how the values of a leader are projected into the command climate. All of this was presented in one seminar meeting incorporating three readings and the results of five surveys done before class.[24] "Points to Consider" included: What are differences among Descriptive Ethics, Normative Ethics, and Meta Ethics? Should Objectivism, Utilitarianism, or Formalism be espoused by military professionals? What is the relationship between moral virtue (personal character) and morally good actions? How is moral character formed? A second lesson asked "Why Study Ethics in the Military?" A third considered ethics and military professionalism. And a fourth considered ethical decision-making in combat, using as case studies My Lai and Beirut.[25]

Course 2, "Politics, War, and Strategy," moved from the level of the personal and individual to that of national-security policy and how it is

formulated. The class began with an examination of American values—
"These we'll defend." These were portrayed in a specially prepared
anthology, "The U.S. Heritage," which condensed a two- or three-semes-
ter political-theory sequence into 100 pages, proceeding without pause
from Thucydides to John Stuart Mill; providing the views of America's
founders through Thoreau; and concluding with the economic theories
of Spencer, Smith, and Marx.[26] Perhaps unexpectedly, special note was
made of the Arab contribution to Western civilization, and the last selection in "The U.S. Heritage" was from Marx's *Communist Manifesto*. In fact,
the last words in the anthology were: "Working men of all countries,
unite!"[27]

Thus, in a little more than six weeks,[28] the class studied the institutions that make U.S. security policy,[29] a project that included a three-day
visit to Washington, D.C.; theories of war, with emphasis on von Clausewitz; and strategies used in the past to implement U.S. policy. Consideration was given to the full spectrum of conflict, with special emphasis on terrorism and the use of nuclear weapons—the two kinds of attack
to which U.S. civilians were most vulnerable. Written assignments
included a 1,000-word essay on a military strategist (a list of sixty-nine
mostly European or American men was provided from which to draw
possible subjects),[30] a similarly short essay on von Clausewitz (twelve
themes were suggested), and a review of a book chosen from the contemporary military reading list.

The mini-American government course was another miracle of con-
densation.[31] Again, absorbing so much material so quickly would seem
to make it difficult to develop enough distance to make independent
judgments. Still, the questions raised were not unsophisticated. For
example, it was noted that the economic base is fundamental to U.S.
security. Accordingly, one lesson was devoted to economics. Then students were asked questions such as the following:

a) What problems are associated with the federal budget deficit? What
   prevents us from having a balanced budget?
b) Can we have stable prices, full employment, and economic growth?
c) Is Third World debt a serious problem? How and for whom?
d) Should the United States have an industrial policy?

Similarly, after just one lesson on "The Role of the Military in National
Security Policymaking,"[32] students were asked:

a) Should the military professional focus his[33] advice only on military factors or should he include considerations of domestic political trends, international economics, etc.?

b) What is the role of the military professional in handling the executive–legislative interface?

c) What should the military professional do if he differs with civilian policy-makers on matters of 1) policy and 2) principle? How do you distinguish between the two?

Attention to the Soviet Union began with Lesson 2.[34] Lesson 2-9 presented the world as Soviet leaders were said to see it;[35] Lesson 2-11 examined Soviet propaganda efforts and U.S. reluctance to move ahead in PSYOPS (psychological operations); Lesson 2-30 considered Soviet nuclear strategy and compared it with U.S. nuclear thinking; Lesson 2-34, looked at East–West issues based on the assumption that the West is committed to maintenance of international stability while the Soviet Union "remains committed to revolutionary change of the world's political and economic order"; and, finally, Lesson 2-35 considered the role of the Soviet Union in supporting wars of national liberation in Third World countries and how the United States had responded and should respond. The lesson considered both the East–West military balance and economic issues such as access to markets and resources. The Soviet Union would also be the subject of lessons in later courses. Although some readings depicted the Soviets as highly successful—for example, as manipulators of international peace movements and as sponsors of international terrorism—others suggested Soviet vulnerability (such as a 1983 Rand Corporation study that set forth the thesis that the United States could force a change in Soviet behavior by outspending the Soviets on defense).

History was seen as important to the study of strategy (about which so much has been written that "readers must be highly selective to avoid wasting their time").[36] The opening of five lessons on strategy involved a comparison of the strategy of Napoleon and of Frederick the Great.[37] It was von Clausewitz, though, who provided *the* text for strategy. In a first application, students participated in an exercise in which they replayed the U.S. Civil War. They moved on to study twentieth-century continental, maritime, and air-power strategies, and then to strategy based on nuclear weapons. The lessons of World Wars I and II were considered, including the effects of technology, logistical requirements, and management of coalitions. Also considered were limited war (Korea and Vietnam were the exemplars),[38] revolutionary war (Mao and Lenin), terrorism (as transformed by sophisticated technology and global communications), low-intensity conflict, the evolution of nuclear policy (including the development of the NATO nuclear "umbrella" (or "pall"), deterrence, arms control, and the Military Reform Movement.[39]

Although no outside speakers were scheduled, twenty-seven lectures were presented over the forty lessons. In 1984–85, listening was considered an appropriate and primary form of learning.[40]

Course 3, "Planning and Decision-making"; Course 4, "Military Forces and Doctrine"; and Course 5, "Leadership of the Army and Management of Army Systems" were dedicated to "preparing for war."[41] The three-month sequence took students into mid-January. The task became one of learning their job. Abstraction and speculation ceased to be the order of the day.

The first eight lessons in Course 3, "Planning and Decision-making," introduced students to the arcanities of the Pentagon and the Joint Chiefs of Staff[42] and, in particular, to the Planning Programming and Budgeting System (PPBS), the Joint Strategic Planning System (JSPS), and the Joint Operation Planning System (JOPS).[43] Emphasis was given, first, to the role of the chief of staff of the Army and his relationship to the Office of the Secretary of Defense, the Joint Chiefs of Staff, and the Unified/Specified Commands, and second, to how the planning processes worked in reality.[44] A number of guest lecturers were used to provide the practitioners' point of view.[45] Six further lessons centered on jointness and on operations planning. The course concluded with a case study of the previous year's joint "insertion" of U.S. troops into Grenada (Operation Urgent Fury).[46]

Course 4, "Military Forces and Doctrine," concerned large (corps and higher) operations. It examined force organization, capabilities, and doctrine. Although some emphasis was given to Army Air-Land doctrine, the doctrine, organization, and missions of the other services were included in the first week of study.[47] The study of joint campaign planning (including command and control, sustainment, and intelligence)[48] was supported by a field trip to three military installations,[49] by a case study of the Inchon landing during the Korean War, and by a two-day computer-assisted exercise in which the United States and the Soviet

Union squared off in Central Europe.[50] A set of optional mini-lectures on the Soviet Union and a closed-circuit noon TV series, much of it on the Soviet Union, were presented during the period of the course. So was a series of movies, including *Command Decision* (1948), *Battleground* (1949), *Midway* (1975), and *Reds* (1981).[51]

Course 5, "Leadership of the Army and Management of Army Systems," dealt with familiar subject matter but at a level students would not have encountered previously. Thus, the written assignment for the course was a 2,000-word "white paper"expressing one's philosophy of command, leadership and management.[52] Students were specifically told that "a dusted-off, reworded statement of ideas you may have worked out as a company or battalion commander" would not do. The assignment is "not for what you once were," but "for what you will be"—for example, Army chief of staff or director of the Defense Intelligence Agency. At the end of the year, "vignettes" were selected from these student papers and published in a small pamphlet. Items were clustered under "Command," "Leadership," "Management," and "Potpourri." Two examples from each category follow.[53]

Command
Preparing soldiers for war is a function of leadership. Sustaining readiness is a function of management. Leading and managing in a military organization is a function of command.

The key is for your soldiers to know that none of them can top you in dedication, commitment, positive attitude, and the never-ending quest for excellence.

Leadership
Command without leadership is hollow and becomes a crutch. Engagement without leadership is sterile and is doomed to failure. But quality leadership reduces the need ever to exercise the first and promotes exercise of the second. Thus, Command, Management, and Leadership, these three—but the greatest of these is Leadership.

I believe one can lead only to the degree by which the led allow you to lead them, or in other terms, you lead only to the extent the subordinates allow themselves to be led. All of this happens (or doesn't happen) through the medium of TRUST.

Management
There is no better way to begin a foot race—or commit the energies of subordinates—than to have an objective mind.

As the rulebook grows fatter, ideas grow fewer. Individuals made to feel like cogs in a machine will soon behave like cogs in a machine.

Potpourri

Perhaps the words of Oliver Wendell Holmes will better express the need for an internal look at one's self. "The great thing in this world is not so much where we stand, as in what direction we are moving."

Guts is the endurance and nerve to keep going when life is not easy. . . . We must have the guts to admit we made a bad decision. We must have the guts to listen to bad news without shooting the messenger. We must have the guts to take bad news to a shooter of messengers.

My favorite: "Don't do dumb things because of 'they.' "[54]

"Management"[55] was described as organizing a variety of Army systems, including force development; research, development, and acquisition; logistics; finance; personnel; training; installation management; and mobilization. In this course, the objective was to achieve understanding of the need for, and the means toward, achieving horizontal integration of these systems. Guest speakers included the undersecretary of the Army, the vice-chief of staff, a division commander, and several academics.

Because Training and Doctrine Command (TRADOC) develops Army doctrine, is responsible for force design, and sets training requirements, it has a crucial role in institutionalizing institutional change. Thus, special attention was given to this command.[56] Information management merited a lesson of its own, as did the Army Family Action Plan. Mobilization issues were covered in two lessons and an exercise.

On the last day before the Christmas holidays, an exercise was run on "force integration"—the bringing together of all of the (Army) systems studied in order to achieve a change that corrected a deficiency. After the holidays, two more exercises reinforced the principles of force integration.

With Course Six, "Regional Appraisals," gears shifted to a geographically based examination of U.S. interests, policies, and strategies.[57] For this purpose, the globe was divided into five regions: Europe and the North Atlantic; Asia and the Pacific (with India almost undiscussed); the Middle East (including North Africa and southern and southwestern Asia, including Turkey); Latin America (including Canada, so better called "The Americas"); and sub-Saharan Africa. Each seminar was also divided into five groups (one for each region) so that three students from each seminar would become "expert" on the political, social, economic, and military trends of one region. This was done by studying intensively in regional groups, rather than in seminars, for a week. The regional courses began by considering each region from the perspective of U.S. interests. Then an effort was made to see the regions from the point of view of the Soviet Union[58] and from the point of view of those living in the region. Next came a discussion of problems, trends, and issues, followed by the development of a proposed U.S. strategy for the region. When the seminars met together again, the regional strategies developed by their members were presented to the whole seminar. The seminar then discussed how the strategies interacted, weighed the strategies' relative importance, and reflected on nonmilitary strategies that could affect military strategy. When the seminars then endeavored to design an overarching, or global, strategy, the difficulty of reconciling resources and competing demands quickly became apparent.

A film series and regional panels with the IFs enriched the curriculum, but some parts of the curriculum seemed simplistic. For example, the "sociocultural relations" between the United States and Latin America were described as "love–hate": "Latins generally envy and seek to imitate our life style while resisting our materialistic and organizational styles."[59] However, hard questions were also raised—for instance, "Does the 'special relationship' between the United States and Israel help or hinder the search for peace [in the Middle East]?"[60] And "What were the benefits of European colonialism for Africa? What problems did this prolonged presence create?"[61] "Should the United States be more responsive to regional countries' desires for a New International Economic Order?"[62] "To what extent are peace movements in Europe an expression of European misperception of U.S. security interests in the region? Do peace movements represent a valid minority in Europe which cuts across national boundaries?"[63] In discussing NATO, an analysis was offered of differences within the organization both between the United States and Western European countries and among different Western European countries.

Courses 7, 8, and 9 moved to the application of power—or, in Clausewitz's formulation, "the conduct of war."[64] In Course 7, the subject was nuclear war.[65] In Course 8, it was limited war. And in Course 9 it was (classic) theater warfare.

In fact, Course 7 was not so much about the conduct of general (strategic) nuclear war as it was about the development of U.S. policy concerning the use of nuclear weapons—and ethics was of such concern that one invited speaker was the Archbishop of New York.[66] The war under consideration was a massive nuclear war in which thousands of targets would be hit and hundreds of thousands of people would be killed in a very short period of time. This war was different from many for which the military planned in that it was not one that the military sought to "win" but one that it sought to prevent. Further, the war was focused on one nation that also possessed a nuclear arsenal and understood that arsenal as essential to deterring U.S. action directed toward it.

An analysis of U.S. targeting policies was examined in detail; so were possible USSR targeting strategies. The problem of destabilizing deterrence if actions were taken to defend against the effects of an attack was studied.[67] The final element of the course was a three-day political–military simulation in which students were confronted with a nuclear-crisis scenario and had to make decisions acting as the National Command Authority (NCA).[68]

Discussion of the moral implications of using nuclear weapons either for war fighting or for deterrence occurred. Also, the question of the impact of peace movements on nuclear policy was considered.[69] Other issues included the difference between tactical and strategic nuclear weapons, the possibility of escalation from the former to the latter, the possibility of a demonstration use of a nuclear weapon, and the definition of victory at the completion of a strategic nuclear war.

Course 8 addressed planning for a limited war in an "immature" theater and operations against insurgents in a revolutionary war.[70] The method was one of planning exercises. The first was for a limited war lasting three days and was focused on the U.S. Central Command.[71] The second was a five-day exercise involving a war of insurgency. Students' strategic appraisals of Latin American and experience from the U.S. Southern Command were used in the second exercise.

The purpose of the exercises was to review the three planning systems (JSPS, PPBS, and JOPS), then to use them to allocate resources and create an operation plan using knowledge gained from the regional appraisals.[72] Particular emphasis was given to assessing mobility. Sustainability was another fundamental concern in the "barebase" environment of the exercise. Other considerations included support from host nations, and the political, military, and economic responses of third parties.[73]

The response to insurgencies, which was considered the most likely form of conflict for U.S. forces for the foreseeable future,[74] required understanding of the U.S. Security Assistance Program and the concepts and doctrine for Internal Defense and Development (IDAD). The major text was *Field Manual 100-20, Low Intensity Conflict*. Here, doctrine held sway. The setting for the exercise to consider how the United States could best "offset" the "exploitation" by the Soviet Union of instability in Third World countries was, as noted earlier, Latin America. Of particular concern were "limitations and advantages of a democratic form of government"; "moral and ethical concerns for planning in a revolutionary war environment"; the role of assumptions; the role of allies; and which nonmilitary considerations would be compelling.

Course 9 involved the big one, the classical one, the familiar one—operations in a war theater. The task involved translating political guidance into operation plans for a major conflict. The "mature" theaters considered were Korea (small) and Europe (large). Planning involved both joint (the different U.S. services) and combined (U.S. with other nations') forces. The assumption made was that the United States would be responding to invasions from North Korea or from Warsaw Pact countries, respectively.[75]

Korea and the concept of "forward defense" were studied first. A case study of Operation Overlord, the World War II invasion of Normandy, then laid the groundwork for the study of NATO's organization and its planning for a possible invasion of Western Europe. It also retaught the lesson that, regardless of how conscientious the planning, the situation becomes fluid once combat begins. "Fog" and "friction" derail plans; intelligence, communications, logistics, and more do not deliver as scheduled.

In 1985, NATO strategy was the same as it had been since 1967: nuclear deterrence, flexible response,[76] and "forward defense." After that strategy was adopted, the U.S. Army developed the doctrine known as Air-Land Battle, which involves using aircraft to take the conflict far forward of the line of battle. Some viewed this doctrine as provocative, as excessively offensive. Debate over the appropriateness of NATO strategy was active during 1985, but there were few indications that any new strategy could be agreed on. Thus, the old prevailed. Course 9 concluded with a four-day exercise, NATO 2000.[77]

Course 10 was the capstone designed to bring the work of eight months to bear on a single problem. The view again was global. (The course was titled "U.S. Global Military Strategy.") It began with a three-day trip to New York to make a series of small group visits to a broad spectrum of U.S. institutions, including the *New York Times*, multinational corporations, and government institutions,[78] but also to visit the United Nations. This was followed by the final, five-day exercise. Its two tasks were (merely) to construct a *global* military strategy for the United States for the year 1991 based on current and predicted capabilities, and to critique current (unclassified) defense policies based on those capabilities. Because there was clearly a mismatch between commitments and capabilities, there was no "school solution." Thus, it was noted that "initiative and intellectual self-reliance" would be needed.[79] The strategy devised by each seminar was then briefed to another seminar and to a visiting senior expert, who could conceivably take good solutions back to the Office of the Secretary of Defense for consideration.

Finally, mention must be made of the Military Studies Program, a required year-long individual or group project. Four options were available: to do an oral history; to pursue a group study of a military problem; to pursue an individual study of a military problem; or to prepare an analytical essay suitable for publication in a professional journal. Due at the end of the year, these projects and papers caused many a student headache.[80] Some titles for papers prepared in 1986 suggest the great variety of subjects: "Graves Registration," "Family Power: Its Impact on Unit Readiness," "The Cost of Sweden's Neutrality," "The Ingredients of Military Genius," "The Strategic Defense Initiative—Do We Really Need It?" "Rear Battle at Corps Level—Are We Prepared?" and "The Military Retirement System."[81] Interestingly enough, virtually nothing was done on the Soviet Union, on nuclear policy, or on ethics—topics that were all central to the common core. Perhaps students felt saturated.

The common curriculum was followed by ten weeks of advanced and elective courses. In most cases, these met for one three-hour block each week. Three hours of preparation were assumed for each hour in class. With a four-class load, each student then had a forty-eight-hour-per-week commitment. Among the many complementary programs, the Military Family Program was the most extensive. There were six other special lecture series: two on history, one on ethics and professionalism, one on strategy, one on command, and one on management. There were also monthly staff rides to Civil War battlefields.

The year concluded with the week-long National Security Seminar, in which civilian guests were invited to discuss military and national-security strategy with the students.

The 1984–85 curriculum regularly used the lecture format and ambitiously condensed what one might think merited a whole course into a single lesson—for example, the lessons on American values, American government, and ethics. Ethics is a theme woven into a number of other lessons, as well. Its importance is understandable: Those charged with taking human life (potentially on a vast scale) need to feel justified in their actions and to have accepted their duties in advance of any call to action.

The message from the Department of Command, Leadership, and Management was that senior leadership carried new responsibilities and required new skills and information. Its coursework proceeded from exploring oneself to the study of effective interpersonal relations to managing an Army and leading a combined (not just a joint) force. Perhaps the most convoluted and perplexing lessons were those that tried to explain how the Army runs and the management philosophy, policies, and procedures within the Department of Defense.

Not surprisingly, the offerings from the Department of National Security placed great emphasis on the Soviet Union, as well as on nuclear weapons and strategy.[82] The department was also responsible for the Regional Strategic Appraisals, which in 1985 received the highest student ratings of the ten Common Overview courses. Students rated the course on the conduct of nuclear war the "most thought-provoking."[83]

The Department of Military Strategy, Planning, and Operations taught four of the ten core courses (but not the one on strategy). Its primary focus was planning—and planning based on the real forces and capabilities of the U.S. military. Thus, the class paid visits to a number of U.S. bases (posts, yards, stations). After teaching the planning process, the department asked students to apply their knowledge in two exercises, one for limited war and one for (putting down) revolutionary war.[84] This was followed by a study of theater-level planning looking at Korea and at Western Europe and by more exercises.

Carlisle students were kept very busy, and mostly they did the same thing at the same time, whether that was attending a lecture, meeting in seminar, or participating in an exercise. Some of their courses used a Carlisle-prepared textbook that contained required and supplemental readings. These texts offered a variety of mainstream views, without the burden of reading a series of books.[85] Each lesson ended by posing a series of questions. These seemed to imply that having studied the lesson and read the readings, students now knew enough to have an opinion—even on issues on which experts do not agree. Essentially, the students were constantly being briefed; they were being given shorthand versions of a wide range of contemporary information (in four phases with eight themes and organized into ten courses). In the future, they would not disgrace themselves or the USAWC by never having heard of Somalia or Afghanistan, or PPBS or JOPS, or the congressional staff or committee system. Once briefed, moreover, students were not only assumed to be entitled to an opinion, they were also assumed to be ready to act, even if only by preparing a paper or by participating in an exercise.

Again, students were exposed to many of the complex issues, events, and policies faced by national policymakers whom they might have to advise in the future.[86] They learned (or, perhaps, relearned) that resiliency and adaptability were two important characteristics of a senior officer.[87] Further, there was explicitly stated support for questioning and for making independent judgments. Nevertheless, there was also a strong tendency to seek certainty and consensus. This was reinforced by the regular use of exercises that forced students to reach a conclusion by requiring them to take action. Action, at least temporarily, puts an end to inquiry.[88]

After only one week of focused study of a region (which students might or might not have studied before), students were asked to construct a strategy for that region—then collectively to construct a global strategy for the United States and to include in that strategy not just the military component, but also political, economic, and psychological elements. Again, academics have no set time for arriving at a truth they are pursuing, and sometimes they are considered exceptionally clever if they unearth not a truth but a paradox. In contrast, service personnel face the possibility of being called to act at any time. They may even have to take grievous action knowing that they do not know all that they need to know.[89] Thus, one can feel some sympathy for the Army War College's approach of "skimming," then, without hesitation, designing a course of action. Conclusions reached by a group after a week's study should not, however, be mistaken for anything but relative expertise. The question then is: In broadening officers' views, does the war-college curriculum lead students to think they "know" even when experts acknowledge that they themselves do not?

The student "issue" alone would have provided a year's worth of work, but the thirty-three weeks of the common core included a variety of additional texts and readings. Then there were four ten-week elective courses, a host of guest lectures,[90] a number of exercises, and games, movies, field trips, panels, and a final paper. It would be easy indeed for a conscientious and curious student to be "fire hosed" all year long. When drenched, it would be easy to lose track of the instruction in the "Curriculum Pamphlet" to be initiating and sensitive to the political, economic, and societal factors that influence the nation's security.

7 The Curriculum in Transition, 1989–90

THE CLASS OF 1990 attended the Army War College in interesting times. If one expected the curriculum to be responsive, but not yet to have relinquished the verities of the past several decades, one would have it about right.

THE TIMES

The class of 1990's political experience featured the presidency of the popular Ronald Reagan, who talked tough about the Soviet Union (the "Evil Empire"), raised defense spending, championed the MX missile, and launched the "Star Wars" Strategic Defense Initiative. But Reagan also made an agreement with the Soviet Union to dismantle all missiles with a 300- to 3,400-mile range.

Reagan was also committed to putting down Central American insurgents. However, he faced a Democratic House of Representatives that disagreed with that policy. This led to the Iran–Contra affair, in which the administration sold arms to Iran, then used that money to support insurgents in Nicaragua. Neither the selling nor the supporting was legal. Convictions, overrulings, and pardons followed.[1]

In addition, the situation in the Persian Gulf was tense. In 1987, thirty-seven U.S. sailors were killed on a ship in the Gulf by an Iraqi missile. Iraq called the incident an accident, and the United States did find that its naval officers had been negligent. Then, in 1988, a U.S. Navy ship, also accidentally, shot down an Iranian commercial flight, killing hundreds.

Elected president in 1988, George Bush was responsible for the decision to invade Panama and to bring its head of state to the United States to face drug charges. The invasion occurred shortly after the class of 1990 had gathered. But an event with far greater impact was the tearing down of the Berlin Wall and the need that created to rethink almost everything that had been assumed about the Soviet Union.[2] A second major event was Bush's decision to wage joint and coalition war in the Persian Gulf—but not with Iran. Instead, Iraq, which had invaded its neighbor

Kuwait, was the foe. This occurred shortly after the class graduated. The two things that most directly affected the Army War College curriculum, though, were the passage of the Goldwater–Nichols Act and publication of the Skelton Report.[3]

THE CORE CURRICULUM

The library's "student [book] issue" previews the year. Between 1985 and 1990, the materials given to the students on arrival had not decreased in quantity or perceptibly changed in quality. There were, however, some detectable differences. The "issue" contained more government documents and reports, which the students were invited to keep, and fewer books, which would have to be returned. Gone were Dean Rusk's *The American Revolution and the Future,* Bernard Brodie's *War and Politics,* Samuel Huntington's *The Common Defense: Strategic Programs in National Politics,* John Keegan's *The Face of Battle,* and even Harry Summers's *On Strategy: The Vietnam War in Context.* Some of the now absent books—such as those by Huntington and Keegan—became "study room" books. There was a slight shift favoring more readings in texts prepared by the Army War College departments and fewer books. This meant reading shorter pieces, but it also made it possible to include excerpts from a wider range of material.[4]

The Soviet Union and nuclear warfare no longer commanded the attention they had enjoyed in 1985. Further, the perspective was no longer bipolar; it had become "global." Warfare was now assumed to be both joint and combined, and was now considered across the whole spectrum of types of conflict. It was almost as though the response to a diminished threat was an expansion of geography and of varieties of war. This meant that topics for study were increased; time for doing so was not.

In describing the college's mission for the class of 1990, the "Curriculum Pamphlet" made explicit two purposes that the college has tried to balance since its founding.[5] They were: 1) to develop senior leaders; and 2) to conduct strategic studies.[6] In addition, the school's philosophy of "rigorous active learning" and the importance of maintaining an atmosphere of "professional military scholarship and camaraderie" were emphasized.

The intended transformation over the course of the year included preparing students to:

- Set the ethical climate
- Work in highly ambiguous environments and deal with problems with no clear-cut solution
- Assess the future and plan for the long term while executing in the present
- Be self-motivated, innovators, and initiators of policy
- Be fit—physically, mentally, morally[7]

To emphasize the rigor and graduate level of the curriculum, the students were explicitly warned, "The curriculum is designed to be provocative. There are at least two sides to every issue you will address at the War College, and there are no school solutions." The curriculum was intended to "cultivate the art of intelligent questioning"; "unexamined acceptance of assumptions and the status quo is neither expected nor desired." The seminar experience permitted the exercise of "the fine art of assenting and dissenting logically, tactfully and convincingly."[8] The message was clear: This was a year for different behavior.[9]

By 1990, the core curriculum had been reduced from 1985's ten courses to only four courses, a week of orientation at the beginning of the year, and the National Security Seminar the week before graduation. The first three courses—"The Senior Leader," "War, National Policy, and Strategy," and "Implementing National Military Strategy"—made up the four months before the Christmas break. From early January to mid-April, two sessions of elective and advanced courses were offered.[10] Course 4, "Global and Theater Strategy Application," occupied the six weeks preceding the end-of-year National Security Seminar. The content of these courses will be summarized later. The New York City trip was part of Course 2 but followed it in the schedule.[11] The Washington, D.C. trip became a spring event.

Each year, certain special themes are selected for emphasis. For the class of 1990, those themes were Ethics of the Profession, including ethics in peace and in times of war;[12] Landpower in Military Strategy;[13] Joint and Combined Planning and Operations;[14] and Operations at the Lower End of the Conflict Spectrum (that is, low-intensity conflicts, or LICs), a new theme.

Course 1: The Senior Leader

In the description of Course 1 we find the first specific reference to "volatility, uncertainty, complexity, and ambiguity"—or VUCA—which has since become a regular part of the USAWC vocabulary.

Self-assessment and preparation of a Development Guide[15] remained the first task. This was followed by an examination of group processes and of the management of stress; leadership in large, complex organizations; ethics and professionalism;[16] and wartime leadership, including the use of history, and stressing the effect of combat on its participants.[17] The written requirement for the course was a 2,000-word essay in which the student imagined himself or herself in a particular senior role, then detailed what she or he must do to prepare to hold that position.[18]

The course began with consideration of the results of the Leader Effectiveness and Adaptability Description (LEAD-Self) testing and a reading of the Army Field Manual on senior leadership. Although the latter represented Army doctrine, students were told to read it critically. The next lesson used information gathered from three- and four-star generals to discuss executive and indirect leadership. The message was that good leadership has different characteristics at different levels— and that what makes for good leadership at one level may actually impede leadership at another. The next subject was "Generalship and Genius."[19] The topic was first tackled through a set of seven readings, with some emphasis on how a genius uses staff and a good deal of emphasis on leading in wartime. "Genius" was later examined through student-prepared biographies. Finally, a practical approach was represented by performing a mock selection board to get students thinking about how to make selections that would produce the desired kind of leadership.[20]

The work of Malham Wakin, a trained philosopher and then an active-duty Air Force colonel, was used as the basis for a discussion of how a leader sets the ethical climate for a large organization and how the imperatives of the American character and of the military profession affect decisions senior leaders must make. This was followed by a discussion of professional and personal values.[21] Two lessons then considered the role of ethics in combat. The first study was of My Lai.[22] Issues considered were background and organization of units; units' training; leadership; the operation; and reporting and investigation.[23]

The second case study involved the fire bombing of Dresden by the allies in World War II.[24] The trial and execution of Japanese General Tomoyuki Yamashita after World War II was also examined. The last case study was a critical one. The issue was command responsibility. General Yamashita was hanged because he "should have known." However, decades later, during the My Lai trial of Captain Ernest L. Medina, the military judge ruled that a commander was responsible only if he *did* know and failed to intervene.

The complexity of being an effective senior leader was emphasized by the fact that MacArthur's formulation of the Army's duty as being one of "winning our wars" was clearly not adequate in an age of adversaries armed with nuclear weapons. Then, the *real* responsibility of the military might be said to be to *deter,* not to win, a war. More complexity comes from the need to understand second- and third-order effects of command decisions and the fact that, at the seniormost levels, the military cannot ignore the political foundation of the assignments given to it. Senior leaders must also face the possibility that the guidance given them by civilian authorities may be unacceptable. The question, then, becomes: What is the soldier's compelling ethic—faithful execution of guidance, or "betraying the nation" by following that guidance? Finally, students were asked to consider how the lack of combat experience *of many senior military leaders* might affect their competence.[25] The course concluded with students' biographical reports on senior wartime leaders and with a lesson on the importance and challenges of senior staff service (an assignment many students would receive in the near future).[26]

Course 2: War, National Policy, and Strategy

The core curriculum's second course placed the military in context. That context included consideration of the nature of war and of the international political system; also, at the domestic level, it included consideration of the nation's ethical and legal foundations and of the political and governmental institutions and policies built on them—particularly those institutions involved in the development of national-security policy. Further, it used a variety of theorists (Clausewitz remaining central and Sun Tzu never overlooked) to examine the history of strategy. Special emphasis was given to strategy in the nuclear age—including strategies of deterrence and arms control.

In the introduction to the lesson on the international political system,[27] students were given an important message: They were told that the U.S. system, a part of the international system, works through "bureaucratic politics: conflict, bargaining and compromise." "We do what we can agree on," but "Multiple sources of power and decentralized decision-making in a democracy are a challenge to the 'rational' development and execution of national policy and strategy. Effective participation in the bureaucratic arena requires the power of expertise. That is why you are here."[28]

Importantly, the military was examined in the context of the nation's total power. The point driven home was that the military is only one of four kinds of power. The others are economic, political, and socio-psychological. Each student was required to brief and to write an essay on one of these four kinds of power.[29] A good deal of guidance and numerous bibliographic references were provided to the students as they undertook an analysis of what might have been unfamiliar forms of power.

To further enhance officers' understanding of the role of the military in a democratic society, the domestic "environment" in which strategy is formulated was studied.[30] That domestic environment was said to include the economy, politics and government, and values and traditions.[31] To consider values, each student was asked to develop a statement of national purpose based on assigned readings (including the U.S. Constitution). Then seminar members developed a consensus statement of national purpose based on the individual statements of students.[32]

The Constitution was assigned a second reading to examine what it says about foreign policy and war powers. To understand legal restraints on the use of military power further, students studied the War Powers Resolution (Public Law 93-148, 1973), and international law and norms, including just war theory. They were then asked to consider possible conflicts between their oath to defend the Constitution and other loyalties (family, friends, conscience, religion). They were also invited to debate the wisdom of the War Powers Resolution and to ask whether the U.N. Charter's statement on the use of force was "realistic." Doubt was encouraged, but neither the time nor the materials were available to assuage doubt.

Attention was given to other domestic influences on national-security policy by having students set up "task forces" to study science, education, and school reform; welfare and poverty; health care; environmental concerns; the war on drugs and crime; and budget options and spending priorities. Each task force prepared a policy paper outlining the issues and problems and identifying options; it then made a recommendation for action. Again, specific readings were required of the whole class, and additional readings are assigned to the subgroups. The three selections on education and school reform were by William Bennett, Chester Finn, and John Chubb, who are among a group of scholars closely identified with conservative Republican positions.[33] The discussions on welfare, housing, and health services appear to have been more balanced.[34] One problem in selecting articles may have been that, in an effort to give "critics" of U.S. culture and institutions a voice, the selections were made from the right, but the right had already taken control of the executive branch and was preparing to do the same in the legislative branch. Thus, the authors were no longer really critics; rather, they were associated with the government. Because students cover topics in such a short time and work in a consensus and recommending model, the faculty bear heavy responsibility for the range (and lack of range) of views represented in the articles chosen.[35]

One purpose of the lesson on domestic issues and on the varieties of national power was to demonstrate not only that education, science, economic growth, and so on are important to the nation's security, but also that they represent competing (budgetary) interests. And they do not compete only with one another; they also compete with the military.

U.S. values affect what is acceptable as strategy. However, it is U.S. interests[36] that were said really to drive foreign policy, and those interests were said to be global in nature. Thus, at the USAWC, the first step in studying U.S. security was to assess the global environment, particularly threats to the United States, but apparently neutral trends were also weighed.

In appraising the realities of the global environment, the Soviet Union remained the central concern—but it was a Soviet Union with its hands full domestically, and one with radically new policies put in place by Gorbachev.[37] Issues that had gained in importance since 1985 were the strong economies of Asia and Europe and the debt-ridden economies of the Third World. At this point, students were asked to examine one of six geographic regions and to determine U.S. interests there.[38]

Queries to the students included: Should competitiveness (implies winning) or interdependence (implies cooperation) be the basis for the definition of U.S. interests in the future? Does the Soviet Union as a global military power have a right to a role in regional security based on its national interests? Does the American tendency to personalize governments and leaders lead to a view of the world based on friendships rather than interests?

Block 3 of Course 2 turned to the subject of the national-security-policy process itself. It considered the players and their roles (including that of the military); it examined how policy is developed both routinely and in periods of crisis; and it reviewed the elements of U.S. national power as analyzed in the students' essays on the four varieties of power.

The National Security Act of 1947 and the Goldwater–Nichols Defense Reorganization Act of 1986 were discussed as the legal framework for the formulation of policy. It was noted that the president's leadership in foreign policy is usually well supported and generally endorsed, even in the case of the Vietnam War. Then, although the president remained the major player, Congress began to assert itself.[39] Also, the media became more critical. Even within the executive branch, differences surfaced among the Department of State and Department of Defense, the National Security Adviser, and the intelligence communities. Presidential leadership became an exercise in difficult and extensive persuasion.

The information on the players who formulate national-security policy is brief (even terse), but the questions are serious. "Does the influence of the Department of Defense and Joint Chiefs of Staff on national-security policy carry too much weight? Or not enough?" "Who is or should be the president's principal adviser on foreign policy, the Secretary of State or the National Security Adviser?" "What should a military officer do if he differs with civilian policymakers on matters of policy or principle? How do you distinguish between the two? When, if ever, in recent years do you believe senior military leaders should have resigned? What effect, if any, would this have had?"

Again, after a single lesson on the intelligence community, students are asked: "Should the intelligence community engage in covert operations? Why or why not?" "Should the CIA be allowed to participate in domestic counter-intelligence activities?" "Is the organization of the American intelligence community optimum, effective, or flawed?" Discuss."[40]

After discussing the tensions within the executive branch and between the executive branch and Congress over foreign and defense policy, a case study of the Iran–Contra affair was presented as a "valuable negative." This was followed by a discussion of the media—a profit-making enterprise that enjoys special First Amendment protection.[41] The questions posed were not easily answered. "How will support for future military actions be affected by unrestricted television coverage? Can there ever be another popular war fought by the United States if the public receives untrammeled electronic media coverage?" "Is increased regulation of the media necessary? If necessary and desirable, who should do it? The government? Can self-enforcement work?"[42]

The historical study of strategy is the subject of Block 4. It approaches the topic through theory, history, and applications of a model based on an analysis of "ends, ways, means." The first application or exercise involved developing a military strategy for the North and for the South early in the U.S. Civil War. Next, attention was given to post-World War I formulations of land, sea, and air power, all of which were relatively developed by the beginning of World War II. World War II strategy was analyzed in both the European and Pacific theaters; that strategy had to expand to encompass joint and combined forces, consideration of the kind of postwar peace desired, and, most important for that peace, strategy in a nuclear age.

Block 5 considered U.S. strategy after World War II. For almost half a century, that strategy revolved around defending the nation and Western Europe from a Soviet Union with nuclear arms. The crucial questions for the class of 1990 may have been whether the Cold War was over and whether previous strategy, previous analyses, previous organization, and previous weaponry remained relevant. These questions, however, were not tackled.

The case study of Korea brought consideration of limited war (as opposed to absolute war), war termination, and the political control of war to the classroom. This was followed by a Vietnam case study. Together, the case studies demonstrated that war occurs over a spectrum, and that limited wars and multifaceted low intensity conflicts (LICs) were directly linked to the possibility of nuclear war. The military's lack of enthusiasm for LICs shows through, but it is also duly noted that insurgency and counterinsurgency, anti- and counter-terrorism, and peacekeeping and peacetime operations are in the U.S. military's future and must be prepared for.[43]

Course 2 concluded with a block on deterrence, nuclear strategy, and arms control. Thus, even as the Soviet Union was dissolving, the big issues of the recent past continued to absorb a large part of the curriculum. After reviewing the theory of deterrence, the very concrete issues about targeting under the U.S. Single Integrated Operational Plan (SIOP)[44] and possible and comparable Soviet plans were examined. Further, a European critique of the theory of flexible response and escalation helped students understand that even our strongest allies do not always agree with us on strategy.

Arms control (nuclear and conventional) was depicted as a practice that could either enhance or decrease security. The focus was on both U.S.–Soviet disarmament negotiations and those involving NATO and Warsaw Pact countries. Soviet strategic thinking and the changes underway in that thought were also considered. Although a Cold War perspective still dominated, there was acknowledgement of change in the Soviet Union, and the question was asked: Is this merely a changing threat or an opportunity? Both the controversy about the security issues surrounding Reagan's 1983 Strategic Defense Initiative—that is, would it lead to a stronger defense or to nuclear destabilization?—and questions about its feasibility and cost were examined. Again, it was noted that our allies did not necessarily agree with the initiative, and that the Soviets saw it as offensive in nature and a violation of the Anti-Ballistic Missile (ABM) Treaty. A variety of points of view were offered, but SDI was taught as a part of existing policy.[45]

Course 2 concluded with lessons on the connection between strategy and planning—planning being the subject of the third of the four core curriculum courses. Students reviewed the current national military strategy of the United States and learned the basics of the JSPS and the force-sizing process. They also examined the role of land power (and the Army) in current strategic debates described as dominated by two perspectives: "maritime strategy" and "coalition defense."

Course 3: Implementing National Military Strategy

The third of the four core courses moved from the formulation of strategy to its implementation. Here one has the acronym experience.

The essential acronyms are: CINCs (commanders-in-chief of the unified and specified commands), CJCS (Chair of the Joint Chief of Staff), JOPS (Joint Operation Planning System), JSCP (Joint Strategic Capabilities Plan), JSPS (Joint Strategic Planning System), NCA (National Command Authority), OSD (Office of the Secretary of Defense), and PPBS (Planning, Programming, and Budgeting System).[46] Although much of the course involved exercises, short, formal papers were also required, some of which become part of an anthology distributed to faculty and students.

The course began with a description of the missions and organization of OSD, the JCS and its chief, the CINCs, and the military services, with a discussion of what is required to achieve unity of effort. The curriculum also included analysis of jointness requirements and doctrine both as an outgrowth of the Goldwater–Nichols Act of 1986 and because of their contribution to unity of effort.

The next lessons focused on the support and capabilities provided to the CINCs by each of the four services. This involved a description of the organization, roles, mission, and capabilities of each service, including weaponry and the structure and training of its forces. After brief accounts of the other services, some fifteen or sixteen lessons were devoted to how the Army prepares to support the CINCs.

The Army, like the other services, is responsible for organizing, training, and equipping—in short, for the readiness of its troops. In its planning, it assumes a vertical framework of strategy, operations, and tactics; horizontally, its planning can encompass a whole theater. As a first step, the USAWC asked students to participate in an exercise in which they took the roles of their counterparts—Soviet staff officers working in the current context, a context that included a new Soviet "defensive doctrine," force reductions, arms control, departure from Afghanistan, the acceptance of on-site inspection of nuclear sites by U.S. personnel, *glasnost*, and *perestroika*. Although the Soviets still had 5 million men under arms and some 10,000 missiles pointing at the United States, our military knew about and was trying to assess the strains within the Warsaw Pact, even including ethnic tensions and drug and alcohol problems.[47]

The services prepare the troops, but it is the CINCs who do the planning for war and who do the commanding in war. The catch is that the CINCs' plans and the nation's strategy create "requirements." The civilian government then provides resources to the services, which creates "capabilities." However, the "capabilities" created rarely match the CINCs' "requirements."[48] Much of the learning process at the Army War College, then, involves learning how to cope and where to cut so the "four pillars of defense"[49] are least affected. The subject was pursued, then another exercise was conducted—one on budget cutting.[50]

The Army has always considered the Air Force and the Navy as advantaged in budget presentations to Congress[51] because of the colorful and concrete requests they can make for awesome equipment and advanced technology.[52] The Army basically finds it hard to intrigue listeners with its Functional Life Cycle and Force Development System, which, simply put, tells how many people are needed in the Active, Guard, and Reserve components of the Army, in what proportion people should be trained in particular specialties, and what percentage should be in combat, combat support, and combat-service support.

Another exercise designed to reinforce learning about the Army's personnel and training systems considered the ramifications of greatly expanding the numbers of military personnel—for example, by creating a National Service Corps. (Clearly an exercise since budgets were being cut.) Included were recruitment, retention, and quality-of-life issues. Next was a lesson on logistics—a massive and complex effort when one remembers that ours is a global military, that it believes it must be prepared for "full spectrum" fighting (nukes to counter-insurgency), that it must be able to respond quickly enough to participate, and that it must be able to sustain itself until a satisfactory outcome is achieved.

The next set of lessons involved joint, near-term planning by the warfighting CINCs both for peacetime (deliberate planning) and for crises (time-sensitive planning). This meant applying an already designed system and giving attention to such items as mobilization plans—of both Reserves and new recruits—to mobility, and to force projection. It also meant developing a risk assessment.

Elaborate planning activity is required to bring the different Army elements together in a coherent system;[53] an even more elaborate system brings the different services under the larger rubric of the national military strategic plan and the JOPS.[54] Special attention was given to "time-sensitive" (crisis) planning and to mobility issues. The Mayaguez crisis was the case study for time-sensitive decision-making. Again, this planning was not just Army planning; it was joint planning involving JSPS, PPBS, and JOPS.

In World War II, the United States had a War Department. After the war, it had a Defense Department. But defense has been taking place farther and farther from our shores. Indeed, our European strategy is called "forward defense." The hope is that it works as deterrence. But it also requires an actual capacity to respond, which requires pre-positioning or rapid deployment. In 1990 (before the Gulf War), planners were pleased with the military's modernization but far less pleased with its capacity for rapid deployment.[55]

The Chair of the JCS has responsibility for assessing threats to the United States and for proposing national-security objectives and the military strategy and force capabilities necessary to support that strategy. Thus risk assessment is (or should be) the foundation for the entire planning process. However, in 1990 there was no reconsideration of "risk," no reconsideration of probability, just a continued assumption that the United States should maintain its strength. If it did, it could do whatever was needed, even if requirements and capabilities were "mis-matched." The focus, then, was on seeking to continue to increase capabilities—not on reassessing risk.

Exercises to consolidate learning followed the lessons on planning. One exercise involved the restructuring of an infantry division to a mechanized division, which included the elimination of one brigade. The assignment was not just to achieve the goal, but also to assess the impact of such restructuring in a variety of arenas and to the "second and third" order. A second exercise involved crisis planning for an overseas deployment.

The last set of lessons, Block 4, concerned campaign planning and theater operations. The scale was large, but the plan for a massive effort was not the only thing 1990 planning called for. Indeed, the first lesson considered LICs, which included peacekeeping operations and antiterrorism and counterinsurgency missions. (Peacekeeping and antiterrorism were new since 1985. Anti-terrorism got the bulk of attention because it was considered the most difficult.) The method involved mastery of Field Manual 100-20 on LICs (1988) and the study of three cases: Venezuela, El Salvador, and the Philippines. The possibility that drug interdiction could become a fourth category of LIC was also raised.

Special Operations Forces (SOFs) are a special, strategic instrument under the command of a CINC that can be used across the spectrum of conflict; they can be vital to both Air-Land Battle and to low intensity conflicts. SOFs can be especially valuable when the use of conventional forces is inappropriate, infeasible, or premature.[56] Students studied F 31-20, "Doctrine for Special Forces Operations," but did not engage in either case studies or exercises related to this topic.

The remainder of the course was directed to the study of the theater-level campaign and to the planning of such a campaign. The first lesson examined command and control—the ways in which organization, command relationships, and information-acquisition and decision-making processes affect the exercise of authority and the giving of direction. Emphasis was given to the need for centralized control but decentralized execution of strategy. The effect of personality and personal style on command was discussed, as were the difficulties of joint and combined campaigns. Finally, how the Soviet Union managed command and control issues was examined.

Neither Napoleon nor Hitler got "sustainment."[57] The U.S. Army hopes never to make their mistake by incorporating "sustainment" requirements into the earliest planning. The lesson itself is typical. Each individual prepared a set of "sustainment principles" based on the readings. The seminar was then divided into two groups, which consolidated the views of group members. Then, each group presented to or briefed the other; finally, the seminar examined the case study of the Russo-Japanese War to see whether the principles they had developed explained the events of that war.

The topic of deception had a lesson of its own. In the massive organization for Air-Land Battle, deception may seem an unlikely element of planning, but strategists see it as having had great value historically, and Army Field Manuals, Bulletins, and other writings highlight its importance. Traditional lack of support for its use was explained by the difficulty of achieving deception, especially at the theater level; the question of ethics was also taken into consideration.

Another topic commanding a lesson of its own was intelligence collection, which has as its primary purpose Intelligence Preparation of the Battlefield (IPB) to identify the enemy's "center of gravity" that, if successfully attacked, will lead to a "satisfactory" conclusion. These lessons rely heavily on Army Field Manuals and authoritative documents. It was noted that even in combined efforts, intelligence remained "a national responsibility." Thus, the question was asked, "What ethical implications are inherent in the dissemination restrictions on intelligence within alliances or among one's own forces?"

Only then did students begin to think about the duties of the CINC, to think about how strategy is translated into plans and into operations, and to think about how to obtain the capabilities (personnel, equipment, mobility) necessary to execute plans. The CINC is the commander of a theater and gets his direction from the NCA through the Chair of the JCS, and in combined action, from alliance authority.[58] He must also consider the media and the combination of U.S. military forces available to him. His duty is to develop campaign plans that lead to the realization of, the practice of, the "operational art."

Following these three core courses, students participated in two eight-week blocks of advanced courses, taking four courses in each block. Students had a choice of some fifty or sixty courses from which to select seven electives. The eighth course was required. It was "Regional Strategic Appraisals."[59] The regions were: the Soviet Union and Eastern Europe, which was still seen as presenting "the most serious threat to the United States. Containment and the principles of strength, dialogue and realism remain key policy considerations as the United States cautiously observes the limited change occurring in the Soviet Union";[60] the Middle East, where past policy has been governed by support for Israel's security, access to oil, and the minimization of Soviet influence; Asia, or the Pacific west of Hawaii, including Japan, China, Korea, Vietnam, Thailand—all the way to Pakistan and India—which was seen largely as a location for U.S.–Soviet competition; the Americas; and sub-Saharan Africa, "a mystery to most Americans" and likely to remain "towards the bottom of the list of United States global interests."

Again, the electives ranged from skills courses, such as writing for publication, to small research seminars. The elective courses were arranged under five themes: National Security Policy and Strategy; Regional Studies and International Security Issues; Military Strategy, Doctrine, Operations, Planning, and Wargaming; Raising, Equipping, and Sustaining an Army; and Command and Leadership. Students were expected to "balance" their selections.[61]

One special program was also (in part) an Advanced Studies course: the Advanced Warfighting Studies Program. This program for selected students, who must be approved by the faculty and the commandant, runs from mid-October through April. It counts as an Advanced

Course in each of the two terms but is an add-on from October through December.[62]

Course 4: Global Theater Strategy Application

The school year neared its end with the fourth course of the core curriculum, "Global and Theater Strategy Application." This was followed immediately by the National Security Seminar and by graduation. Course 4 synthesized all that had gone before. Students first developed global and regional military strategies. They then participated in a force-planning exercise in which they detailed the requirements (and risks if requirements were not met) for executing their strategies. Students were introduced to "the World of 1992" (near- and midterm campaign planning being the requirement, second- and third-order effects of each decision being highlighted). Scenarios were presented for low-, mid-, and high-intensity conflicts, and it was the students' job, through analysis, simulation, and exercises, to work out appropriate policies.

The four-day low-intensity-conflict exercise involved terrorist and guerrilla activities in the Philippines and Central America.[63] It emphasized the military's supportive role, applications of nonmilitary forms of power, and the other U.S. agencies active in the region of a LIC. The six-day mid-intensity conflicts used Saudi Arabia and Korea as locales for planning a conventional military confrontation at a distance, with two simultaneous conflicts and with combined forces. The eight-day high-intensity scenario was a crisis with the Soviet Union and its allies. Issues included deterrence, first use of nuclear weapons, de-escalation, and war termination. The role-playing and decision-making levels were the NCA, the National Security Council, the Department of State and Department of Defense, the JCS, and the CINCs. Substantial support came from the Center for Strategic War Gaming, located in a 1761 mill.[64]

THE MILITARY STUDIES PROGRAM

Like the core curriculum, the yearlong Military Studies Program was required of all students. Unlike most of the rest of the curriculum, the Military Studies Program involved mostly individual and written studies.[65] Topics were selected as early as August, and papers or projects had to be completed by late March. A 124-page list of possible topics, with a possible adviser for each one, covered topics that ranged from "The Impact on the U.S. and U.S. Army Chaplaincy Resulting from the Entry of Moslem and Buddhist Chaplains" to "Industrial Mobilization" and "Prospects for an Increased U.S.–Japanese Role in the Defense of Northeast Asia." Topics were proposed from all Carlisle units and from the Army Staff and other Army components. The studies sometimes are published; sometimes they are forwarded to appropriate decision makers; sometimes they win prizes—and sometimes they are a disappointment. Term papers are not part of most officers' recent activities.

It is hard to convey how many and how distinguished were the speakers at the Army War College over the course of a year. The Commandant's Lecture Series alone listed almost one speaker a week (attendance required). Most weeks featured two outside speakers. Most were military. The majority were Army. Still, the list included Barry Commoner, Newt Gingrich, Marine Lieutenant-General Carl Mundy, and Senator Arlen Specter, as well as the Army Generals Norman Schwarzkopf, Gordon Sullivan, and Max Thurman. Students were not, however, exposed to even moderately left-of-center views. One doubts that students were "provoked" by any of the speakers.

The leadership curriculum focused on the senior experience, with particular attention to the human dimensions of combat. An important assignment was the "white paper" presenting a personal philosophy of command, leadership, and management.

Between 1985 and 1990, the "War, National Policy, and Strategy" course was completely revised. The number of lessons was reduced from fifty-seven to thirty-seven; the number of lectures was reduced from twenty-eight to fourteen; the number of study periods was increased from two to eight; and increased emphasis was given to active learning.[66] Soviet studies was increased in 1990 but would be reduced the following year because of the need to give more coverage to LICs, arms control, and countering narcotics. An important theme for the following year would be the future and its requirement for alternative strategic concepts in "the dramatically changed world we are experiencing." Ethics remained a central theme in 1989–90 and was raised as an issue in virtually every lesson.

This was the year Regional Studies Appraisals became a required advanced course; the lengthy bibliographic materials and format provided for regional analyses were also new. The USAWC vision was becoming even more global.

The Department of Military Strategy, Planning, and Operations emphasized the interdepartmentalism of the 1990 curriculum, which contrasted with previous years. Also, making Course 4 almost exclusively applications was new. Still to be developed, though, were further teaching and applications of joint doctrine; in spite of Goldwater–Nichols, much of the curriculum remained very Army. Although there was a high level of satisfaction about using the application course as the culmination of the year's activity, it did run up against end-of-the-year distractions.

Student evaluations of the year are interesting.[67] In assessing the year, 69 percent of the students believed the course load was "about right," although 20 percent found it "heavy." Half found reading and writing requirements about right, but 30 percent believed they should be reduced. The various courses were rated on a five-point scale. In the core curriculum, "The Senior Leader," "War, National Policy, and Strategy," and the Regional Strategic Appraisals were rated 3.5 or higher. "Implementing National Military Strategy" and "Global and Theater Strategy Application" received ratings of only 3.2 and 3.3. The advanced (elective) courses received the highest rating, at 4.2. The National Security Seminar scored 3.5. The New York City trip rated 3.4, and the Washington, D.C., trip rated 3.6. Among the voluntary programs, high scores went to the Health and Physical Fitness Programs, the International Fellows Program, the Advanced Warfighting Studies Program, and the Battlefield Ride Program. Lower scores went to the Military Family Program and the Military History Lecture Series.

Responses to an item querying the degree to which the curriculum fulfilled its sixteen stated objectives ranged from 4.0 (for understanding the role of the military in a democracy)[68] to 3.8 (for thinking strategically and understanding second- and third-order effects) to 3.3 (being self-motivated), with most around the 3.6 mark.

As noted, the war colleges give serious attention to educational methodology and, in particular, to "active" learning. However, when students rated the methodologies, the lowest score went to exercises

(3.0), followed closely by written assignments, both of which are considered "active." The highest went to seminar discussions (4.3), followed by guest speakers. Still, comments made it clear that excellent seminar discussions are difficult to achieve and that such discussions are prone to slip into opinionated debate or passivity. Case studies, faculty lectures, and required reading all scored 3.5. Fewer exercises and less writing were recommended by some 30 percent of the class.[69]

Students thought that grades might have increased "work" but not learning. At their age, rank, and experience, pride and peer pressure were deemed sufficient motivation. Still, a number of students would have appreciated more regular and thoughtful feedback.

Most students found the year valuable. Negative comments about the curriculum tended to focus on guest speakers who gave "Rotary Club" talks and the fact that too many of them were "party men." They noted a lack of controversy, a lack of learning about joint operations, and apparent inconsistencies in the requirements of the Military Studies Program. (They also pointed out that papers had to be completed while students were taking their eight advanced studies courses, which also had writing requirements.)

By 1990, the organization of the core curriculum had been simplified. Instead of ten courses, four phases, and eight themes, the curriculum consisted of four courses and four themes. Both the 1985 and the 1990 curricula began with self-assessment, with consideration of the requirements of senior leadership, and with the design of an individual learning plan for the year. Each then moved to a study of war, to an examination of the U.S. political system, and to consideration of national-security strategy. Clausewitz was basic to the historical study of strategy; in addition, each student presented an analytical, biographical study of a famous strategist.

In 1985, more was done with the study of U.S. values and culture than in 1990; in 1990, there was more material on U.S. government processes and also on domestic issues (ills). Both curricula devoted a large block of time to teaching the arcane and confusing planning process by which national military strategy is translated into personnel, equipment, plans, and action. Both also emphasized the discrepancy between strategic commitments and resources. By 1990, the curriculum had experienced changes due to Goldwater–Nichols, but students still reported inadequate education about "jointness." Materials on the Soviet Union de-emphasized "threat" and emphasized "change" and "the unknown." In both 1985 and 1990, the full spectrum of warfare was reviewed, but nuclear strategy and deterrence received less attention in 1990, whereas LICs loomed large and peacekeeping was introduced. Perhaps, the major difference though, was the expanded period for electives—from the beginning of January to mid-April. Note, too, that electives were the part of the curriculum given the highest rating by students. Finally, although questions were standard in each lesson, it would be hard to describe the curriculum as "provocative."

8   The Peacetime Curriculum

A NEAT COMPARISON would be the curricula for the classes of 1985, 1990, and 1995, and so it was planned. However, I actually spent the 1995–96 year at the Army War College working in the Peacekeeping Institute and the first semester of the year 1996–97 as a student-participant observer with that class as a member of Seminar 2. Thus, it seems only sensible to sacrifice some system in order to capitalize on my experience. Thus, the account in this chapter is a combined account. The core curriculum discussed will be that of the class that graduated in 1997—the class in which I actually participated. But the overview of the year will draw on my observations and the school's records for the class that graduated in 1996. I was also present for this year (and keeping track of events), but I was not a part of that class. The year 1995 will not, after all, be the subject of this chapter.

THE TIMES

By 1996, the world scene was very different from that of 1990. The Soviet Union was no longer a military threat. In fact, the Soviet Union per se no longer existed. However, its nuclear weapons remained a matter of concern, as did the political instability and economic disarray of Russia, the Soviet Union's principal successor state. In fact, it was the weakness, not the strength, of our former adversary that made U.S. officials nervous. This led the United States to become involved in a number of agreements and partnerships with Russia, including the Partnership for Peace, which entailed substantial U.S.–Russian military-to-military relations. Few American or Russian officers could have anticipated such close cooperation with their decades-long nemesis. Few could have imagined officers from the Soviet Union as students at the Army War College, but by 1992, an officer from the former Soviet bloc had enrolled, as had an officer from what was formerly part of the Soviet Union.

In addition, the United States had recently enjoyed great success in the Gulf War (1991). That victory,[1] which claimed the lives of fewer than

150 Americans (in battle), came after one month of bombing and just 100 hours of ground warfare. Importantly, the conflict demonstrated the capacities of several new weapon systems, achieved a combined operation with diverse allies, realized a mostly smooth joint operation among the U.S. services, and provided a morale boost for a military that felt it had demonstrated its full recovery from its Vietnam loss.[2]

However, in short order, the commander-in-chief of that successful war was replaced by President William Jefferson Clinton, who was suspect for his non-service during the Vietnam War, and who promptly stirred up a hornet's nest with his decision to permit open homosexuals to serve in the military. Also, during the next few years the military would experience substantial downsizing. Since the military has such high personnel turnover, this was relatively easy to bring about by reducing the number of new recruits. However, a reduced force also meant that fewer senior officers would be needed, which meant that officers suddenly saw opportunities for promotion diminished. As promotions became more competitive, the "zero defects" problem became a matter for lunchtime discussion.[3]

What soldiers (sailors, marines, and airmen) do in peacetime is prepare. And they prepare for the worst—for the calamitous "big one" (or for two simultaneous regional conflicts). They train for action and expect that action to include the use of force. However, most of the action the U.S. military has seen since 1991 has been small in scale and has involved little force. This is because the U.S. military has been doing a lot of peacekeeping.[4] Sites have included Rwanda, Somalia, Bosnia, Haiti, and Kosovo. Some who see the military as dedicated to "winning the nation's wars" see peacekeeping as distracting, and even as debilitating.[5] Others see it as the only task available, a task that can be a form of training, and as the kind of task the military has frequently been asked to do in the past. They conclude that the services should learn to do peacekeeping well and willingly.[6]

The other issue that captured attention in the mid-1990s was sexual harassment and sexual misconduct. Drama was first injected into the issue by Air Force Pilot Kelly Flinn's refusal to go quietly after lying to Air Force officials about, and continuing, an adulterous affair with the spouse of a married enlisted woman. It gained steam with charges at the Army's Aberdeen Proving Ground of harassment by Army trainers of those they were supposed to be training, and with charges leveled against the Army's sergeant-major, its highest-ranking enlisted man. It culminated[7] with the loss of an officer's appointment as Chair of the Joint Chiefs of Staff because of an adulterous affair he had had a decade earlier while in the process of a divorce.[8]

This, then, was the climate in which the class of 1997 unpacked their household goods, enrolled their children in Carlisle schools, and began their year of "senior military education."

THE PEACETIME CORE CURRICULUM—1995–96–97

In 1995–96–97, the core curriculum was still composed of some one hundred classroom days and lasted from early August to early January. Although some new course content appeared, the global uncertainties facing the nation had not led to a more open and varied curriculum. More than half the students' time continued to be shared and prescribed.[9] Each of the three academic departments continued to teach a core course of approximately equal length. One small difference was that in 1995 and 1996, the three departmental courses were taught sequentially. In 1997 the course, taught by the Department of Command, Leadership, and Management was divided into two sections, becoming Courses 1 and 3 of a four-course sequence. This had the effect of dividing what had been called "Responsible Command" into two pieces: "Strategic Leadership" (with themes related to command and leadership) and "Joint Systems and Processes" (with themes related to management).

Course 1: Strategic Leadership

This course continued to begin with a focus on the individual. Each student was asked to examine his or her strengths and weaknesses and to design an individual learning plan for the year that established both goals and the routes to their achievement. This included the selection of advanced courses, the choice of topic for a research project, skill development, and planned family and community activities.[10] A variety of tests helped the student to understand his or her preferences (Myers-Briggs) and style (Kirton Adaption–Innovation Inventory).[11] Next, attention was directed to the seminar itself and to the building of peer relationships among the sixteen members.[12] Specific lesson titles included Adult and Seminar Learning; Individual Awareness; Group

Dynamics; Creative Thinking; and Critical Thinking—as done both by individuals in isolation and as a group.

In the first day's seminar, self-introductions invariably began with telling about the student's family. (Only one student was single.) The second topic was almost always one's military job and experience; if there was a third, it was hobbies. Another form of introduction occurred early in the term when students came to seminar and discovered cards with their Myers-Briggs scores at their places.[13] The cards were set up facing outward so that class members could quickly register both individual typologies and, very important, those of the class as a whole. Notably, in the entire seminar there was only one "P" who saw "possibilities" in a situation; the rest were all "J"s prepared to "judge" (and, therefore, act). Again, in the whole group there was only one "F" who made decisions based on feelings. The rest were "T"s who relied on reason. This suggested the group would make the many seminar decisions that had to be made both quickly and with little regard for feelings. This prediction was borne out: Seminar uniforms for intramurals were selected in three minutes flat. Also, the Kirton Adaption-Innovation Inventory scores for the group showed that its members were highly adaptive, suggesting that innovation was not going to be a strong point.

The lesson on creative thinking offered specific techniques for overcoming common barriers to creative thinking and discussed how paradigms ("frames") both help to make sense of the world and to limit perception. In Creative Thinking and Critical Thinking,[14] the tenor of the lesson was similar to that offered in business schools. The goal was to improve thinking, but decisions were expected. This differs from what it is meant by creative and critical thinking in a doctoral program, where students have the luxury of deeper and longer contemplation and, although they may have to report, do not necessarily have to decide. The popularity of the two "thinking" lessons was demonstrated by a large turnout for voluntary noon programs on both subjects.

The course then shifted to the strategic perspective.[15] This is really what the Army War College is all about: getting students to see the biggest and longest-term picture; getting them to understand the nature, extent, and relative criticalness of U.S. interests; getting them to understand the nonmilitary forms of power available to pursue national purposes; getting them to expect the unexpected and to perform in an environment that is "volatile, uncertain, complex, and ambiguous";[16] getting them to appreciate the rapidity and magnitude of change and to anticipate future changes in technology, demography, economics, ecology, and, yes, politics.[17]

With the environment changing so rapidly, it was acknowledged that changes in the military were likely to be necessary, so a study of organizational cultures and of techniques for leading and managing change became part of the curriculum.[18] Special attention was given to evolving and implementing a strategic vision. At this point in the semester, the Army's chief of staff addressed the class. The seminars then assessed his performance in light of their discussions about strategic leadership and, in particular, the importance of projecting a vision.[19]

The next concern was ethics. This topic was approached in two ways. One was a discussion of military codes of conduct. It was noted that there was no single U.S. code and no single code for an Army officer. West Point has "Duty, Honor, Country."[20] Officers have an oath of office and a commission. Doctrine is set out in field manuals. And there is the Uniform Code of Military Justice's reference to "conduct unbecoming an officer and a gentleman" and a Code of Conduct for POWs. But there is no single shared code equivalent to, for instance, the Boy Scout pledge. The second approach was to explore the concept of "just war."[21] Two scenarios were provided: One concerned the use of nuclear weapons (where no possibility of discrimination exists and where there is certain to be debate about proportionality); the second considered interventions in operations other than war.[22] The discussion was at first general, then devolved into a consideration of the special responsibilities of the strategic leader who must be prepared to give orders that may guarantee the deaths of American servicemen (and some women), and who will also have to advise the seniormost civilian authorities on military matters.

A strategic leader is also expected to create an "ethical climate" for those under his or her command. Three illustrations were provided of what can happen when a strategic leader fails to do this. They were the killing of Archbishop Thomas Becket by followers of King Henry II of England, the Watergate affair, and the Iran–Contra affair.[23] "Ollieism,"[24] which occurs when a profound desire to please one's superior leads to the breaking of rules and even laws without the superior's specific direction or knowledge, was noted as particularly to be guarded against.

Equally serious were practices that bent, subverted, or overrode policies on the grounds that a senior officer has important duties that must not be thwarted or delayed. Again, setting the climate is seen as the responsibility of the commander, but it is also emphasized that a leader and manager must not get bogged down in conflicting ethical requirements.

Two other topics (lessons) that a civilian might not intuit as important to the curriculum were Group Decision-making and Consensus Building and Negotiations. Both reinforce the point that at the most senior levels, collaboration, cooperation, and agreement—or, at least, concurrence—become crucial to decision-making. It is not a matter of voting and majority rule, or of a solitary individuals' deciding and directing. The reality of high-level decision-making is that it is collective, and it may (or may not) get distorted as it moves through the organization. Further, there are second- and third-order consequences to be considered.[25] Again, the teaching materials were drawn from business,[26] and emphasis was given to better and less better ways of arriving at a collective decision.[27]

Course 1 concluded with an application: reports by students assessing the strategic skills of a historical leader. The list of twenty-four suggested names included Golda Meir and Margaret Thatcher, along with Martin Luther King, Jr., Francisco Franco, Adolf Hitler, and Woodrow Wilson. An "Alternate Sign-up Sheet" of mostly non-"Northern" leaders (which did, however, include Catherine the Great and Elizabeth I) added names such as Kemal Ataturk, Giap, Genghis Khan, and Hideki Tojo.[28] The 1995–97 lists are much broader than earlier lists. In my seminar, choices included Winston Churchill, Henry Ford, Margaret Thatcher (chosen by a man), Kemal Ataturk, Nelson Mandela, and Tecumseh. The female officer chose Hannibal. About a third of the first list were American military officers; the only two chosen were Chester Nimitz and Robert E. Lee. The reports were presented orally and in written form. Directions for the writing requirement of five to seven pages filled eight pages (admittedly widely spaced) and concluded with a logo whose message was "no bullshit."

Course 2: War, National Policy, and Strategy

This course was modified only slightly in 1995–97, although in 1997 the "environment" for strategy was specifically broken down into global and domestic environments (each of which included political, economic, and social trends). Twentieth-century case studies were given more emphasis than previously. Also, the strong emphasis on the difference among national-security policy, national-security strategy, and national military strategy was maintained. Each was examined—first in its present form, and second in its possible future formulations.

The course was an ambitious one, and one that could easily be part of a civilian curriculum. Indeed, three of the first five lessons involved all-class lectures.[29] One was given by Gary Guertner, Ph.D., the chair of the DNSS; one by Colonel Arthur Lykke, USA ret., author of the USAWC text *Military Strategy: Theory and Applications;* and one by Colonel Harry Summers, USA ret.[30]

Block 1, the first of five blocks in Course 2, was titled "War and the National Security Environment."[31] The new international environment was described as permitting a variety of choices for the United States, including isolationism, hegemony (Pax Americana, or primacy), collective security, and pragmatic and selective engagement.[32] What was said to be new to the strategic environment was the power of non-state actors, threats from small states, the transparency created by the cable network CNN and the World Wide Web, and global urbanization. What was said *not* to be new was famine and disaster, ever-changing technology, aggression, and ethnic or religious conflict.

The discussion of "realism" and "idealism" reviewed the assumptions and benefits of each "lens," but did not choose one as more accurate; nor did the discussion exclude consideration of national values[33] and national interests.[34] Values were described as slippery concepts that nevertheless are crucial to policy development and its implementation. Still, as soon as national interests and a national-security strategy have been defined, it is the military's job to develop a military strategy to support the security strategy.

Block 2, "National Security Policy and Decision-making," took on the American political decision-making process, which sets security strategy. The institutions examined were, first and in most detail, the U.S. Presidency, then the Congress, and finally the military itself.[35] Attention was given to the human actors; to the interagency process, with its principal committees, its deputies committees, and its interagency working groups; and to the National Security Council, the National Security Adviser, and the National Security Council staff. Various descriptions and explanations of the decision-making process, such as the rational actor and the organizational and bureaucratic models, were examined, and a case study of the fall of the Shah of Iran was used to assess the usefulness of the different models.

In discussing civil–military relations, time was allotted to consider President Clinton's early difficulties with the military. The nadir of that relationship involved Clinton's effort to legalize open homosexuals' participation in the military, an effort that was publicly resisted by the Chair of the JCS.[36] Discussion occurred, too, about how civilian service secretaries (and even service chiefs) have lost ground to the JCS Chair and his CINCs under the Goldwater–Nichols Act. Still, even with regard to military affairs, the president's primary conflict is rarely with the military; it is with Congress. Further, the mobilization of the bureaucracies of his own executive branch is no mean task.[37] These bureaucracies include the State Department, the Department of Defense, the National Security Council, the Central Intelligence Agency, and often the Department of the Treasury and the Department of Commerce.

The media is not part of the government system, of course, but it is understood as crucial to the military's relationship to civil society. In 1995–97, one whole day was devoted to the media, including a lecture by a distinguished journalist. Also, individual seminars held discussions with a member of the press; thus, there were twenty media guests-for-a-day. The dramatic stimulus for discussion of the effect of the press that year was the suicide of Admiral Jeremy Michael Boorda when he learned that he was to be interviewed by a journalist about whether he had worn ribbons to which he was not entitled.[38]

The block concluded with an exercise: the revision of U.S. policy toward Cuba. The setting was the rendering of a Supreme Court decision that the Helms Burton Act was unconstitutional. The intent was to integrate all that had gone before: that the United States participates in an international political arena; that war is political; that power takes a variety of forms; that strategy entails analysis of ends, ways, and means; that the legislative and executive branches of government have formal and informal ways of working; that the media is a player. In short, that all of the above affect the military's functioning.

Block 3 included "The Domestic Environment; New York City; and the U.N." (a peculiar pairing). After assessing the global environment, it may well be important to take a look at the domestic environment. And many officers *are* from small towns; perhaps they do need to know that the Big Apple is a part of the contemporary scene. But New York City is hardly typical, and the United Nations is anything but domestic.

Actually, the discussion was not of the domestic environment. That would have involved a lesson in sociology. It would have included statistical analyses of, for instance, income distribution, home ownership, church attendance, and health-care coverage. If historical data were used, it might prove or disprove the idea that society was "decaying." Instead, the focus was on "social problems . . . especially as they are manifested in urban American." (U. S. social "ills" were clearly linked to "urban America," as though drugs, AIDS, teen pregnancies, and murders, including multiple slayings, do not occur in small towns.)

The unit considered domestic issues particularly as they were debated in the 1996 (Clinton–Dole) presidential campaign, and outlined the contrasting positions of "liberals" and "conservatives."

It is not clear that the debate structure used for instruction in this unit (with students divided into teams of "conservatives" and "liberals") is the best way to reach either a sound analysis of domestic problems or possible solutions.[39] Also, it is not clear that a study of campaign rhetoric is a good way to grasp the views of the public. Campaigns may ostensibly be pitched to the "American people," but they are actually directed toward a small group of "swing" voters who are not already in one camp or the other. Further, the practice of government is geared to making things work and looks toward compromise. This is quite different from a campaign, which focuses only on winning. Wouldn't Gallup poll data, for instance, tell more about citizens' views than campaign rhetoric, which is cast as a debate between opposites? For instance, most U.S. citizens do not agree with either of the strong proponents in the debate on abortion policy. Amazingly, the subject of social problems and possible solutions was covered in a single lesson.[40]

The trip to New York City was a first for many in the seminar, and the first of any duration for others.[41] The trip involved a visit to Ellis Island, a half-day briefing on urban affairs,[42] a half day of visiting the missions of the International Fellows in the class, one day of small-group visits to a wide range of institutions,[43] and a half-day briefing at the United Nations by a U.S. Ambassador, a military adviser to the U.N. secretary-general, and the representative of the Russian Federation to the United Nations.

The preparation for the briefings included a lesson that assumed the importance of collective security but also concluded that the United Nations was so overextended that it could be overwhelmed and discredited "perhaps forever."[44] Much of the reading focused on the expanded number and versions of "peacekeeping" after 1990. (No note or particular use was made of the Army's own Peacekeeping Institute located at Carlisle.) Website documents provided background on the United Nations and on Clinton administration policy on participation in future peacekeeping operations. Some attention was given to possible reform of the United Nations, but little was said about the United States' failure to pay its dues or the views other countries have about the role the United States plays in the United Nations—views that would not necessarily be flattering. (They include " leader," "deadbeat," and "dictator." Also, although the American public may be unaware, other nations know that the United States has not ratified several U.N. conventions ratified by most other nations. These include conventions on discrimination against women, child soldiers, land mines, and a world criminal court. In fact, many U.N. members perceive the United States as acting not mutually or collectively but manipulatively.)

Block 4 turned to "Case Studies in Twentieth Century Strategy."[45] Finally, the historians had their chance at center stage. The analyses were framed around Clausewitz's trinity: the people, the military, and the government. Clausewitz's themes of war as art or science; the center of gravity; absolute and real war; total and limited war; the role of uncertainty; and the role of genius commanded particular attention.[46] The lecture on strategy by Arthur Lykke, a college favorite, was treated as doctrine on the subject of strategy. All received copies of the slides from his lecture; all also received a text prepared by Lykke.

The study of twentieth-century U.S. strategy began with an examination of three historical strategists: Sun Tzu, Niccolo Machiavelli, and Henri Jomini, men separated by many centuries.[47] A seminar lecture then laid out the developments in warfare and in European strategic thinking in the seventeenth through the nineteenth centuries. With World War I, students were asked to dig in. Warfare changed in that war. Railroads became crucial, although all armies still used horses; airplanes were first used; and the machine gun was introduced. But theory and strategy did not adapt, and the war was fought as a war of attrition— attrition so severe that the United Kingdom, for example, lost 20 percent of all men younger than forty-five. World War I, then, was used as an example of technological change occurring without a revision in doctrine or in military organization. It was described as an "incomplete revolution in military affairs" and an object lesson for discussion.

During the interwar years, theorists began to develop new strategies—but often separately for air, sea, and land power. The strategists can be seen as rivals, for each concluded that the shrinking military dollar should be spent quite differently. Admiral Alfred Thayer Mahan developed the concept of an offensive battle fleet that would engage the enemy at sea rather than cling to the shore. This necessitated globally distributed coaling stations and well-developed long-distance communications. However, even Mahan overlooked what would become the importance of amphibious landings and of submarines. The supporters of air war waxed eloquent about the destruction of enemies' centers of gravity—but included little discussion of the "just war" principles of discrimination, proportionality, and likelihood of success. The strategists of land warfare were determined that a strategy of attrition would not again drive military planning. They saw a need for rapid mobilization, troop mobility (including logistical support), and armored protection (the tank). Land-warfare theorists were also more likely to see the need for integrated planning with sea and air components.

World War II was no surprise. In fact, the United States had prepared a "Victory Plan" by 1941.[48] The lesson, though, emphasized that strategy requires continual adjustment, that it must not be static. Appropriately, the World War II case studies concentrated on how strategies evolved over time.

Waging World War II required cooperation among three strategic leaders with different ends, ways, and means: Winston Churchill, Joseph Stalin, and Franklin Roosevelt. The United Kingdom, the Soviet Union, and the United States agreed, though, that the Axis (Germany, Japan, and Italy) must be fought until defeated; that they must ally to bring about that defeat; and that defeating Germany would take priority. The leaders' strategies for the day after victory, however, were quite different, and the Soviet Union and the West almost immediately cast each other as the new "threat."

By 1950, U.S. Cold War strategy had been codified in National Security Council Document 68, prepared for the State Department by Paul H. Nitze.[49] This document described a United States threatened by, and determined to resist, communism. It concluded that meeting the Soviet challenge through economic and political competition was not enough. The United States had to rearm—even if this meant spending up to 20 percent of the gross national product on defense. The Soviets were no longer an ally but an active adversary. (Note that the Berlin blockade, the fall of China to Mao Zedong, a communist coup in Czechoslovakia, the Russian testing of an atomic weapon, and the invasion of South Korea all occurred at about this time. It was these events— particularly the invasion of South Korea—that made the decision to rearm politically feasible.)

Post–World War II U.S. strategy and resources were focused on Europe (NATO was founded in 1949), but the United States' next two wars were fought in Asia. They were different from the world wars; they were limited wars.[50] The American public and the American military had to come to terms with a new conception of war, in which winning did not imply surrender by, but negotiation with, the enemy. The Korean War was limited to the objective of keeping South Korea out of the communist orbit; it was also limited by policies of not engaging China in a land war and not using nuclear weapons.[51] Vietnam was limited by the means the United States was willing to use in South Vietnam's defense. Eventually, the United States withdrew rather than pursue a too costly or greatly escalated conflict. Needless to say, Vietnam became a major source of sometimes contradictory "lessons learned."

President Dwight Eisenhower, faced with a nuclear enemy, evolved a deterrence strategy based on mutually assured nuclear destruction. At the same time, however, the great powers tested each other through proxy wars, the most important being the conflict in Vietnam, where the leaders of both South Vietnam and the United States (Jack Kennedy) were murdered just as the war heated up. Nine years later, Richard Nixon and Henry Kissinger brought an end to that war with a strategy that was based neither on an assumed monolithic, conspiratorial communist threat, nor on the containment of communism. Instead, it was based on a classic balancing-of-power strategy. In this case, the balancing was of Europe, the United States, the USSR, China, and Japan.[52] Ending a war without winning—and by conventional measures, by losing—was not previously a part of U.S. strategic thinking. Conflict termination has since become a routine part of U.S. strategic thought. To most, Vietnam was a "strategic failure."[53]

With President Ronald Reagan, the classic form of the Cold War was resuscitated. But it came to an unexpected and sudden end. The Soviet Union overreached itself and dissolved. The United States now had to shape a strategy without the existence of a specific threat.[54] Although strategy continued to be based on U.S. interests, once survival was no longer the issue, discussion of the importance of lesser interests was less likely to yield consensus.

The Gulf War has been judged a "strategic success." New doctrines based on new technology, on mobility, and on combined forces were brought together. U.S. weapons and troops trained for a Soviet attack came from Germany prepared. Further, many troops had trained in the desert conditions of the Army's National Training Center. The Goldwater–Nichols Act had been implemented, putting the regional CINCs, not the service chiefs, in charge. Allies, many of whom had even more vital interests than the United States (which, after all, had oil and was not in danger of being invaded), worked in smooth coalition. The people and the military were united in formal votes in the House and Senate in support of the war. Unanimous international support came from the U.N. Security Council. Russia cooperated. Fourteen of the Arab League's twenty-one members joined the coalition. The media reported live but followed military rules. The many requisites of the Weinberger–Powell doctrine were fulfilled. These included having a clearly defined goal,[55] having public support,[56] having all necessary resources, and doing the job and leaving.[57] (The careful planning and execution of strategy was made possible by Iraq's permitting the United States to have all the time it needed to fulfill each step of its preparation.)

Block 5 brought "Current and Future National Security and Military Strategies" under scrutiny. A primary goal of this block was to reinforce the difference between the national-security strategy and the military strategy that supports it. A second goal was to be sure students understood current, formally announced strategies, then to get them to consider how future strategies might differ from today's. Elements of military strategy related to weapons of mass destruction (WMDs) included deterrence, arms control, nonproliferation, and (new) counter-proliferation.[58]

Formulation of the National Security Strategy, a "vision" based on national values and interests that takes into account both predictions of the future and realizable possibilities, is required of the executive by the Goldwater–Nichols Act. The National Security Strategy tends to be a short statement produced by a long and bureaucratic process. The strategy published in 1996 was to "engage and enlarge" the community of market democracies.[59] The National Military Strategy is supposed to support the National Security Strategy, but the military requirements for support are hardly clear;[60] further, commitments appear nearly open-ended.

Strategy was once oriented toward deterring aggression, but many current conflicts are related not to aggression but to civil war or secession. International law is quite clear about aggression but has little to say about secession. In addition, many of the current problems are created by masses of refugees fleeing their countries. Their crossing of national boundaries might be said to violate the sovereignty of receiving nations. Recent remedies for such mass movement of populations, though, have involved violation of the sovereignty of the nation they fled, for example, Kosovo/Serbia. Traditionally, violating sovereignty has been taboo in international law. Those who must develop military strategies are thus mired in an ambiguity not of their making. Congress has mandated that the president provide strategic clarity, but that clarity does not always exist. Even so, Army War College students are asked to be visionary.[61] With no well-defined National Security Strategy in place, their task of developing a support strategy is difficult, and thinking tends to focus on new capabilities, particularly elegant and expensive weapons and technology that will lead to "winning."

The exercise for this block was the seminar's working together to formulate a new National Military Strategy, taking into account such details as jointness, the federal budget, and risks to be taken. A clear step-by-step process for the development of that strategy was provided in an appendix to the course directive.[62] This was followed by a presentation by an admiral, a JCS staff member, concerning the issues being worked on by the staff there. Those included the Quadrennial Defense Review (QDR), the Unified Command Plan (the "constitution" of the armed forces), the Overseas Plan,[63] Operations Other Than War, and new technology.[64] The last lesson in the course looked to the future: the year 2010.[65]

Course 3: Joint Systems and Processes[66]

Joint Systems and Processes is a nineteen-day attempt to make the defense and military bureaucracies and the way they do their work comprehensible. The course is also essential to the fulfilling of phase one of joint education. Its introduction to the multiple, intermeshing Pentagon systems is an essential introduction for those students whose next assignments will be in Washington. By the time the course is completed, all students are expected to know "how the Army runs."

The study of jointness begins with the history of its development, particularly during World War II, when U.S. forces were influenced by their British allies, whose services already planned together. The Defense Reorganization Act of 1947 and its 1949 and 1958 amendments were intended to reduce interservice rivalry and strengthen civilian control. Under Presidents Kennedy and Johnson, there was a proliferation of joint groups. However, these were cut back under President Nixon. Only with the Goldwater–Nichols legislation of 1986 did significant change finally occur. One change involved the mandated teaching of jointness in professional military education; another required joint training and assignments for those seeking promotion to top positions; a third involved increasing the size of the JCS staff to more than 1,600 and placing it under the direction of the Chair of the JCS, who was to provide advice to the executive, consulting the other joint chiefs only as she or he considered appropriate.

Institutions created to enhance joint planning include the Joint Requirements Oversight Council (JROC) and the Joint Warfighting Capabilities Assessment (JWCA) process. The relationship among the various implementers of military strategy—specifically, the NCA (the president and secretary of defense), the OSD, the Chair of the JCS and the JCS Staff, the Service Chiefs, and the CINCs—and the content of the current Unified Command Plan received two days of attention. Care was taken to distinguish among responsibility to advise, responsibility to support, and authority. The distinction among Combatant Command, Operational Control, and Tactical Control and Support was also made clear. In short, the complicated rules of the game were laid out and, one hopes, mastered.

Planning is a military specialty—such a specialty that there is a whole set of systems for planning. The Chair of the JCS's Joint Strategic Planning System (JSPS) concentrates on the "ways" strategy could be implemented. It brings together the services' force-development planning (which produces a Program Objective Memorandum, the POM) and the operational planning of the unified commanders (which yields the

Integrated Priority List, the IPL), and ensures that the two accord with national strategy and JCS direction. The JSPS functions in the midterm and sets forth the ideal. One of its four products is the Joint Strategic Capabilities Plan (JSCP).[67] This represents the marching orders for the combatant CINCs. The JSCP also furnishes service-component commanders direction for the preparation of their Mission Essential Task List (METL).

The Chief's Joint Operation Planning and Execution System (JOPES) concentrates on the "ends." JOPES defines the threat, constructs a strategy, and develops an action plan (sure to be revised once operations begin). JOPES involves both deliberate and crisis action planning and gives guidance to the CINCs.[68]

The Chair of the JCS has two further tools for pursuing jointness. One is the Joint Requirements Oversight Council (JROC), and the second is the Joint Warfighting Capabilities Assessment (JWCA) process. These are designed to permit a view of the total capabilities of the U.S. military and to uncover both redundancies and deficiencies.[69] These tools assist the CJCS in preparing the Chairman's Program Recommendations (CPR), which are presented to the Secretary of Defense for use in planning and budgeting.[70]

The Office of the Secretary of Defense's Planning, Programming and Budgeting System (PPBS) ensures the availability of "means. " It operates in the "nearer term" and allocates resources among the services.[71]

Reality is injected into the account of this intricate, acronymic, and seemingly unintelligible system by noting that what is supposed to happen does not always happen. For instance, although the National Military Strategy is required annually, the JSPS failed to produce it from January 1992 to February 1995.[72] While students read policy memoranda and excerpts from Title Ten, they are again informed that prescribed form is not always followed, and that once action begins, plans must be continuously revised.

When the Army gets down to its own planning, it does so for four different-size forces: the DPG (Defense Planning Guidance) force, the POM (Program Objective Memorandum) force, the budgeted force, and the current force. Once again, one message is that the formal and the actual may be far apart. Overall, teaching at the USAWC seems to emphasize doing things as one is supposed to. One has the sense that the other services think about Pentagon structures and processes as mere vehicles (or impediments) to accomplishing their purpose. A second message is that planning and management are tools for change.

The dizzying array of Pentagon bureaucracies and processes (both made even more opaque to the uninitiated by the use of acronyms) was made somewhat more human by a speaker from the JCS Strategy Division. In his address, the visitor gave Polonius-like advice: Think big. Think beyond. Knowledge is power. So is recommending. Memory is nonexistent. Pace is both that of molasses and a speeding bullet. Build consensus. Choose your battles. Things will change.[73]

After exploring "how the Army works," Course 3 concludes with a study of the acquisition system,[74] the nation's industrial base,[75] logistics, and the federal and defense-department budgets.

Grasping the rules of the many defense systems does not mean that one has grasped the whole picture, though. Emphasis is also given to the importance of thinking through second- and third-order effects and considering the goals of "stakeholders" who influence the system even though they have no official role.[76] The key lesson? The take-home message? That the next challenges will not be predicted; that the United States will face mostly "improbable" challenges.

Course 4: Implementing National Military Strategy[77]

Course 4 remained very similar for the academic years 1995–96–97. One module of five lessons emphasized planning for theater strategic warfare, including planning with partners in an alliance or coalition,[78] planning when an opponent may possess weapons of mass destruction, and planning for effective theater organization, command, and control. The exercise involved planning a campaign in North Africa (Libya) and planning for post-Castro Cuba. The case study was the Arab–Israeli War of 1973.[79]

A module of fifteen lessons examined the organization of a Joint Task Force and support to the CINCs with combatant commands. Seven lessons systematically considered, first, the specific and unique support each service could offer a CINC, and then how that support could best be employed.[80] Senior officers from each service made presentations to the class as a whole, then seminar members (prepped by their services) briefed their seminars on their own services.

A final element in planning is development of the Rules of Engagement (ROEs). ROEs are sometimes seen as limitations on military effectiveness. However, they are also intended to ensure that the purposes of the civilian authority are implemented. Sometimes they are designed to prevent escalation, which means that they could also be described as a force-protection measure. Appropriately, ROEs have political and legal components; they are not only military directives. They become especially difficult, though, in multinational operations because different countries may issue different ROEs to soldiers working side by side. Sometimes ROEs represent an element of strategy and are therefore classified. However, war fighters need clear and useful ROEs. These contrasting requirements can create a dilemma.

A final (applicatory) module focused on campaign plans. Four days were given to the study of Operations Other Than War (OOTW), and to an OOTW exercise involving post-Castro Cuba. The discussion of OOTW suggests that such operations are different and a distraction from "fighting and winning the nation's wars." However, if the military's *real* job is to deter, then OOTW should not be seen as "other" and as requiring a different "mental framework."[81] It is true that political goals may be clearer in OOTW, but all wars have political goals. It may be that an exit strategy has special prominence, and that military organizations must work closely and cooperatively with civilian organizations—governmental and nongovernmental, national and international—but these considerations are part of all strategic-level thinking. Perhaps the issue is not actually OOTW itself, but the fact that many soldiers see these operations as peripheral rather than vital to the national interest. They see their purpose as one of serving more critical needs. If this is the case, the executive, the commander-in-chief, needs to explain better the purpose of each mission, or perhaps reconsider them—to ask what, precisely, is the national interest?[82]

The course concluded with a campaign-planning exercise for a theater war in North Africa, further developing the scenario introduced early in the course.

A new concern was the possible use of weapons of mass destruction against U.S. troops by countries that are unable to match the United States in a conventional military conflict. Planners now assume that some twenty-four countries may have offensive chemical-warfare programs; fourteen, biological-warfare programs; and sixteen, nuclear-weapons programs.[83]

Perhaps the most difficult part of Course 4 was getting students to think about the nature of future wars. The two documents used to help students do this were "Joint Vision 2010" and TRADOC Pam 525-5, *Force XXI Operations*. The doctrine prescribed the following: "protect, scan, strike, strike again, swarm, scatter, and refit." Intelligence and its many sources were discussed as a tricky element but one that is as essential to an OOTW as it is to the planning of a theater campaign. Also, it was noted that in the era of the Internet, new attention must be paid to the analysis of Open Source Intelligence (OSINT), in terms of what we can access and what others can access about us. Much of the future was envisioned as operating in a new technological world, yet students were also warned that the likeliest enemies of the future would be "warriors" whose goal was spoils, who were lawless and without national allegiance, who relished violence and were without regard for order—in short, the antithesis both of our military and of our usually hypothesized opponents.[84]

THE CORE CURRICULUM IN THE SECOND AND THIRD TERMS

The second term's fifty days included three components; everyone participated in two of them: the ten-day Strategic Crisis Exercise (SCE),and the Regional Strategic Appraisals (RSAs). The SCE is an extensively planned and supported exercise involving all the students, most of the faculty and staff, and a number of distinguished invitees. The facilities and support staff at the new Center for Strategic Leadership serve not only the USAWC but also the Army as a whole. Roles in the SCE range from president, ambassadors, and cabinet members, to U.N. and nongovernmental organization representatives. The SCE is a strategic-level, free-play, "research" game that focuses on the period 2020–25. Interestingly, none of the results of the game played in 1997 were anticipated.[85]

As in previous years, seminar students are divided into six regional groupings to develop their Regional Strategic Appraisals. Each group has a minimum of two from each seminar, and each seminar is later briefed by its own members, who have participated in the six different groups. Thus, the students get a global perspective. While students prepared short research papers on a narrow topic, the text for the course was the National Defense University's Institute for National Strategic

Studies's "Strategic Assessment 1995"—not quite, but almost, an in-house text.

In the third term, all students completed a Strategy Research Paper[86] and participated in the week-long, end-of-term National Security Seminar organized for civilian visitors. In the second term, students elected three advanced courses of their choice; in the fourth term, they elected four. Some of the military planning and operations courses extend over both terms.

The advanced courses are clustered under the three academic departments—DCLM, DNSS, and DMPSO—or are sponsored by Communicative Arts, the Center for Strategic Leadership, or the History Institute. In the first term of spring 1997, about sixty courses were listed. Six sections of the Advanced Warfighting Studies Program were enrolled.[87] The other most popular courses were "Personal Affairs Management for Strategic Leaders," "Professional Ethics for Senior Leaders," and "Theater Strategy and Campaign Planning." There were not many takers for "Weapons of Mass Destruction," "Case Studies in Center of Gravity Determination," or "From Eben Emael to Entebbe." There was only moderate enthusiasm for the courses on peacekeeping, and international students made up a high percentage of the enrollees. Toastmasters Club, the Current Affairs Panel, and Directed Study (reading) were among the for-credit options.

The disintegration of the major threat to the United States at the beginning of the decade made it clear that new strategic thinking was in order.[88] But there was not much change at the U.S. Army War College. The students, the faculty, the organization of the college, and the structure of the curriculum closely resembled their counterparts of 1990. The tenor of the core curriculum, though, was different. "VUCA" was still the chosen description of the atmosphere for which officers had to prepare, but they were no longer told simply to "go beyond" school solutions. They were taught how to do so. The goal was "out of the box" thinking, and specific (and popular) lessons on both creative and critical thinking were made part of the first course, which focused on leadership. But the goal was not merely the development of individual brilliance. Another theme that was more fully developed at mid-decade than it had been previously involved the importance of mastering tech-

niques for crafting a consensus and of acquiring skills useful in negotiation. Further, specific consideration was given to the ways in which
large institutions can be changed.[89]

"Vision" became a key topic in 1995–96–97, and regular efforts were
made to think about how wars would be fought in the future—both the
near-future and a quarter-century away.[90] This necessitated consideration of existing and possible technology. The Army, though, does not
have the same delight in high-tech that, say, the Air Force has. Still, the
new curriculum recognized new conditions the students would con-
front as they practiced their profession. These included dealing with
non-state adversaries, such as drug lords, with asymmetrical conflicts
(in which the United States is inevitably cast by some as a bully), with
transparency to a global media (sometimes known as the "CNN factor"),
and with global urbanization.

Ten years after the passage of the Goldwater–Nichols Act, the services
had developed their curricula on jointness and had been accredited by
the Chair of the JCS for Phase 1 of PJE. In terms of domestic issues,
there was still a tendency to look at society's problems rather than to
provide a balanced picture of society. Probably because of the presidential election in 1996, the campaign was used as a framework for current domestic issues, and a debate format was used to consider the positions of conservatives and liberals. Still, the justification for including
domestic problems and possible solutions in the curriculum, as opposed
to studying just governmental institutions and processes, may need
rethinking.

A final and dramatic change involved the Strategic Crisis Exercise.
This elaborate two-week exercise was now housed in a state of the art
facility, the Center for Strategic Leadership. Built at Carlisle, and first
used in 1995, the facility was intended for the use of the Army as a
whole. A permanent staff spends the year preparing for and running
exercises for a variety of groups, although the two-week SCE for Army
War College students, faculty, and staff is the "crown jewel" exercise.

Peace presents the military with a problem. When it prepares for an
agreed-on major threat, it assumes, correctly or incorrectly, that it is also
prepared for lesser threats. When no major threat exists, however, it is
necessary to think concretely and specifically about just what challenges
may still arise. In the United States, it is the duty of civilian political

leaders to set national-security strategy and to approve decisions about the strategy and the nature, preparation, and use of our military. But politicians may or may not fulfill these responsibilities. And if they do, politicians may or may not choose strategies appropriate to the challenges that arise, and they may or may not provide the financial resources required to support their own strategies. With little civilian direction, it is easy to see why the Army War College curriculum places so much emphasis on staying open, on adaptation, and on thinking globally and across the full range of possible forms of conflict.

Military thinking today is probably less straitjacketed than it was in 1985. Senior officers know that they must reconceptualize the world, but they have received no clear mandate from their civilian "masters" about how to do so. Military personnel have been reduced, but there is little agreement about what else is no longer needed. After all, it is far easier to say we must now be able to respond to "rogue states," to terrorist attacks, and to challenges in urban areas than it is to say we no longer need this, or that, or the other.

The military is sometimes caught between its "can do" ethic and expansive governmental commitments. "We can do anything," is constantly, if mostly silently, modified with, "But we can't do everything." Thus, the military plans both for major conflicts and for disaster relief, peacekeeping, and OOTW. Indeed, the SCE encompasses every contingency. But even as the Army contemplates future warfare, it finds it difficult to entirely put away Cold War strategies, doctrines, and toys. Preparation for two major regional contingencies has dominated its thought since World War II. That conceptualization is proving hard to relinquish.[91]

9 Army War College Administrators and College Policymakers

A DISCUSSION of some of the strains, contradictions, and problematic elements of the USAWC curriculum will be the subject of the next and concluding chapter. Some recommendations for change will be made. However, for change to occur, someone must have the capacity to take decisive action. This chapter will describe the various individuals and organizations that have a role in deciding the USAWC program. It is not clear that any single "decider" is positioned well enough to initiate a reformulated curriculum, but it is clear that it deserves "creative and critical" thought.

The president of the United States, the commander-in-chief, has not usually concerned himself with professional military education (PME); the secretary of defense has it as one of his many responsibilities and has occasionally commissioned studies about how it might be improved. The civilian secretaries of the services also have not been noticeably proactive when it comes to monitoring senior military education. Nor was Congress—until recently. In recent years, however, there have been two congressional initiatives that have significantly affected the war colleges. The first was the Goldwater–Nichols Act of 1986, which was designed to reduce interservice rivalry and to require joint planning and action among the U.S. services. The second was a rather critical 1989 report undertaken by Representative Ike Skelton, Democrat of Missouri, who chaired the Panel on Military Education for the House Armed Services Committee.[1] Both initiatives will be discussed in this chapter.

The uniformed military *has* concerned itself with the education of its officers. Both the chiefs of each service and the Chair of the Joint Chiefs of Staff have conducted reviews.[2] However, it is the Army chief of staff, who is most likely to review, monitor, and recommend changes in the education offered at the Army War College (as do the chiefs of the other services for their war colleges). The Army chief visits Carlisle early in the term to address the class. Further, he is likely to have graduated from either the Army War College or the National War College. He is

almost certain to have opinions about the education that is being conducted (or should be conducted) there. And, significantly, the chief
selects the commandant.

Just where does the Army War College fit in the Army's chain of
command? Some think it should report to Training and Doctrine Command (TRADOC) because TRADOC is responsible for all the other
Army schools. However, others argue that what must be accomplished
at the Army War College is not training but education, and that its students must think beyond doctrine. They aver that the problems
addressed at the Army War College necessarily deal with the unan-
swered and unanswerable; doctrine cannot suffice. Although the debate
sometimes resurfaces, the latter argument has thus far prevailed. The
Army War College commandant reports to the Army chief of staff; he
does so through the deputy for operations. He does not report to
TRADOC.[3]

The administrative structure of the Army War College will be discussed later. In brief, though, the college's commandant is the boss on
the spot.[4] His views, like those of the chief of staff, are likely to be experienced as directives. He has two deputies. One is an Army officer
administrator who is said to "own the class" because he manages the
many details of its year at Carlisle. The second is a foreign-service officer, an ambassador, with less-defined responsibilities.[5] The academic
dean, an Army officer, is primarily an administrator. Formal decisions
at the Army War College are mostly the collective work of the Academic Board (more later). The faculty, which understands itself to
govern the academic curriculum (and sometimes claims to govern the
school itself) at civilian universities and colleges, does not think of itself
as responsible for governing the Army War College or for governing the
curriculum.[6]

The Goldwater–Nichols legislation had a strong impact on curriculum changes in 1985–95. It is a good place to begin an analysis of the
different "deciders" (for the War College) and what they have decided
recently.

GOLDWATER–NICHOLS

As late as World War II, there were two service secretaries. One was
called the secretary of war. He directed the Army and the Army Air

Corps. The second was the secretary of the Navy. His responsibilities included the Marines, the Navy, and, during wartime, the Coast Guard. After the war, several of the leaders of that war—most notably, Dwight D. Eisenhower—concluded that the military services should be unified. Indeed, Eisenhower was so committed to this belief that he gave the Army War College's building at Fort McNair to what was to be a National War College. The Navy resisted unification vigorously and successfully. Not only did unification not occur, but a new service, the Air Force, was created.

Instead of closing down its War College as anticipated, the Army had to reopen it (at another site) in order to give its officers the same chance at senior schooling that was offered to officers in the other services.

Even though the services remained separate, some steps were taken in the direction of unification. One was the creation of a secretary of defense over the separate service secretaries. A second was the creation of the Joint Chiefs of Staff. A third was the creation of separate, joint military educational institutions. These included the Armed Forces Staff College, the Industrial College of the Armed Forces, and the National War College. All were established in 1946. The first two schools were newer renditions of existing institutions. The National War College was a wholly new institution.

In 1946, the plan was to eliminate the service war colleges. By 1950, however, it had become clear that the new schools would be add-ons. The Industrial War College had become equivalent in level to the service war colleges, and a new service war college, the Air War College, had come into existence. The National War College was intended as a capstone institution, one that students attended after attending one of the other war colleges. Things continued to evolve, however, and by the 1960s the National War College had become an alternative to, and equal with, the other schools. Thus, the joint school, which was supposed to displace the service schools and then become pre-eminent, became different, but not "higher."

No meaningful move toward more jointness occurred until almost thirty years later. Then it would be at the initiative of Senator Barry Goldwater, Republican of Arizona and a Reserve Air Force general, and Representative Bill Nichols, Democrat of Alabama and a World War II veteran. The precipitating events were the bombing of a U.S. Marine barracks in Beirut in which almost 250 Marines were killed and for which

Nichols (and others) blamed, at least in part, a Byzantine command structure; and the almost simultaneous invasion of Grenada by U.S. troops
that revealed grave problems in the capacity of the services to work
together. For instance, they found that the services' communications systems were not interoperable. Calls for "reform" had been in the air for
some time, but as is often the case, a precipitating event (in this case, two
events) was needed to overcome institutional resistance and inertia.[7]

A former Chair of the Joint Chiefs of Staff, David Jones, had publicly
called for reform of the JCS. Also, both the Senate and House Armed
Services Committees had been considering a variety of reforms. Think
tanks, including the Center for Strategic and International Studies (CSIS)
and the Heritage Foundation, had done studies. President Ronald Reagan had appointed David Packard to head a presidential commission
on military reform.[8] But when Senator Goldwater and Representative
Nichols teamed up with Senator Sam Nunn, Democrat of Georgia, and
House Armed Services Committee (HASC) Chair Les Aspin, Democrat
of Wisconsin, inertia and opposition were finally overcome. The result
was Goldwater–Nichols.

There are probably only a handful of devoted readers who have actually perused the 900 pages of the Goldwater–Nichols legislation. Its
essence, though, is jointness, and it includes a variety of provisions
designed to both encourage and require joint behavior and thinking. The
following are among the bill's chief provisions. First, the Chair of the
JCS is to be a uniformed officer who is *not* his service's chief of staff. (The
other four members of the JCS are the respective heads of their services.)
Second, the chair has specific responsibility for advising the secretary
of defense, the president, and the National Security Council. He is to
do so from a joint perspective. Third, the CINCs report directly to the
chair, placing him or her in the operational chain of command.[9] Fourth,
a sixth member was added to the JCS, a four-star vice-chairman whose
special duty is to represent the views of the CINCs.[10] Fifth, the Joint Staff
(composed of more than 1,000 officers) was placed directly under the
chief.[11] Thus, the nation's top military officer and the commanders of
war-fighting troops were all to have identities beyond those of their
service. In the parlance, they were to be "purple suiters."[12]

Powerful incentives to joint identity were built into the legislation.
New personnel policies tied promotions, assignments, and education
to joint duty.[13] For example, it was decreed that no officer could be pro-

moted to flag rank (general or admiral) unless she or he had experience in a joint assignment. Further, new flag rank officers were required to take capstone, which would emphasize working with the "other armed forces."

The legislation also created a new category of officer, the Joint Specialty Officer (JSO), intended to provide a set of officers with both service and joint expertise. These officers were to alternate their assignments between service and joint tours. The legislation also stipulated that JSOs were to be promoted at the same rate as officers on service staffs, and that half the joint slots were to be filled by them. To ensure that joint assignments were not short-term, token assignments, the legislation specified two years as the tour length for general and flag officers, and three years for other officers.

Goldwater–Nichols was also attentive to the content of professional military education. The secretary of defense, with the advice and assistance of the Chair of the JCS, was to "periodically review and revise the curriculum [of the joint schools] . . . to enhance the education and training of officers in joint matters."[14] After graduation, 50 percent of the students at joint schools[15] were to go to joint assignments. Then, after completing a joint tour, they would be qualified as JSOs.

The service schools[16] at both the command and staff and war-college level were to offer joint education "from a service perspective," but their curricula were to have "a strengthened focus on joint matters and preparation for joint assignments." The goal of Goldwater–Nichols has been called "nothing short of a change in the culture of the officer corps," because "schools transmit, interpret, and share culture."[17] The new legislation required that that culture be very different from the one then in place. To ensure change, the curricula of the service war colleges related to joint education became subject to a formal, somewhat onerous, accreditation process. The Chair of the JCS was responsible for that accreditation.

THE SKELTON REPORT[18]

The following year HASC Chair Les Aspin appointed Representative Ike Skelton, Democrat of Missouri, to chair a Panel on Military Education. The panel's charge was to review Defense Department plans for implementing the educational requirements of Goldwater–Nichols, and to assess the ability of the PME system to develop "professional military strategists, joint warfighters, and tacticians." The committee also assumed for itself the responsibility for weighing and making recommendations about the quality of education offered at military schools.[19]

The Skelton Committee concluded that, in the future, senior military leaders would not only have to have both command and staff experience but also service and joint experience. Further, it stressed the importance of senior leaders' having a genuinely "joint perspective"—that is, one that viewed the other services not from the perspective of one's own service but from a higher vantage point, one exemplified by a unified commander, a CINC, or the Chair of the JCS.[20] The panel believed that genuinely joint education should be conducted by "an authority independent of any service" and by multiservice faculty for multiservice students. Thus, to facilitate joint education, the panel recommended that the joint schools have a student and faculty service mix of one-third, one-third, and one-third.[21]

It also proposed that the service war colleges have a faculty and a student body composed of one-half host-service students, and one-quarter each from the other two services.[22] The report also recommended that an accrediting process be set up so the service schools could demonstrate their compliance with Goldwater–Nichols. This process would involve giving (or denying) schools credit for supplying what was to be called Phase I of joint education (that which every officer needed to know). To complete Phase II of joint education, however, a service war-college graduate would have to attend a short course at the Armed Forces Command and Staff College, a joint institution.[23]

In addition to considering requirements for joint education, the Skelton Committee devoted considerable attention to its other charge: assessing the ability of PME to develop "military strategists, joint war fighters, and tacticians." Well, actually, the focus was on what it takes to develop strategists.

In doing this, the committee first provided a definition of strategy: "the link that translates power into the achievement of objectives." Next it proposed "national *security* strategy," the product of a political process, as the appropriate subject for focus by the National War College. It then urged "national *military* strategy"[24] as the appropriate focus for the service war colleges. It went on to note that, in thinking broadly and over the long term, strategists must think about much more than how to deploy and use military resources. They must also consider such things as arms control, finance, and relationships with allies.[25]

The characteristics the panel attributed to strategists included being analytical; being pragmatic; being innovative; and being broadly educated (including in history, international relations, political science, and economics).[26] With candor rare among most advocates of education, the panel noted, "Few officers possess all of these attributes. It is rare to find individuals capable of a high degree of conceptualization and innovation. . . . Fortunately, the objective of the PME system is *not* the creation of a *large*[27] pool of military officers who are strategists on the order of a Mahan. . . . [O]nly a small number of genuine theoretical strategists are needed."[28] It concluded that the goal of the war colleges should be to identify and nurture that small group with the potential for being theoretical strategists, and to improve the quality of strategic thinking among senior officers generally, even if most would function principally as problem solvers, or as applied strategists. The panel also stressed the importance of using the few "bona fide" strategists well—of ensuring that they were assigned to slots where their special expertise would be of benefit.[29]

There was nothing timorous about the panel's approach to its third topic—the quality of PME. It first considered faculty. The panel reported that throughout its inquiry, it was told that much of PME learning was the result of student exchanges in the classroom. Indeed, it found "the extent of dependence on student exchanges as an educational device in some schools . . . disturbing." At least one witness called that dependence "an indictment of the faculty." The panel expressed its belief that the task of the faculty was to teach, not to "facilitate."[30] To do so, it said, faculty must be expert, whether that be in operations (largely drawn from experience) or in specialty fields (based on education) such as intelligence or foreign-area specialties. Further, the panel argued that expertise was not necessarily linked to age or rank. Therefore, faculty did not have to outrank students; they did not have to be role models (as it is assumed they must be at the service academies). Expertise, it said, can be sufficient to command respect.[31] The panel even argued on behalf of a secondary specialty as a military educator, which would permit officers to alternate education assignments with those in their military specialty. These faculty would mostly have doctorates earned at civilian schools.

Again, the Skelton Committee made a strong argument in favor of expertise. To achieve that expertise, the committee recommended that incentives be created that would make a faculty assignment more attractive to uniformed officers. Such incentives could include credit for a joint assignment, enhanced opportunity for a future command, an opportunity to obtain a Ph.D. from a civilian school, or even a realistic chance to obtain a star based on expertise as an educator.[32] It found the practice of using new graduates as faculty "unreasonable."[33]

The panel also urged increasing the proportion of civilians on the faculty to perhaps as much as a third and using distinguished chairs as a recruitment device. It recognized that, to attract high-quality civilian scholars, the colleges would have to provide an environment that promoted academic freedom and was supportive of critical, scholarly research.[34] To attract high-quality civilian faculty, military schools would also have to offer competitive salaries. (It is not clear that the committee understood just how expensive the best senior faculty are.)[35]

The committee further recommended more tests, more short papers, more term papers. It urged careful grading and more detailed feedback to each student related to his or her analytical performance, research techniques, and writing skills. These are onerous tasks, and faculty were also expected to do counseling, and lead discussion groups. Further, these recommendations not only involved a substantial commitment of time; they also involved skills that officers who are temporarily assigned to faculty positions—positions that might be short in length and unrelated to the officer's past or future career—simply might not have. Similarly, the idea that a Ph.D. is "desirable"[36] for military faculty teaching at a war college seems unnecessary in some subject areas. In making recommendations, one must consider scarcity versus availability.

High-quality students are also important. The Skelton panel found that student selection was satisfactory for three of the services, but that this had not been true for the Navy until recently. It urged the Navy to stay on course.[37]

The committee even included a section on pedagogy. Echoing every educational theorist, the committee called for "active learning." This was said to include reading, writing, and seminar discussion.[38] Virtually any listening activity was defined as passive, including lectures,[39] panels, and films. Further, the panel seemed to believe that "active" learning was best guaranteed by rigorous grading. And exams—especially essay exams.[40]

An assumption was also made that there was more active learning in elective courses than in the core curriculum that at that time made up three-fourths of the curriculum at the National War College and Industrial War College, and 85–90 percent of student hours at the Army, Naval, and Air war colleges.[41] There was also a strong endorsement of simulations and war-gaming.

The committee made a number of specific recommendations for a total "realignment" of PME.[42] For example, it found the de facto interchangeability of joint and service schools to be wrong. It believed that the two kinds of schools had important but different missions. Further, it argued that the primary mission of each war college involved the use of combat forces, and that this should receive primary emphasis. Leadership, management, and fitness might be important, it said, but they should be treated as secondary. It argued (unsuccessfully) that the National War College should be for officers who had already attended a war college. The committee also recommended that the Chair of the JCS have a director for military education. In part, the committee's recommendations were to insure coordination and to end both overlap and gaps in PME.

Two questions specifically directed to the Army were: Would co-location with other schools (at Leavenworth) not be beneficial and economic? and, Does the fact that all other Army schools report to TRADOC not create miscommunication, contradictions, or, at least, inefficiencies? (The Army's implicit answer was "no." It did not change location or alter the reporting relationship.) The report specifically criticized the Army War College curriculum for its lack of focus and insufficient emphasis on national military strategy.[43] It noted that only 22 percent of its faculty then had doctorates (the lowest among the war colleges); further, it observed that the college lacked military faculty who were "front runners" and civilian faculty who were "magnets"—that is, who would attract others of great expertise.[44] Finally, it criticized the fact that the college had had extremely rapid turnover in commandants. As the Skelton Report was being written, however, the incumbent commandant, General Howard Graves, had been asked to make substantial changes and had indicated that he might stay as long as four to six years in order to accomplish them. He stayed fewer than two.

THE ARMY CHIEF OF STAFF AND THE COMMANDANT

The Army chief of staff selects the commandant and sometimes has a close relationship with him. He may issue formal or informal guidance as to the curriculum or other aspects of the Army War College curriculum, or he may entrust the institution to the commandant and focus his energy elsewhere. Even if supervision is light, the chief and the commandant are in a senior–subordinate relationship. The Skelton Report's only critique of commandants (and presidents) was their short tenure. It did not see a problem with excessive advice from the service chief; instead, it declared that he should protect the commandant from unnecessary input into the curriculum from the Army's various branches and agencies, because this led to a disjointed and thin curriculum. Although the commandant is spared the task of outside fund-raising, he (no shes yet) does have to lobby internally for his budget and can play an important role in faculty recruitment. Most notably, the commandant plays a larger role in the shaping of the curriculum than one would find in a civilian school.

THE ARMY WAR COLLEGE ACADEMIC BOARD

Most significant decisions are taken—or, at least, ratified—by the Army War College Academic Board. This internal board "plans, establishes and evaluates academic policy, programs and procedures." It considers the college's "educational philosophy, instructional methodologies, curriculum design . . . and related issues." It is also the vehicle for the faculty to raise issues for consideration by the college's leadership.[45]

The Academic Board burnishes the mission statement and the curriculum's enduring themes. It considers the special themes selected for emphasis each year. It fulfills an important evaluative role not only of the year's program, but of each and every course—even of each and every lesson. Still, the board is advisory to the commandant. When it sets policy, it does so "IAW" (in accordance with) the commandant's guidance. It also transmits "guidance and directives from higher authority."

The board, which meets once or twice a month, is chaired by the dean.[46] Other members are the college secretary,[47] an administrative position; the chairs of the three academic departments and the chair of Corresponding Studies; the directors of the Center for Strategic Leadership, Military History Institute, Strategic Studies Institute, and Army Physical Fitness Research Institute; the director of academic policy, and the senior representatives of the Navy, Marines, and Air Force.[48]

There is not a lot of flexibility in the schoolyear. The curriculum pamphlet for the class that enters in August is published by March. Directors of each course in the core curriculum brief both Department of the Army officials and college officials soon thereafter. Library requests are prepared in April, and guest lecturers are secured by May. All of this activity is launched by the commandant's guidance for the year issued in January.

That guidance is derived from extensive evaluation of everything done during the previous academic year. It can be quite specific.[49] For example, the 1985 guidance for the year 1986 directed that the ten courses for 1985 be reduced to seven. It also directed that each Complementary Lecture Series be limited to no more than three speakers; conferences and symposia were to be restricted to six over the course of the year, and they had to be linked to the curriculum; 8:00 A.M. was established as the starting time for core courses; and course directors were instructed to be prepared to discuss written assignments required in their courses and to be ready to describe the standards they expected, the criteria that would be used in evaluation, and the type of feedback students would be given. Three field trips were approved for the class: a force-capabilities field trip; a trip to New York City; and a trip to Washington, D.C.

A final group that advises[50] the commandant on the affairs of the USAWC is the recently appointed Board of Visitors. It was thought that this civilian body would be particularly helpful as the school prepared for accreditation by the regional accrediting association.

THE MILITARY EDUCATION COORDINATING COMMITTEE

The commandants, presidents, and directors of all intermediate and senior colleges meet once a year with the Joint Staff's director and deputy directors for military education and joint history as the Military Education Coordinating Committee (MECC). Other officials from the Defense Department and CINC representatives may also attend. The conferees discuss academic matters, coordinate their curricula, and respond to concerns of the JCS. The Chair of the JCS makes his views known in an "Officer Professional Military Education Policy" document. That document, issued in March 1996, emphasized (again and still) jointness and vision.[51] Special areas of interest may be identified by the JCS. The colleges are not required to incorporate these in their curricula, but they are expected "to evaluate each issue for inclusion."[52]

OTHER INFLUENCERS AND COMMENTATORS

The Center for Strategic and International Studies (CSIS) in Washington, D.C., offered a study chaired by former Secretary of Defense (now Vice President) Dick Cheney titled "Professional Military Education: An Asset for Peace and Progress" in the spring of 1997. Its primary recommendations were even further attention to joint education, training, thinking, and operating; better preparation for the ethical dilemmas that face military officers (specifically, it urged the services to "establish a comprehensive, sequential program of mandatory ethics instruction at each level of professional military education"); more comprehension of and competency in the technological advances of the Information Age; and strengthening preparation for "Operations Other Than War." The CSIS report also recommended expansion of the education system to encompass more officers through correspondence and distance learning. The theory was that rapid change requires education for most senior officers. The contrasting view is that only a small percentage of colonels and captains will, in fact, become generals and admirals and that the war-college curriculum should be aimed at that select population.

At any given time, someone somewhere is probably studying PME even if the reports prepared rarely rise to the level of public notice. For example, shortly before the CSIS study was issued, the JCS had prepared an internal study titled "A Strategic Vision for the Professional Military Education of Officers in the Twenty-first Century" (March 1995). It, too, focused on jointness; it also argued the importance of more officers' receiving in-residence war-college education. Similarly, the Naval Postgraduate School and the Office of Naval Research hosted a two-day conference on professional military education in January 1998. Considerable attention was given to the need for officers to be able to make decisions about technology and to use it in operations. (Interestingly, the Navy, which has placed the least emphasis on the importance of war-college education, does give its officers the most technical training. Pilots do not have to build or fix their planes; Naval officers do have to know about their ships.) A second point discussed involved the importance of learning from "old warriors," because fewer and fewer officers actually have had combat experience. In particular, importance was attached to learning not just from others' experience but also from their failures. The particular kinds of failure enumerated included failing to adapt to changing conditions and technology, failing to understand foreign cultures, and failing to take into account geopolitical and economic factors. There was also discussion about the importance of emphasizing "the place of the military in a democratic society."

Conferees may have been agreed on the importance of PME, but they did not reach agreement on the percentage of officers who should receive PME or the content of that PME, especially how much time should be given to technical literacy. One thing they did agree on was the need to review the career pattern of officers. At present, there is probably not enough time in an officer's career for him or her to meet all current requirements for operational and command experience—that is, for service-staff duty, for joint duty, for civilian master's degrees, and for Command and Staff and War College education.

As compared with civilian graduate-degree-granting schools, war-college decision-making has three characteristics. First, it is relatively responsive to outside influences and authorities, including the executive and legislative branches of the federal government, alumni, and service organizations, among others. Second, directives tend to come from the top down, and decisions are likely to need ratification from levels higher than that at which an action is to take place. Third, many decisions are collective. This is true at the level of the course, where twenty faculty members may participate in its design and teaching, and at the level of the Academic Board that reviews and approves every element of the curriculum.

This is almost antithetical to the decision-making in a civilian college, particularly with regard to curriculum content. There, each course is very much the responsibility of the individual faculty member who teaches it. Larger decisions, such as the content of a major or requirements for a degree, may be collective. However, the collective is not composed of senior administrators or officials. It is composed of subject experts, the members of a department or a school faculty committee, or, perhaps, a faculty senate. In a civilian school, administrators do wield the power of resource allocation, but de facto decisions concerning curriculum content and degree requirements come from the bottom up—even if some formal ratification occurs at a higher level. Decisions by civilian faculty groups may be influenced by the skill of individual advocates, but their power of persuasion is based on expertise, on specialization. Although student demand may play a role in civilian schools, the many kinds of evaluation collected by the Army War College, which solicits the opinions of students, former students, employers of former students, and faculty, play a less important role. Again, at a civilian school, much more deference is paid to individual expertise. Collective decisions are far less frequent.

In civilian institutions, there is great continuity among faculty, and egos can get invested in research topics, courses, readings, and curriculum. Often, there is a tendency to go along with others' definition of their intellectual domain as long as one's own work and research are protected. Continuity can lead to stagnation. However, a saving grace for colleges and universities may be the premium colleges place on research, on discovery, on the new. This means that change is expected and assumed to be an advance.

At the war colleges, and especially at the Army War College, there is rapid turnover among faculty and leadership. Few vest their lives in developing the school. Officers may be good at making decisions and working cooperatively. But the Army War College, which seeks to produce good strategists—individuals who can think broadly, deeply, and into the future—does not seem to be able to strategize about itself. Major changes seem to require a powerful, external influence such as the end of a war, an act of Congress, or a congressional report.

Conclusion

In 1957, John W. Masland and Laurence I. Radway concluded that war-college education lacked rigor and critical, analytical thought; that decisions there were based on consensus rather than thought; and that, "in spite of stress upon the importance of individual initiative, none [of the colleges] appear willing to let the student alone for long periods of time."[1]

In 1973, Bernard Brodie wrote that war-college education was "too brief, too casual, comes too late in life and keeps the military consorting with each other." He believed that the few strategic thinkers in the military with analytical and reflective minds were not to be found among either war-college teachers or students and that military advisers tend to "give without hesitation assurances that are well beyond their qualifications and knowledge."[2]

In 1990, Martin van Creveld found that war-college students were not prepared to study and were not given a high-quality education. He recommended expert faculty, a two-year program, and attendance by a younger and more select group of officers.[3]

In 2000, Eliot Cohen said, "Officers spend as much as a third of their careers in classrooms. Yet what goes on there receives remarkably little attention from civilian leaders." Further, he wrote, "Civilian leaders need to review and, if necessary, overhaul the military educational system, particularly for senior officers."[4]

This volume has provided a detailed account of the Army's war-college year. The intent has been to provide so full an account that readers can come to their own conclusions about the validity of such critiques. Still, three issues that are deeply embedded in the curriculum require discussion. The first concerns the degree to which the war-college year is training as opposed to education, and which of the two it should be. The second involves an assessment of what is taught and what is learned about civil–military relations. And the third involves an exploration of the relationship between preparing for war and achieving peace.

TRAINING AND EDUCATION

Army War College students do write research papers, and some of these are published. Also, the Strategic Studies Institute, which is located at Carlisle but reports to a deputy chief of staff, regularly publishes monographs, and the Senior Service Fellows (who are assigned to the Army War College but are actually in residence at civilian institutions) also do some research. Nevertheless, the Army War College is primarily a teaching institution. The questions, however, are: Does that teaching seek mastery of the known (training), or does it teach the tools to deal with the unknown (education)? Does the college's teaching efficiently communicate information, or does it stimulate sound thinking?

In the beginning, the Army War College was clearly military and a school. The subjects were military, and the students and faculty were military. Work was collaborative, and officials seemed to know what they wanted done and how it should be done. Their confidence was reflected in the fact that, for years, all students followed the same curriculum. Electives did not appear until the late 1960s; as late as 1985, three-quarters of the curriculum was prescribed.

Beginning in the 1950s, the description of Army War College goals began to sound more like the goals of a civilian academic institution. Words such as "contemplation," "creativity," "growth," "thought," and "wisdom" began to appear in institutional literature. By the 1970s, the Army War College had begun to experience outside pressure to emphasize the "college" in its title—that is, to remake itself to resemble more closely a civilian graduate school. Three things contributed to this pressure. The first was Vice Admiral Stansfield Turner's transformation of both the curriculum and teaching methods at the Naval War College. That new curriculum expanded the number of electives and assigned hundreds of pages of reading each week; students were required to write papers and take exams; and the best 20 percent and 5 percent of them, respectively, were graduated with "distinction" and "highest distinction." Also, more civilians and more Ph.D.s joined the faculty, and the Navy received permission to award a civilian-accredited master's degree to its graduates. In short, the Naval War College became very like a civilian school and was praised for doing so.

The second event that created pressure to civilianize came in the mid-1980s. The Skelton Committee's hearings and subsequent report made it clear that the committee doubted the rigor of war-college education; it strongly recommended more civilian faculty, more Ph.D. faculty, exams, and grades.[5] The fact that the Naval War College had already moved in this direction may have given the committee confidence that it was not trying to stretch a military school to fit a civilian, Procrustean bed.

The end of the Cold War also created pressure to revise war-college curricula. Even if one's impulse was to train, it was hard to know for what one should train in such an uncertain time. As a result, "education," preparation for the unknown, moved even further toward center stage.

An argument can be made that training for senior leadership is indeed the appropriate war-college function—that there is new information senior officers should have, that there are new skills they should acquire, that savvy about how things "work" and a well-filled Rolodex will make them more effective in their next assignments. A full schedule, a core curriculum taught to officers by officers, exercises, the provision of meticulously prepared course directives describing every lesson and its objectives, program completion by virtually all participants—all of these are characteristic of training. But the USAWC seeks academic accreditation by a civilian agency,[6] and its aspirations sound like those of a civilian institution. Indeed, they often sound like those of a liberal-arts graduate program when they might more appropriately be compared to those of a professional school.

When the war-college year is measured against the ideal civilian education, it falls short. This needs to be recognized if the goal is in fact education rather than training. Let us assume that the goal of education is to stimulate individuals to habitual, critical, and creative thinking.[7] One must first ask: Is it possible for the Army War College to achieve that goal with a faculty composed largely of fellow officers without Ph.D.s who will soon rotate to other assignments? In a civilian graduate program, virtually all faculty are Ph.D.s. They are specialists whose work is their career—for some, their life. Even if they are young, faculty members command intellectual respect. Near-peer, short-term faculty may be compatible with training. Indeed, teaching what one has recently learned can be a very effective way of ensuring retention. But can such faculty educate? Even if they are able and hardworking, can they be expected to know the newest literature? Can they provide analytical feedback on students' work? Can they help students tease out assumptions and test the logic of arguments? Can they help them see that what matters is not a fact or event, but "of what" that fact or event is "an instance"? Education involves hierarchy. Students should be able to learn more from a faculty member than from one another.

One reason it is hard to develop an exceptionally able faculty is that so many faculty are required. Each of the twenty sixteen-student seminars is staffed with a team of four.[8] The seminars meet three half-days a week, but their function is not just to teach. They are also social and administrative units. Each seminar has a chair (chosen ahead of time by the faculty team of four[9]). She or he serves in many ways, among them by (unobtrusively) taking roll at mandatory events, including seminar meetings and required lectures; maintaining appropriate decorum in the seminar; appointing committee members for class activities such as the Gift Committee, the Yearbook Committee, and the Jim Thorpe Day Committee; and choosing others to fulfill seminar responsibilities, such as security, for sponsorship of the two International Fellows and for social events. Announcements and discussion can consume a substantial amount of seminar time, too. Announcements about an Eagle Scout Court of Honor, the Christmas Tea for Carlisle senior citizens, and the Gettysburg staff ride illustrate the range of items formally raised to each student through the seminar. The multiple functions of the seminar help to explain why it is so central to the war-college year, and, more important, why it would be difficult to eliminate or change it—even if it is determined that it is not particularly conducive to the development of individual, critical, and creative thinking.

The seminar system is also supported by the conviction that "active" learning is the best learning, and that seminar discussions and group exercises are therefore the best forms of pedagogy.[10] Note that these are both interactive, group activities. Reading and writing are accorded some pedagogical merit. These, however, are individual activities, and the more individual the work, the more variable the content and quality of learning—and, not incidentally, the more burdensome conscientious evaluation. The question not addressed is: Is group activity or individual study more likely to lead to education's goal of habitual, creative, and critical thinking?[11]

Lectures by experts, a favored pedagogy in civilian schools, are almost derided. They are considered passive and therefore of low efficacy.[12] Why? Can't officers sit still? Or is it possible that civilian schools are as irrationally wedded to the lecture as war colleges are to the seminar? Or is it that the best pedagogy for training is different from that of education? Does group participation enhance training, while attendance at lectures coupled, with individual study and research, better stimulates thought?

An important element in military culture is uniformity. This helps to explain the use of a core curriculum that is thoroughly organized and that provides detailed objectives for every lesson. Curriculum changes do occur from year to year, but no experimenting is done within a year—for instance, by having half the class follow the core curriculum organized by seminar while the other half pursues a more civilian-like program of lectures and research seminars.[13]

Other program elements reinforce the idea that the war-college program is more training than education. First, although the pace of the core curriculum permits mastery (as would training), it does not leave time for the exploration associated with Whitehead's stage of precision (as education would require). One result is that abstract thought, controversy, skepticism, and originality are not central to war-college culture.

It is also important to note how programs are evaluated. The Army War College routinely collects extensive feedback.[14] But its evaluation is largely a matter of collecting opinions from participants: students, faculty, graduates, employers of graduates. Neither the faculty nor the curriculum is assessed by outside experts. In a civilian institution, faculty promotions require letters from outside reviewers. Usually, faculty members do not know who has been asked to review them. Also, curricula and programs are periodically reviewed by outsiders. At the Army War College—almost ironically in an institution that is structured so hierarchically—there is almost no recognition of hierarchy based on intellectual expertise.

Academic freedom is a cherished value in civilian academic institutions. This can involve controversy and sometimes creates difficulty for administrators.[15] In an environment such as the USAWC's, which is so driven by cooperation, consensus, and collective decision-making, it is not surprising that the issue rarely arises. Indeed, although students are urged to get out of their "comfort zones," there is very little in the curriculum or environment to make officers uncomfortable. The civilian student (later a faculty member) who described her colleagues as able and hardworking was surely correct. But perhaps more important, her comment that they had "no idea how different" they were may help to explain the bland curriculum.[16]

Again, much of the USAWC program seems to fit the definition of training. It is not really designed to teach students to think independently, to ferret out assumptions, or to test claims for logic and evidence. However, the program is by no means confined to the transmission of agreed-on facts. It does not merely convey information and skills. It is intended to expand students' vision, to prepare them for change, to teach them to function well in civilian and even foreign settings. This is why VUCA is so regularly invoked as reality. It *does* try to prepare officers for the unknown—but by expanding their experience rather than by teaching research methods, or by asking students to examine worldviews that are different from their own. Suspended judgment, the pursuit of the contrary and the novel, and the testing of logic and weighing of evidence characterize the optimum environment for an education that seeks to stimulate thought. That is quite different from the USAWC environment.[17]

Officers have to be prepared to act. One can appreciate that they have a need for certainty that the civilian scholar does not. One can understand why so much time is devoted to planning and to learning the rules of the game. Thus, even if the institution and its leadership speak of their mission as education, the fact is that the USAWC does not really wish to challenge students' fundamental assumptions or to create immobilizing doubt. Nor does the curriculum concentrate on raising students' technical proficiency, as might a civilian graduate degree in engineering or accounting. Instead, the curriculum is designed to train students to act effectively in an expanded, changing, and more heterogeneous environment than they have worked in before. In sum, a civilian education tries to make students more critical and creative by narrowing the field and creating doubt. USAWC training tries to make students more effective by expanding their view and increasing their assurance.

Should the military emulate and further imitate civilian education? Yes, if the goal is to develop a set of military intellectuals. Those who now exist are not concentrated at the Army War College. Indeed, when I asked one canny general where the Army's "brains" were located, he replied that they were aides to generals with an eye for talent. If education is the goal, though, the USAWC should reduce the size of its classes and select faculty and students based on their intellectual interests and capacities.[18]

However, if the goal is to bring senior officers up to speed for a new set of responsibilities, one is talking about training. And training may be what is wanted. After all, would the country be better served by a set of individualistic, creative, and critical senior officers who know that they do not know, but who also know that those who command them don't know, either? Or is there some danger that officers who receive a civilian-accredited master's degree may become overly confident of their knowledge? For instance, will they believe that their Regional Studies program has made them geographical area experts? And how would either of these outcomes—skepticism or excessive confidence—affect officers' acceptance of civilian leadership and control? Indeed, what are senior officers' current views about civilian control?

CIVIL–MILITARY RELATIONS

At the Army War College (and at the other war colleges), only one lesson a year is specifically devoted to civil–military relations. Nevertheless, students perceive civil–military relations as one of the most important parts of the curriculum. In 1990, when USAWC students were asked whether the curriculum had achieved its objectives in some sixteen areas, "Understand the role of the military in a democracy" won hands-down. The precise nature of that understanding is important, because some of these students will win stars and the most senior command and staff positions. What are they taught about civil–military relations explicitly? What messages are implicit? What do students believe, regardless of what they are taught?

Let us look closely at the USAWC's 1998 curriculum. The one lesson on civil–military relations raised two questions: 1) Has the military become more politicized, more conservative, and more Republican since the advent of the All-Volunteer Force; and 2) Is participation by the military in decisions regarding the use of force more likely to encourage or discourage the use of force? No firm answers were provided,[19] but the lesson did address two debates that were then prominent in the media.[20] The lesson also included a case study of a conflict between the Army's leadership and President Dwight Eisenhower. This established the point that the civil–military relationship is not necessarily smoother just because the commander-in-chief was once a general.

Several other lessons had civil–military themes. One titled "National Values" involved reading the Declaration of Independence and portions of the U.S. Constitution and the U.N. Charter. Just war theory and international law were also discussed as embodiments of society's values—and as possible constraints on military action.

A second lesson, "The President and National Security," described the roles and structure of the various executive-branch units charged with national-security responsibilities. The lesson also described the president's burden of crafting a coalition to support his policies. At a minimum, that coalition was said to include the public, the Congress, and the president's own executive-branch bureaucracies. The message was: He may command the military, but the President's other support has to be courted and won—again and again.

A third lesson considered the role of Congress in national security and the military's relationship to Congress. The complicated and political workings of Congress were described, and attention was given to the War Powers Act and to the Iran–Contra episode, in which some military officers violated the law and the intent of Congress (probably with the tacit consent of the chief executive) and were convicted and later pardoned. A take-home message was that policy is the product of a complex and extended political process.

"National Security and the Media" directed students' attention to the most problematic civilian–military relationship—a relationship for which there are no well-formulated and agreed-on rules. The media was understood as having a special constitutional status but also as an institution pursuing profit and sensation. It was seen as both a potential constraint and a potential force multiplier. Taken together, the USAWC lessons imparted a fairly conventional message about the military's subordinate relationship to civilian authority.

But were there implicit messages? And if so, were they reinforcing or contradictory? The American government lessons have the potential to cut both ways. Knowing more about the actual workings of the federal government can lead to an appreciation of the complexity of a process that permits broad participation and whose legitimacy comes not from outcomes or policies but from participants' following an agreed-on, democratic process. Knowledge could also lead to impatience with, and even disdain for, government's apparent inefficiency, irrationality, and tolerance of self-interest.

A second set of messages also seems likely to cut two ways. These derive from the emphasis on ethics throughout the USAWC curriculum. The lessons and discussions about ethics emphasize the importance of hewing to a high standard of personal integrity; they also emphasize the importance of creating a "climate" so that others behave well. The officer's professional code does include acknowledgement of civilian authority, but there also seems to be an implicit message that officers are more ethical, more moral, than civilians.[21]

A related, implicit message about the military's moral superiority does not involve individual behavior. It concerns the relative morality of the military as a whole—for instance, the military has no tolerance for drugs, unlike civilian society, which is seen as "in decay."[22] When civilian culture is described as in decay because it is individualistic, undisciplined, and hedonistic, no connection is made to the Declaration of Independence and its ringing phrases honoring the individual, liberty, and the pursuit of happiness. Officers need to be made more conscious of the fact that their values of the group, discipline and sacrifice are almost antithetical to the enduring and fundamental values of the society they have sworn to protect and to serve.

The field trip to New York City may also deliver an implicit message that U.S. society is decaying or disintegrating. The trip involves a visit to a variety of flourishing public and private institutions, but it also brings officers face to face with a variety of social ills by including, for instance, a visit to a prison. Also, the 1990 USAWC curriculum specifically discussed a number of society's deficiencies—for example, in public education–then asked officers to propose remedial policies. Is it wise to teach the men and women who wield our weapons that they are individually and collectively better than, rather than just different from, the rest of us? And why should they be asked for recommendations on domestic issues?

Finally, the effort to get officers to think strategically and to prepare them to work with foreign officers in combined operations, with civilians in government and in private organizations, and with a variety of others, such as U.N. officials, suggests that senior officers do need to be more than soldiers. One formulation is that they should aspire to be "warrior–statesmen." This seems to imply that their skills and experience should be used in realms beyond those of national security. Indeed, one officer has argued that officers' problem-solving abilities should be put to use in solving a host of social ills, including health policy, drugs, the environment, and even civil rights.[23] The author in question appears to believe that social problems can be approached and solved apolitically by experts. One does not have to see the United States as following the path of a Chile or a Turkey (democratic allies whose militaries have decided to "rescue" their nations from civilian governments) to think that it is not good for the military to believe that it is not only more moral, but also more competent, than civilian government.[24]

All the war-colleges teach civil–military relations, but they emphasize different themes.[25] At the Air War College, the focus is on leadership during wartime and on the problem of fixing responsibility (and the different views that officers and civilians may hold on this issue).[26] Related questions were posed in a case study involving General John D. Lavelle, who was relieved of duty for issuing orders that contravened the Rules of Engagement issued from Washington, D.C., and who filed false reports to conceal this action. The study did nothing to suggest Lavelle had been in the right; however, one question asked whether the officer who disciplined him had been "too idealistic," and no questions were raised about the responsibility of the officers who knew about, and may even have participated in, the breaking of rules and filing of false reports. (The disobedience was revealed in a letter written by an enlisted man to his Senator.)

In discussing "ethical dilemmas" at the Air War College, the question was explicitly raised as to whether U.S. society is "in decline." The clear, if implicit, answer was "yes." Great emphasis was given to the importance of always telling the truth, even in the face of temptation—for example, while testifying to Congress about budget requests.[27] One written assignment asked students to prepare a brief for foreign officials on "the role of the military in a democracy." Another asked students whether they believed a challenge to traditional civilian control existed. If they did, they were asked to cite three pieces of evidence opposing their position; if they did not, they were also asked to provide three reasons in opposition to their position. Finally, the Air Force teaches its students that they have a responsibility to educate the American public. In particular, this seems to revolve around budgetary needs to produce new and better aircraft and technology.

At the Naval War College, civil–military relations are approached less as a matter of constitutional principle or professional ethics than as a complication requiring intelligent cooperation in order to create a sound working relationship. At the National War College, the curriculum gives more attention to the workings of the federal government and the variety of ways in which military officers participate in it than do the other schools. Several well-subscribed elective courses, including "The Soldier and the State" and "Military Professionalism and Civilian Control," provide a historical account of civil–military relations and tackle current issues head-on. The latter include appropriate justifications for and modes of dissent; the role of the military in decisions to use force and what kind of force; the role of retired officers and military interest groups; the military's responsibility in conflicts between its two masters, the Congress and the president; and comparisons of the role of the military in the United States and in other countries. Both courses carefully examine the principle of civilian control in a variety of contexts. Both, though, are electives. They are not required.

The Marine War College has heard from both Supreme Court Justice Anthony Scalia and the North Carolina historian Richard Kohn when it explores the civil–military relationship in conjunction with its "Constitution Day." "Discussion topics" handed out at the seminar presented by Kohn and Scalia, however, formulated an officer's responsibility as being either that of a Doberman pinscher brought out of his cage when threats emerge or of a professional with "the right, indeed, the obligation to speak his or her mind ... and to be heard not only in the councils of both state and war, but to be heard in public so that military views can be part of public discourse." Clearly, students were not expected to identify with the first position. Whether the second option was understood as proper is not clear, but participation in the public discourse, as described earlier, is surely political, not professional, and therefore unacceptable.[28]

Finally, many of the students at the Industrial College of the Armed Forces are civilians, and the concern of the college is the civilian economy and its capacity to support military operations. Students study the economy and, in particular, defense-essential industries. This curriculum takes explicit account of the mores and ethical perspectives of various cultures and considers how best to elicit cooperation among them. This involves cross-national cultures, but it even considers a variety of

U.S. subcultures in a lesson titled "Ethics and Organizational Cultures: When Military, Business and Engineering Cultures Meet."

Suggestions that teaching at the war colleges implicitly imparts the belief that the military is both more moral and more able than civilians are disturbing. Are there further grounds for disquiet? Let us look at some recent survey findings about war-college students' beliefs about the military's role in U.S. society.[29]

One question concerned compliance with civilian directives. War-college students were asked whether it was appropriate to carry out a civilian official's "unethical but legal" directive. Eighty-eight percent were prepared to place their ethical judgment above the directive of a civilian authority—even while acknowledging that the order was legal. However, 62 percent thought it *was* appropriate to carry out a civilian's "unwise" request.

Students were then asked about the appropriateness of a variety of alternative noncompliant actions. In the case of an "unethical but legal" directive, 37 percent thought they should try persuasion, but if that failed they should follow the directive. Half thought it appropriate to inform other officials; three-fourths thought it appropriate to appeal to a higher authority, even if it meant leaping the chain of command; 85 percent thought it appropriate to report the matter to an Inspector General or to a Judge Advocate General officer; and half thought it appropriate to leave service or to refuse the directive and accept a court-martial.[30] Obedience to civilian authority clearly cannot be assumed to be automatic.[31] Responses to the appropriateness of alternatives to following an "unwise" act were lower but probably higher than civilians, who perceive the military as a command-obeying hierarchy, might expect. In sum, "civilian control" may be accepted, but a belief in the appropriateness of *not* complying is startling high. Further, support for noncompliance based on an ethical, personal judgment was far higher than for noncompliance based on a professional judgment that a directive was unwise.

A second question involved the military's understanding of its role as an adviser to civilian authorities. More than 80 percent of students thought their role was, indeed, to "advise" on decisions as to whether to intervene with force abroad. However, once a decision was made, 80 percent believed they should "advocate" or "insist" in discussions about the rules of engagement, and 86 percent said they should "advocate" or "insist" to ensure that clear political and military goals were established. Sixty-two percent, though, said that officers should "advise" only on the content of the goals. Even though students are taught that military strategy is but one element in national-security strategy, and that military power is but one form of national power, these views suggest that too many officers believe that once a commitment to the use of force is made, they alone, as professionals, should determine how that force is organized and applied. One hopes that they do not believe that decisions about the use of nuclear weapons are theirs rather than the president's. Why, then, should the president not make other decisions, as well, including on the selection of bombing targets and the rules of engagement? The president rightly takes into account the possibilities of diplomacy, the commitment of allies, and the views of the U.S. public. Officers who feel entitled to "insist" may be overlooking the larger picture, including the principle that their commander-in-chief has the right and responsibility to decide, including the right to be wrong.

Eighty-seven percent of war-college students agreed that members of the military should not criticize a senior member of government.[32] However, a third believed it appropriate to criticize American society, and almost 40 percent believed they could publicly express political views, "just like any other citizen." Although such views might be compatible with holding a low rank and with the understanding that the opinions are clearly those of the individual, one would expect officers who are being prepared for senior positions to understand that, simply by virtue of their position, they are *not* "like any other citizen."

Two-thirds of the students surveyed believed it proper to advocate publicly for military policies that the military believed to be in the best interests of the United States. Unfortunately, the question was not entirely clear as to whether such advocacy should be restricted to policies in accord with civilian direction, or whether the military should publicly advocate for policies it believes to be in the best interests of the United States even when civilian authorities do not agree with them.[33]

About a third of the respondents thought the military should have more influence in deciding policy vis-à-vis other countries. One might think that foreign policy is the purview of the State Department, but one seasoned commentator has described the U.S. military as having a "penchant for a parallel foreign policy."[34] This is illustrated by ever more extensive military-to-military contacts and the use of those contacts for political purposes, as well as by the military's public opposition to issues such as U.N. conventions on land mines, child soldiers, and a world criminal court. (In the last instance, officers actually attended the U.N. conference to lobby against the proposal.)

President Bill Clinton's relationship with the military was difficult, and some would say that he did not really try to control it. But President George Bush could not get the military to do a bottom-up review at the end of the Cold War, and President George W. Bush has faced similar unresponsiveness to proposals for review, for base closings, and for changing planned weapons procurement.[35]

Again, officers may agree that the political is taboo, but their responses to these items suggest that many war-college students do not appreciate the fact that providing professional advice does not involve "insistence," and further that once an officer goes public with advice that is contrary to the views of civilian authorities, he or she has by definition acted politically.[36]

Yes, there should be concern about war-college students' views of the civil–military relationship, even though 93 percent of them believe civilian control is "safe and secure." Historically, many officers were so eager to avoid being political that they did not even vote. Today, a large minority (40 percent) believe they should publicly express their political views "just like any other citizen." They are wrong. Those to whom society entrusts its weapons are not like any other citizen. They act for the citizenry at the direction of the citizens' elected leadership. It is not the military's responsibility to criticize either elected officials or those who elected them. Politicians and citizens are unlike the military. The former are appropriately compromisers; the latter are appropriately individualistic seekers of pleasure. The military appropriately submits to the judgment of the latter as expressed through the former.

Again, even if war-college students are correct that there is no current danger of usurpation, they seem to lack consciousness of two quite different dangers. One is the erosion of civilian control based on officers' insistence on supposed military expertise and on the ethics of their profession. The other, less discussed danger is erosion caused by civilians who, thoughtlessly or by calculation, try to politicize the military. The military must think about how to respond if politicians try to use it to advance their own or party interests.[37] In short, officers must be better educated about the subtleties of civilian–military relations, and they are likely to have to educate civilians about them, as well. Most important, they may have to educate the very civilians who purportedly control them.

WAR AND PEACE

Does today's Army War College fulfill the mission that was proclaimed at its founding a century ago? Does it preserve the peace by preparing intelligently and adequately to repel aggression? Or has its preparation reduced prospects for peace? Or has the military and the security environment so changed that a new mission is in order?

The U.S. military today is different from that of a century ago in three important ways. First it has become something our founding fathers warned against: a standing army, a large and generously funded peacetime force. Apart from being expensive, standing armies develop their own interests. They can be seen by others as provocative, and their availability can lead to their use (at home as well as abroad) when a lack of availability might have led authorities to other strategies and to the use of other forms of power. President (and former General) George Washington specifically warned against a standing army when he left office. President (and former General) Dwight Eisenhower warned against the influence not only of the military but also of the "military–industrial complex." We had a large military during the Cold War. When it was over, we did reduce the military's size, from about 2 million to 1.4 million. But our defense budget remains larger than the budgets of the next ten big-budget militaries combined—and at a time that no nation threatens us.[38] Our Army definitely stands.

Second, it is a professional force. There is no talk of Cincinnatus leaving his plow. Those who wear uniforms today do so by choice. They include few from society's elite and few from the lower class. The Army is self-selected, selective, middle class, and conservative. It is an army in a democracy, but it is not representative even of young men.

Third, it is an imperial army. Its reach is global—on land, in the air, and on and under the sea. The U.S. interests it protects extend far beyond defending the homeland from aggressors. The United States has reacted to acts of aggression by one state against another; we have also acted when we were concerned about stability and the balance of power, and even when we were merely appalled by a government's treatment of its own people. NATO's Cold War purpose was clear, but its might has been employed only once—in a civil war within an already disintegrated small country.[39]

The standing, professional, imperial U.S. military does indeed seek to preserve peace by being prepared. But being prepared can be effective either by deterring others, thus preserving peace, or by winning, thus imposing peace, and both deterrence and winning are different today. Deterrence was a well-understood and effective policy that kept the homeland safe for the second half of the twentieth century, but with the collapse of the Soviet Union, the United States began a new form of deterrence that is not focused on protection of the homeland. That is peacekeeping. Often, this has not been the classical U.N. peacekeeping based on consent, impartiality, and the use of force only in self-defense. It has been more like imperial policing and has been seen by some as intervention, as supportive of one side or the other, and as implicitly or explicitly threatening force. For the most part, the U.S. military has not been enthusiastic about peacekeeping,[40] partly because it sees itself as made up of fighters not policemen. The military has expressed its reluctance in terms of being asked to do something that is not its function and that detracts from being prepared for its "real" duties. It does not perceive peacekeeping as a deterrent, as a way to prevent more calamitous conflict. But there is a second reason for the military's reluctance. Although the military is surely prepared to sacrifice in defense of the United States, its contract with America does not call for sacrifice for any oppressed people, anywhere, anytime. Thus, even if it does not say so, the military may doubt that some peacekeeping missions have been vital to U.S. interests. Indeed, military actions of the past decade have not been given a rigorous examination for interest. That may be why civilian leaders have been so anxious to avoid casualties, and why the military may rightly think, "If it isn't important enough to risk and sacrifice, why am I being asked to do this job?"[41]

Winning is different today, too. After World War I and World War II, the enemy surrendered, the victors dictated the peace, the defeated were occupied, and, in the case of Japan, the nation's institutions and government were dramatically altered. In the second half of the twentieth century, however, the United States became involved in conflicts in which the doctrine of pursing peace by victory was replaced by a doctrine that required limiting U.S. military response to avoid a wider war.

Thus, the U.S. military found itself being asked to sacrifice lives in conflicts in which victory was not the goal. Such a policy is in complete accord with Clausewitz's dictum that war is policy by other means, and also with USAWC teaching that the military is but one instrument of power used by the government to secure the national interest. However, the military was not comfortable with civilian limitations. The military commander in Korea was fired, and soon after the U.S. loss in Vietnam, a new policy related to the use of force was developed. Called the Weinberger–Powell doctrine, it committed the government to the use of force only under certain conditions. These included the setting of clear and achievable goals; the public's support of the action; the provision of all necessary means to achieve the goal; and a specific exit strategy.[42] When a campaign is undertaken to meet only "achievable" goals, the assumption may exist that victory will bring peace. Unfortunately, this has proved untrue both in the Gulf and in Kosovo.[43] Because the military plays an important advisory role in any decision to go to war, it is important that military strategists anticipate second- and third-order effects of military action—in particular, that they study the nature of the peace likely to follow. Is a winner-imposed peace, such as that in Germany and Japan after World War II, more likely to yield a sustained peace than one based on a negotiated settlement that may require continued monitoring and enforcement? Again, the USAWC studies war. It needs to study peace, as well.[44]

Anticipating war's aftermath is difficult, of course. For instance, few expected years of Cold War deterrence to suddenly become victory in 1989–90. But even if events have not been anticipated, one might think that dramatically altered circumstances would lead to an immediate reassessment of threats to the United States and of the military requirements needed to meet them. That has not happened. Instead, the resources intended to deter the USSR were put to use almost immediately in the Gulf. And those same resources were quickly deployed after the bombing of the World Trade Center and the Pentagon, even though they were not designed to punish the kind of terrorist conspiracy responsible.

Most would describe the Gulf War as a victory. It was, however, different from any war the United States had fought before. First, some describe the United States as having been a mercenary, because our allies, who were more dependent on Middle East oil or were more threatened by Iraq than we were, paid for the war.[45] The U.S. taxpayer felt no pain.

Second, the war was large but asymmetrical, and we were able to fight it with near impunity—that is, with very few American casualties.[46] In the next war, Kosovo, and later in Afghanistan, impunity actually became part of U.S. planning. We sought to win a war without casualties. One does not dishonor Americans who did die in the Gulf when one says that the very low ratio of American-to-enemy deaths raises "just war" questions about proportionality and discrimination. Third, because of instant television coverage, the views of ordinary citizens may have assumed a larger role in military thinking than they had before. Even Clausewitz described "the people" as part of the "holy trinity" (with the government and the military) whose unified effort is necessary to the successful waging of war. However, it is important to remember that, although these three elements identify with one another within a nation, each to some degree also identifies with its enemy counterpart.

Thus, one government appreciates the stability provided even by an enemy government—and Hussein and Milosevic were left in place. Similarly, one military may appreciate the role of the other—militaries are, after all, the ones who bear the duty of killing and of risking their lives. Less appreciated may be the fact that civilians may identify with *their* counterparts, too. They appreciate, first, what little control ordinary civilians have over their governments and militaries, and second, they realize that civilians are in grave danger if war breaks out. Civilian casualties, whether targeted or collateral, have become the norm. Officials receive special protection, and militaries can fight back, but civilians are vulnerable, even if the attack on them is only indirect—for example, through the destruction of a nation's power grid or by embargoing its trade. Today's media makes it possible for ordinary citizens to see and discriminate between military action directed against another government and military action directed toward people like themselves. In the end, the citizenry becomes the arbiter of war and peace. It may have little direct influence on the decision to go to war, but the citizenry decides whether a war will continue. Today's media enables citizens to register their views more quickly and effectively than in the past.

Citizens register their views with the officials responsible for giving direction to the military. Although responsible, those officials are likely to lack military experience. This worries the military, which fears being given unwise directives and inadequate support. But the other side of the coin is a civilian government that defers too easily to the military and that takes the military's "Can do!" ethic literally.[47] Further, as noted earlier, civilian guardians may try to use the military to electoral advantage, and quite apart from inexperience or self-interest, civilian guardians charged with the responsibility for security may seek to provide a 100 percent guarantee (impossible to achieve) that can lead to the elevation of low probability threats, to overspending, to overpreparation, and to the curtailment of civil liberties.[48]

Although it would probably be too unsettling to change the language of the USAWC's formal mission, it might be possible to change the college to help it meet its aspirations. And it might be possible for the war college to act as a badly needed catalyst for changes in thinking about military strategy, structure, and procurement—changes that many critics have supported but that have thus far proved impossible to implement. Inertia, resistance, and interest have all played a role in defeating efforts to remake the military. The inertia, resistance, and interests have come partly from the military, but they also have come from defense contractors and elected officials protecting constituency interests. The events of September 11, 2001, may finally provide the motivation needed for some action. The forces and weapons designed to support a security strategy based on Europe and prepared for a short but violent war—with the possibility of having to fight a second major conflict simultaneously—were shown to be woefully inadequate to prevent September's devastating attacks.

A crucial change would involve faculty capacities and functions. Efforts to hire more Ph.D. and more civilian faculty have not changed much. Hiring retired officers who have earned a Ph.D. while on active duty does not raise the standards or open the atmosphere. More faculty need to be engaged in the profession. They need to do research that is submitted to peer review and to design courses that create "discomfort." To do this, core faculty members at least would have to be relieved of some of the myriad duties now assigned to them. At present, many faculty members function like graduate assistants; as such, they could easily teach two seminars rather than one. This could be done by reducing seminar meetings to two mornings a week and having half meet on Monday and Wednesday and half on Tuesday and Thursday. It should also be possible to invite distinguished visiting faculty for a year—not just scholarly friends but experts who are critics. Outside experts should be invited to review the curriculum. Experiments should be tried: Have four individuals separately design each core course and teach it to five of the twenty seminars. Let students see that experts disagree or, at least, find different items salient. Use more experts—and those with controversial views—in the speaker series. Have an "honors" seminar or two for those who really want to use the year for intellectual growth. Don't try to get the whole class through a master's program; make that program available to a limited number of students, and to only the best students. Make the year a challenging one but not a requirement for career success.

"The best" are always in short supply, but the Army's chief of staff needs to ensure that a critical mass of the Army's most creative and critical thinkers can always be found at the USAWC. The chief needs to nurture their talents and to protect those whose creativity or criticism makes waves. All institutions, even the Army, need intellectual provocateurs. Their ideas or views may not prove to be wholly true, but the stimulus they give to others will enhance the whole.

Finally, a goal of impunity can be understood to sully a fundamental part of our military's code: sacrifice. In recent years, there has been some reluctance on the part of the military (especially the Army) (which *is*, nevertheless, prepared to make sacrifices for the nation) to use force in situations that were not clearly in the nation's interest, or that were not clearly "worth" dying for. But the possibility of impunity raises an entirely new issue: When one can be personally safe, what is worth killing for? The traditional tenets of just war have led to little restraint.[49] Let me propose a simpler rule developed by Albert Camus while serving in the Resistance during the occupation of France in World War II: "Be neither a victim nor an executioner."

In our determination not to be a victim, we must be careful not to become executioners. Our military guardians' job is to be prepared for war. It is not their job to make policy or to criticize civilians in government or civilians collectively. It is the job of our civilian guardians to protect us, but not to overprotect, overspend, overprepare. It is not necessary to seek impunity. Overpreparation can lead to overreaction and can also be provocative. Citizens must guard their civilian guardians; civilian guardians must guard the military guardians. And our military guardians must be loyal to their professional ethic. This includes thinking about how to ensure that their preparation does preserve the peace and that it is not actually *"the real war"* with battles "only a sort of public verification of the mastery gained during a 'peace'-interval."[50]

Notes

INTRODUCTION

1. *The Federalist* nos. 90 and 92 attribute the question "Who shall guard the guardians themselves?" to the Roman Senator Juventus. This volume will concern itself only with military guardians. Note, though, that there are numerous checks on possible police oppression and exploitation. The jurisdiction of the police is local; their weaponry is limited (no nuclear weapons or land mines, few tanks and grenade launchers); their pay and social status are only middling; and their action is subject to a variety of formal and informal checks from, for example, the judicial system, the press, and watchdog organizations such as civilian review boards and the American Civil Liberties Union.

2. A majority of officers enter through the ROTC. Also, it is important to remember that although this book examines officer education, only some 15 percent of military personnel are officers. Most of the military are enlisted.

3. Some officers attend civilian schools instead of or in addition to command and staff school or a war college. Also, officers' rapidly rotated assignments provide them with a wide variety of on-the-job education.

4. Under the U.S. Constitution, Art. 1, Sec. 8, the elected president does so as commander-in-chief. Elected legislators do so through their power "to raise and support Armies," "to provide and maintain a Navy," and "to make Rules for the Government and Regulation of the land and naval forces," as well as through their responsibility for declaring war.

5. Some might argue that the military came close to mutinous behavior during President Bill Clinton's first administration over the issue of permitting homosexuals to serve in the military. However, the president's plan to implement such a policy was vigorously opposed in Congress as well as by the military, and Congress passed legislation barring service by open homosexuals—legislation that Clinton then signed.

6. For the case of France, see John Stewart Ambler, *Soldiers Against the State* (Anchor Books: Garden City, N.Y., 1968).

7. That senior civilian and military leaders have not been strangers to each other is shown by the fact that eleven of our presidents, roughly a quarter, have been generals. More than a dozen others served in the military. John Adams and Thomas Jefferson did not but played major roles in the Revolution. Only two presidents had an opportunity to serve (that is, they were young adults when the country was at war) and did not: Grover Cleveland and Bill Clinton.

8. Law and tradition, however, separate them from the avowedly political.

9. If an officer is selected for general or admiral, she or he does attend a six-week "capstone," course which is sometimes irreverently referred to as "Charm School."

10. An Army officer who becomes a general stops wearing the insignia denoting his or her branch (specialty). All branches become a general's concern. It is not clear whether the colleges actually retool narrowly focused students, or whether they encourage and further develop those who have been successful specialists but have maintained a broad perspective.

11. For Root's vision of an army war college, see Harry P. Ball, *Of Responsible Command* (Carlisle, Penn.: Alumni Association of the U.S. Army War College, 1994), 57–61.

12. Except for the Panamanian "operation" and the Gulf War, the conflicts mentioned had anti-communist roots and were related to the larger Cold War.

13. A study based strictly on five-year intervals would be tidier, but as I was on campus with the class of 1996 and was a participant observer with the class of 1997 during their study of the core curriculum, there is some elision in the discussion of the post-Cold War curriculum in order to take advantage of my experience.

CHAPTER ONE

1. In peacetime, the Coast Guard is a civilian service under the Secretary of Transportation. In wartime, its command is transferred to the Navy. It has an academy but not a war college.

2. Humor is an important part of military culture. Although jokes can hardly be said to provide "the truth," those that persist are likely to be ones that listeners (those who pass the stories on) recognize as offering insight.

3. Carl H. Builder, *The Masks of War,* Rand Corporation Study (Baltimore: Johns Hopkins University Press, 1989), 5. Much of the discussion in this section is drawn from Builder, who based his work on an analysis of the services' approach to strategic planning. In Builder's analysis, the Marines are not treated separately from the Navy, because they are a combat unit of the Navy and derive their support from the Navy. But one should make no mistake. The Marines *are* different from the other services. (Sara Lister was driven from her position as an Army assistant secretary for describing the Marines as "extremists" in a remark at an academic conference. The language was ill chosen, perhaps, but again the Marines *are* different.) Among other things, they are younger, fewer are married, and they have the lowest retention rate. But perhaps the simplest thing to say is that the Marines seem to take literally things that the other services hold as ideals. They may come closest to the stereotype of the military as patriotic, order-obeying, fierce, and sacrificing. Builder's volume compares and contrasts the services in such fine details as the decor of their Pentagon corridor, the chapels at their academies, and their academy mottoes.

4. A tiny percentage of the Air Force flies, and those who do are largely officers. Thus, in the Air Force the endangered make up only a small percentage and are elite personnel. In the Navy, officers and enlisted are all in the same boat (ship). In the Army, junior officers and junior enlisted personnel are the ones most exposed to danger.

5. When I suggested this to one officer, he rejected my argument out of hand. I argued that members of the military by definition were not the competitive, economic men of democratic and capitalist lore, but were altruistic, socially contributing, even communitarian. I thought I had surely won the day when I reminded him, that he, a devoted church-goer, tithed. (He gave 10 percent of his income to his church.) With vigor he denied that tithing was the result of either generosity or a feeling of community. Tithing, he said, was an order—God's order—and he obeyed orders.

6. Lieutenant-General (then Major-General) Claudia Kennedy, who reached the highest rank ever achieved by an Army woman, described the Army's altar as "combat," arguing that the one-third of the Army in noncombat slots had a greatly reduced chance of ever becoming generals: Statement made at the "Strategic Leadership Workshop on Women in the Military," U.S. Army War College, March 2, 1996. Kennedy later became a public figure when she accused a fellow general of sexual harassment, an accusation that the Army investigated and found credible.

7. Builder, *Masks of War*, 25.

8. Ibid., 27.

9. Although the Army Air Corps eagerly abandoned the Army to become the Air Force after World War II, the Army still flies planes. In fact, it has more planes than the Air Force, but they are not technological wonders. They are helicopters, reconnaissance aircraft, and planes that fly in close support of ground troops. The Navy also has an air force of its own, and some would say that the Marines are its army.

10. Costa Rica is the only nation that has no army, but it is a tiny country and has a large police force.

11. Builder, *Masks of War*, 107.

12. The Naval Academy Prep School, the Navy Adjutant General School, a Senior Enlisted Academy, a Chaplains School, and BOOST, a program to give enlisted personnel the opportunity to become officers, are also located at the site. In addition, a new Naval Warfare Development Command, which includes responsibility for Naval doctrine and for fleet battle experiments, recently moved to Newport.

13. U.S. Naval War College Catalogue (1998), 1. This view is similar to that of the Army War College's founder, Elihu Root, who declared that the way to prevent war is to prepare for it.

14. Ibid., 4.

15. International students and correspondence students do not receive degrees. (Correspondence students' work typically takes three and a half years.)

16. For a more complete discussion see U.S. Naval War College Catalogue (1998), 46 f.

17. Command Presentation, 1998. See also U.S. Naval War College Catalogue (1998).

18. Electives are graded pass/fail.

19. The top 5 percent graduate "With Highest Distinction." The next 15 percent graduate "With Distinction."

20. Civilians make up roughly half the faculty in two departments. Military officers predominate in the Department of Joint Military Operations: "College of Naval Warfare Joint Professional Military Education Self Study," May 1998, App. E.

21. "Naval War College Self Study," 1994, 35, 37.

22. The other six schools within the university are the Marine Corps Command and Staff College, the Officer Candidate School, the Staff Non-commissioned Officers Academy, the Basic School, the Amphibious Warfare School, and the Command Control and Communications Systems School.

23. Beginning in the summer of 1997, a minimum of 20 percent of the military-service student body at service war colleges had to come from the non-hosting service, and one student had to come from each of the two non-hosting services (the sea services are treated as one) in each seminar: *Officer Professional Military Education Policy* CJCSI 1800.01, Chair of the Joint Chiefs of Staff, Washington, D.C., March 1996, B-2. In addition, the mix of military faculty at the senior colleges must comprise no less than 25 percent from non-hosting services, with a minimum of 10 percent from each non-hosting service.

24. The other colleges have academic-freedom policies, but the Marines' policy is especially prominent, even insistent.

25. Change does not come easily, however. The college's "Standard Operating Procedures" manual lists fifteen standards to be examined before any change is made in the curriculum (p. 6-2). These begin with Commander's Guidance and Intent and Marine Corps Order 1553.4 and go through to "common sense and experience" and "available resources."

26. The importance of knowing opponents' capabilities and intentions is emphasized. To learn while keeping one's mind open and supple, the Marines emphasize seeing things from a variety of viewpoints. Thus, during the study of the Pacific Rim, for example, the class might travel to Washington, D.C. for full-day briefings on the region from several different sources, such as the Department of State, a retired CINC, and the Brookings Institution.

27. Just as Montessori education requires extensive and meticulous arrangement so that children can make "spontaneous" discoveries, the Marine Corps takes enormous care to try to create "independent" thinking. Lengthy instruction is given to faculty on how to design a course, beginning with objectives that include the level of learning, and moving on through the design of "courseware" (including methodologies, references, readings, calendar, support material, and a syllabus), and ending with a "class card" for every class meeting that details precisely what is to happen and why during that period.

28. The "Course Director's Task List" lists thirty-nine items.

29. The curriculum involved a significant increase in rigor and the quality of instruction. As part of its new curriculum, the Air War College also shifted from six to thirty civilian faculty.

30. All of the war colleges seek to broaden their officers, to make them more sophisticated, and to help them grasp the political context in which they work. But the concept that officers are to be "statesmen" has a hint of usurpation, of overstepping into the realm of the civilian and the political.

31. Curriculum Catalog (1997), 1. Again, there is a "we know better" element to this curriculum and a certainty that, even with the demise of our Cold War opponent of many years, preparations for war should go undiminished.

32. The assumption seems to be that we should dominate the world. Also, contrasting "liberal" with "realist" and contrasting core values such as democracy and human rights with "interests" seems peculiar. The spirit of the catalogue is assertive; there is little questioning. It is very different from, for instance, the Marine Corps catalogue.

33. The other is the Industrial College of the Armed Forces. Other university components are the Information Resources Management College; the Institute for National Strategic Studies; and, in Norfolk, the Armed Forces Staff College. The Inter-American Defense College is at Fort McNair but is not part of the NDU. Also, the six-week "capstone" course for newly selected generals and flag officers is based at NDU, although this group, like the Marine Corps War College students, travels extensively.

34. *Report of Self Study,* Process for Accreditation of Joint Education (PJAE), 1994, p. 32.

35. In addition to its own college program, ICAF is responsible for the Defense Acquisition University's "Senior Acquisition" course. The students in this program are fully integrated into the ICAF program. Their special course is obtained through the Advanced Courses. ICAF was founded as an Army school in 1924 (to be sure, the lessons learned from World War I were not forgotten). It became a joint school in 1948.

36. "Consideration of Others" is another thread woven through the curriculum to emphasize the diversity of our society and the strains that may arise under conditions of stress.

37. Civilianization of faculty is important for stability. Between 1978 and 1991, ICAF had nine commandants.

38. "ICAF Strategic Plan," Faculty Handbook (1995), 15.

39. Those requirements involve preparation in "jointness" and are discussed further in Chapter 9.

40. This 1989 report on military education was prepared by a subcommittee of the House Armed Services Committee under the direction of Ike Skelton, Democrat of Missouri. It is discussed in Chapter 9.

CHAPTER TWO

1. The German empire was not formed until 1871. Independent Prussia had developed a sophisticated military-education system years before.

2. For more on the Prussian system, see Harry P. Ball, *Of Responsible Command*, rev. ed. (Carlisle, Penn.: U.S. Army War College Alumni Association, 1994), 1–6.

3. Ibid., 14. The Navy's growth coincided with the general acceptance of Captain Alfred Thayer Mahan's naval doctrine, which called for an aggressive, seagoing Navy that could, at a minimum, control the approaches to the Central American isthmus.

4. That issue will not be addressed here.

5. Ball, *Responsible Command*, 22–3.

6. The Military History Institute, located at the Army War College in Carlisle, is appropriately housed in Upton Hall.

7. Ball, *Responsible Command*, 29–30.

8. The Army describes the levels of its activities and analysis as tactical, operational, and strategic. The last is the most comprehensive.

9. The Artillery, Infantry, and Cavalry Schools closed during the Spanish–American War. This was appropriate. In peacetime, the military prepares; in wartime, it fights. Some might argue that our military over-prepares, but if it is not preparing, what should it do during peacetime? One possibility is national service, as it performed in running the CCC camps during the 1930s (see n. 32). Another possibility would be to demobilize to a much greater degree than we did at the end of the Cold War. Deep demobilization was the previous U.S. pattern: Drafted soldiers were rarely reluctant to go home. However, today's volunteer-professionals would be likely to find that kind of demobilization less appealing.

10. Ball, *Responsible Command*, 42.

11. The war against Philippine forces was more challenging.

12. There was no Secretary of the Army. There was a Secretary of War and a Secretary of the Navy. This organization continued through World War II. After that war, the Department of Defense was created, with three service secretaries (Army, Navy, and Air Force) serving under a Secretary of Defense.

13. Ball, *Responsible Command*, 48.

14. The Navy had had a war college since 1885.

15. The planning problems set for war-college students and military staff reflect leaders' best estimate of the possible future direction they might receive from elected officials. Although some planning problems may seem obvious, the public might be surprised (and instructed) if it were to learn about the range of contingencies for which our military prepares.

16. These three purposes are continuously referenced, although they are not as firmly engraved on the hearts of war-college graduates as are "Duty, Honor, Country" on the hearts of West Point graduates.

17. For details, see Ball, *Responsible Command*, 93–6.

18. Ibid., 134.

19. Ibid., 141.

20. An extraordinarily high percentage, due, of course, to the huge expansion of the Army during World War I: Ibid., 137.

21. The Army has an elaborate "lessons learned" system that, if it were conducted candidly, made public, and read, could be extremely valuable.

22. Ball, *Responsible Command*, 149–50, 166.

23. The first class of "The Second War College," the class of 1920, had 75 students: ibid., 158.

24. In 1922, Leavenworth became the Command and General Staff School. Its program was reduced to one year and became selective and competitive. (Only 250 officers were to attend each year.) A number of students failed to complete the course. Individuals also failed the War College—for example, in the class of 1922, almost a quarter of the students did not receive diplomas. This large number, however, would not be typical. Today, virtually all students complete the year successfully.

Instruction at Leavenworth was to encompass leadership and administration of units up through the level of the corps: Ball, *Responsible Command*, 185, 191. Discussion would go on (and on) as to whether there was a "gap" to be filled by the War College in preparing individuals to command large-scale (above corps) operations, or whether the college could safely focus only on strategic issues.

25. This authorization was for an army roughly three times the size of the pre-World War I force. Although there was strong isolationist feeling in Congress and among the public, an army of this size was clearly intended for use abroad: Ball, *Responsible Command*, 147, 167.

26. A 1923 mission statement specifically directed the War College not only to train officers for command and staff for Corps Area and higher commands, but also to prepare officers for General Staff duty: Ibid., 195.

27. History is one of the areas that has been moved in and out of the curriculum.

28. Ball, *Responsible Command*, 211.

29. Ibid., 212.

30. The offending book had actually been submitted to Pershing for review: Ibid., 215.

31. Ibid., 221 f. Personnel and procurement would also be the choices made in the downsizing of the 1990s. It should also be noted that in the 1930s, the Army was required to undertake yet another task for which it had not prepared. President Franklin D. Roosevelt ordered it to enroll 274,000 unemployed men in the Civilian Conservation Corps, then to establish them in work camps. This was to be done even more quickly than the Army had mobilized troops for World War I: Ibid., 223.

32. Ibid., 240 f. Soon thereafter, a series of plans called the Rainbow Series were developed, which abandoned the traditional U.S. strategy of passive continental defense for a more aggressive strategy.

33. In fact, it so reduced the eligible pool that some slots went unfilled: Ibid., 251.

34. Ibid., 288. Civilian academics might argue that minimizing distinctions between students and faculty represents an anti-expert, anti-academic tendency.

35. Ibid., 284. The committee method worked by dividing a problem into separate questions that were to be researched individually. The group then met to analyze and discuss what had been learned and prepared a written report with conclusions and recommendations. This report was presented orally, or "briefed," to a designated audience.

36. Under the Truman Doctrine, the United States was committed to fighting communism everywhere and to assisting nations that faced a communist threat,whether it was foreign or domestic.

37. By 1957, twenty weeks of the curriculum would be devoted to international affairs and national-security problems. The academic year would also be increased from thirty-seven to forty-three weeks. In addition, in 1960 a cooperative program would be set up with George Washington University in Washington, D.C. . to permit students concurrently to earn a master's degree in international affairs: Ball, *Responsible Command*, 319 f, 505.

38. By 1957, the time allocated to war planning would be reduced to eleven weeks.

39. Atomic weapons and long-range missiles had brought new complexity to planning.

40. Ball, *Responsible Command*, 292–3.

41. Nuclear weapons and strategies related to them stimulated interest in national security among civilian academics, who had tended to ignore the military as a research subject.

42. The journal, which would be called *Parameters*, would begin publication twenty years later, in 1971: Ball, *Responsible Command*, 314, 506.

43. A chief of staff can influence curriculum powerfully through directives sent to the commandant, which are forwarded to the dean and then issued to the faculty, most of whom wear uniforms and only temporarily serve on the faculty. Civilian academic leaders find it more difficult to manipulate a school's curriculum.

44. John F. Kennedy was elected president in 1960.

45. This was the case at West Point. Ball, *Responsible Command*, 363.

46. Ibid., 370–1, 383–5. Electives began in 1967–68, and the extension/ correspondence program began in 1968–69.

47. Ibid., 392. During the Vietnam War, the reserves were not activated. Draftees gave only two years of service, individuals served in Vietnam for only one year, and college students were exempted from the draft. All these policies would be questioned in postwar analyses.

48. Vietnam technically was not a war, and in some libraries you will find nothing at all in the database under that topic.

49. Within a few years, an arrangement would be made with nearby Shippensburg State College that allowed Army War College graduates to enroll con-

currently in a master's degree program there. At the time, more than half of the students at the War College already held master's degrees: Ball, *Responsible Command*, 409.

50. Ibid., 394. A study done by the Center for Strategic and International Studies in 2000 suggested that "disappointment" in senior leaders may be hard to eliminate: Center for Strategic and International Studies, "The American Military Culture in the Twenty-first Century" (2000), xxii, 68–71, 79–80.

51. Ball, *Responsible Command*, 400.

52. As Davis was undertaking his assessment of the Army War College, Admiral Stansfield Turner was radically and quite publicly changing both the curriculum and method of instruction at the Naval War College: Ibid., 418. For an extended discussion of Davis's reforms, see ibid., 410–18.

53. Ibid., 430. Note that the first black students graduated in the class of 1963. The first women graduated in 1969. The first female faculty member, Evelyn P. Foote, taught in 1979: Ibid., 505–7.

54. This program certainly aimed at expanding the views of the Army's future leadership rather than at training them for specific professional behavior: Ibid., 437.

55. Ibid., 446.

56. Ibid., 445.

57. The IF program is discussed in more detail in Chapter 3.

58. Ball, *Responsible Command*, 453.

59. Ibid., 460.

60. Harry Summers, *On Strategy: A Critical Analysis of the Vietnam War* (Novato, Calif.: Presidio Press, 1995).

Clausewitz is probably best known for his assertion that war is a continuation of policy by other means. The Army, however, derives a number of lessons from his *On War*, including the concept of the "fog" and "friction" of war and the importance of the "trinity" of government, the military, and the people.

61. In large part to increase officer retention.

62. Ball, *Responsible Command*, 138.

63. Ball describes this method as assisting practitioners to become very good at what they were doing, but with "no assurance that what they were doing was correct": Ibid., 141.

64. The commandant and his faculty were all World War I veterans.

65. This curriculum would remain in place until the school was closed at the beginning of World War II.

66. Richard A. Chilcoat, "The 'Fourth' Army War College: Preparing Strategic Leaders for the Next Century." *Parameters* 25, mo. 4 (winter 1995–96): 3–17.

CHAPTER THREE

1. Note the changes in geography, positions (often alternating between command and staff positions), and units. Typically, officers proceed to bigger units. An infantry platoon has twenty to forty members and is composed of

several squads. A company is composed of platoons and has sixty to 140 members. A battalion is composed of companies and may have as many as 850 personnel. A brigade (composed of battalions) may have up to 2,000 members. (Ordinarily one would not receive a brigade command until after completing one of the war colleges.) Larger units are the division, the corps (up to 50,000), a Field Army, and an Army Group.

To complicate things, the Infantry, Artillery, and Cavalry (tanks) branches do not always use the same nomenclature. For example, an Artillery company-level unit is called a battery. And the number of personnel in units varies a great deal by branch (Colonel Karl Farris, USA, ret., e-mail to the author, June 22, 1999).

2. This portrait is of the in-residence class. The USAWC program is also offered through correspondence to selected students. This is a two-year program with two two-week summer sessions. Many of the correspondence students are reservists or members of the National Guard, but others are active-duty officers who pursue the program while fulfilling other full-time duties. The correspondence class may suffer a 30–50 percent attrition rate, but completion is supposed to "count" in the same way that it does for in-residence students. A group of some forty Senior Service College Fellows are also considered members of the USAWC class as far as items such as the yearbook and class gift are concerned, but after an orientation at the War College they spend their year at a civilian institution, such as the University of Texas or Massachusetts Institute of Technology, or at an agency such as the U.S. Department of Health and Human Services or even the Institute of Peace.

The Army War College also provides several short courses, including a two-week Adjutants General National Security Seminar for senior National Guard officers; a six-month Defense Strategy Course (correspondence); a one-week Reserve Component National Security Issues Seminar, held in Washington, D.C.; and a one-week Senior Reserve Component Officers Course for general and flag officers.

3. USAWC classes are larger than those of the Naval, Air, and Marine war colleges. Some Executive MBA programs and Harvard's Kennedy School do offer an intensive year of training to mid-level professionals. However, the only other group education at this level—that is, education for people employed together in the past who can expect to be employed together in the future—are two federal government programs: one for executive-level members of the civil service, and the other for State Department personnel.

4. Recent downsizing truncated some careers. Nevertheless, retirement by age fifty was not atypical for many officers. Often, this means a somewhat difficult transition to civilian employment.

5. Twenty is a magic number, because in that year, the war-college class was organized around twenty seminars with sixteen members, and the equal-distribution policy, or the uniform seminar policy, required one Air Force and one sea-service member per seminar.

6. Military-to-military contacts of this kind can facilitate combined efforts under the North Atlantic Treaty Organization (NATO), the United Nations, or

other collective sponsorship. Such contacts may also serve an intelligence func-tion. There is also some argument that foreign officers can learn professional skills and values, such as respect for civilian authority, from our military. Also, there may be some anticipation of military sales to militaries that have worked with us and know our equipment. One remote but harrowing scenario involves militaries of several countries deciding that they know better than their civil-ian governments and acting together outside the limits of civilian authorization. Indeed, one of the required core texts at the USAWC that year was Bob Wood-ward's *The Commanders* (New York: Simon and Schuster, 1991). Woodward states that when William J. Crowe, Jr., was Chair of the Joint Chiefs of Staff, he set up a secret, private communications channel to his Soviet counterpart, *without clear-ing it through the administration* (p. 6; emphasis added). The purpose was to avoid "accidental" war or war derived from missteps or misinterpretations by politicians. Two years later, this hotline was made legitimate. But the questions of whether Woodward was right (that the two military heads acted collusively and without authorization) and, if he was, whether there was anything wrong with such an action were not raised in any seminar discussion that I know of. When I raised the question with individuals, they did not find it troubling, although it was not clear whether they were not troubled because they assumed Woodward was wrong or because they thought it was wise to avoid placing too much confidence in civilians/politicians.

7. Because the other war colleges also enroll international students, the degree of military-to-military interaction is significant.

8. During the year, they are also excluded from a very limited number of lec-tures and exercises for security reasons.

9. These data and those that follow apply only to U.S. students.

10. See the summary in the General Accounting Office's "Operation Desert Storm Evaluation of the Air Campaign," GAO/NSIAD-97-134, June 1997.

11. Seminars followed a distributive principle that required each to have two IFs, one civilian, one sea-service officer, one Air Force officer, one National Guard or Army Reserve officer, one combat service support officer, one combat support officer, and one combat arms officer. Thus, nine of the sixteen slots were filled by category. Also, only ten of the sixteen could be Regular Army officers.

12. The divorce and deferred-family rates are probably lower for war col-lege students than for civilians with similar levels of education and income. Three-fourths of the students were married at the time, and three-fourths had children. The two groups were not perfectly congruent.

13. "Geographical bachelors" are individuals who came to Carlisle alone, leaving their families elsewhere.

14. This is the source of the stories about Students A, B, and C presented earlier.

15. Students are encouraged to have family members take the test, too. The idea is that family relations can be improved if members' responses can be bet-ter predicted and understood. I did this. It does make one more tolerant when one realizes that a husband's preference for reading a book to dancing is real

and not perverse, or that a daughter's impulsive decisions are just how she makes decisions and not merely a backlash in response to one's own deliberation over carefully executed decision trees.

16. After scoring, individual MBTI results are shown on a card that is placed next to one's name card in the seminar room. Thus, seminar mates should have a leg up on how best to deal with one another.

17. Seminar handout (fall 1996).

18. If each of the sixteen types were evenly distributed, which they are not, each box would contain 6.25 percent of the population.

19. Many friends wondered what a nice girl like me was doing at a war college. My MBTI explained it perfectly. As an "E," I was willing to plunge into a new social milieu; as an "N," my professor self could hardly wait to explain it; and as a "TJ," I was as logical and structured as the best of them.

20. The 4 percent and 4 percent selection rate was stated by a commandant, but official inquiries about the rate yield a variety of responses, most of them less selective. Also, as noted in Chapter 2, Corresponding Studies is a written course that includes two in-residence summer blocs. A significant number of these students do not complete the course, but those who do receive the same credit as those in the resident course.

21. A briefing or brief is a highly stylized presentation in which information is imparted clearly and confidently. It is almost always accompanied by a slide or overhead presentation. There is no fumbling for notes, no hesitation. The speaker "stands up, speaks up, and sits down." Most officers are good briefers.

22. The same name (but perhaps a different color) is used for the main auditorium at the Army Command and Staff College at Fort Leavenworth.

23. The auditorium has two sections of 240, seating 480.

24. As in the medical field, the military approaches its tasks rationally and systematically and armed with as much data as possible. However, although both professions employ science as far as they are able, both see the highest practice of their profession as involving "art"—something that goes beyond the mere use of logic and facts. Also, note the use of "strategic"—a central theme that will be repeated again and again.

25. Some may have doubts as to the degree to which these themes become an actual part of the college experience, but those who plan orientation programs always have high hopes.

26. Still other Army officers attend the other five war colleges. Thus, although many Army colonels will have had a "third tier" of PME, its content and the environment in which they have worked will be quite varied. In fact, if one hundred Regular Army officers attend the other war colleges or are chosen as Fellows and 185 attend the Army War College, a third of the senior Regular Army officers will have had quite a different experience from the other two-thirds. This may suggest that it is not so important to have a standard, shared curriculum at the USAWC itself.

27. Since passage of the 1986 Goldwater–Nichols Act, "jointness" has become a formal requirement and a bureaucratic accrediting burden for military pro-

grams. Its purpose is to end inefficient and even dangerous rivalry among the services. This is examined in more detail in Chapter 9.

28. Cooperation among the services, with civilian agencies, and with allies differs from cohesion, which is part of any effective military unit and is an essential element in all military training, beginning with basic training, the first level of military education.

29. Indeed, students are told again and again not to settle for "school solutions."

30. See also n. 26.

31. Manuals and training are valuable because they make it possible for an institution to function effectively even when there is rapid rotation of personnel.

32. This, of course, is part of rising to the top of any institution. Faculty who become university administrators have to grasp the purpose, not just the content, of their institutions and its rules. They must also learn to operate in a larger and nonacademic environment. The Swiss psychologist Jean Piaget demonstrated that, as they mature, even little boys playing marbles learn the purpose of rules and the need to modify them to fulfill the game's deeper purpose, play.

Change may be particularly hard to initiate in a conservative institution such as the military. However, once a course is chosen, there is a distinct advantage to being able to order altered behavior.

33. Most faculty are fellow officers, do not have Ph.D.s, are themselves recent war-college graduates, and have been faculty for only a short time. Thus, students are teachers not just because they are experienced, but also because the faculty does not possess deep expertise. This will be discussed further in Chapter 4.

34. The duties of a course instructor will be discussed in Chapter 4.

35. Attributed to J. F. C. Fuller in the orientation brief.

36. Similarly, although successful officers are generally a competitive lot, they are instructed that the USAWC year is to be one of cooperation, not competition—that collegiality is to be the norm. This is probably made easier by having distributed (or "one of each") seminars. If a whole seminar were composed, for example, of colonels who were nurses, each would likely be gunning to become commander of the Nurse Corps. Distribution means that one is not likely to be interacting actively with one's direct competitors for assignments and promotion. Competition may also be reduced by the USAWC's policy of not giving exams or grades.

37. Reputations earned in a graduate seminar can follow one for years. Twenty or more years later, estimates of a full professor's accomplishments can still be influenced by the opinions about his or her ability that former graduate seminar classmates hold.

38. In *Ideology and Utopia* (New York: Harcourt Brace, 1968), Karl Mannheim describes the impact of generations on social views. He sees twenty-year-olds, forty-year-olds, and sixty-year-olds as having different views because of their age, but he also notes that people who have experienced major upheavals such

as a war or depression share views. He notes, further, that when individuals share imprinting events at the same chronological age, they are an especially cohesive generation.

39. Their "successes" would include smaller operations in Grenada and Panama and recent operations in Bosnia, Kosovo, and Afghanistan.

40. The memory of Vietnam and the experience of the Gulf war and of Kosovo may also have created a generation that places great emphasis on "force protection," believing that it is both wise and possible to prosecute a war successfully while incurring few casualties.

41. Alfred North Whitehead, *The Aims of Education and Other Essays* (New York: Free Press, 1967).

42. Whitehead is very much a proponent of "active" learning, but it is active thinking, not physical experiencing, that he means. He is also an advocate of the importance of self-stimulation and self-learning. For him, the ultimate goal is not the accumulation of information, or even learning how to learn, but acquiring the *habit* of learning.

CHAPTER FOUR

1. Typically, there are only twenty civilian students in a class of more than 300. In a 1996 study, the USAWC listed about a quarter of its faculty as civilians.

2. In the USAWC self-appraisal, ABDs ("all but dissertations") were counted as Ph.D.s, but in compiling the data from the self-appraisal for purposes of this discussion, I have listed ABDs in the master's degree category. In fact, an ABD has done a good deal more course work than the master's degree holder, but she or he has not demonstrated the ability to do and report a major piece of research.

3. In 2001, the chair in Corresponding Studies was civilianized. A retired colonel with a Ph.D. in history was appointed as chair.

4. SSI faculty are typically employed on three-year contracts. They do not enjoy the protection offered by academic tenure, although their work may deal with potentially controversial subjects. Although no issues of academic freedom have been raised recently, one would expect a certain amount of self-censorship—although even that may not be necessary. SSI faculty are likely to be selected (and self-selected) to have pretty much the same assumptions and come to pretty much the same conclusions as those for whom they work. In a civilian institution, academic freedom is highly prized, but even if a tenured faculty member's basic salary is secure, to do research she or he usually must compete for funding from a variety of government and private institutions. In that sense, civilian faculty, too, have "masters."

In 1999, a decision was made to make SSI "more Army relevant." Seven of its nine civilian faculty left or retired. Some felt that the SSI's mission had been changed from providing impartial strategic analyses to advocacy of Army positions and policy. The new director is a retired Army colonel.

5. The commandant appointed in the summer of 1997 has a Ph.D. in history from Duke University. His successor obtained a Ph.D. from the University of Wisconsin.

6. When an officer is going to be assigned as a faculty member to West Point, she or he is given the opportunity first to obtain a master's degree in the relevant field. Officers are not likely to be given further subject-matter education as a prelude to being assigned as faculty to the USAWC, even though the students there will be mature and probably will already have graduate degrees.

7. For example, a "historian" is assigned to each seminar as part of the teaching team. This does not mean the faculty member has a degree in history, although many do.

8. Because so many faculty are given only three-year assignments or appointments, and because not all of them complete those assignments, turnover is high. In fact, at the Academic Board meeting of November 25, 1996, faculty turnover for one core course was reported as 45 percent for that year and predicted as 58 percent for the next year. This high rate is partly explained by faculty who retire early when attractive civilian employment materializes. Also, in general, officers can retire at will. Enlisted personnel sequentially reenlist for specific periods of time.

9. Semipermanent employment that can be ended for cause and that is designed to protect academic freedom—that is, it is a protection for an individual justified by the benefit to society of permitting wide and sometimes unpopular inquiry.

10. Typically, candidates do not know who has been asked to evaluate their work, and at least some of the letter-writers should have had no previous connection with the candidate.

11. In public institutions especially, some percentage of raise money may be allocated across the board. Also, some moneys may be allotted to "compression." Compression occurs when first-year faculty are brought in at a higher salary than other recently hired junior faculty. Few senior faculty achieve large raises without resubmitting themselves to the national market, and being prepared to change institutions if they are made an offer elsewhere and their home institution does not match it.

12. Further, although virtually all schools have degree requirements, those requirements tend to involve the taking of certain *kinds* of courses—for example, mathematics, artistic creation, language. Courses are rarely prescribed on the basis of their content. For instance, American history used to be a standard requirement. This is no longer the case. And even if one American history course is required, one student might take "The Civil Rights Movement," another "Patterns of Colonial Immigration," and yet another "The Labor Movement in the United States." There would be no overlap at all, no shared content, but each course would fulfill the requirement.

13. Eight a.m. (even 7:30) seems very reasonable to people who schedule meetings in the military. And the time a meeting is scheduled for is the time that

meeting begins. In fact, more than once I attended meetings at the USAWC that began not on time but early, because everyone was prepared and there.

14. There is a feast-and-famine element to the teaching. When one's department is offering the material in the core curriculum, one is absorbed much of the day every day. When one's department is "off," many other duties remain.

15. Students' communications skills are tested soon after arrival. A class in remedial writing is made available to seventy-five students. The bottom third in the testing are offered the opportunity to take the course; the bottom twenty-five students are strongly urged to do so. The editor of *Parameters*, an Army journal published at Carlisle, estimates that 20 percent of the students need remedial work, and that only 20 percent are able to prepare a publishable paper, even though all are required to write one.

16. The duties involved as escort fill three pages in the handbook. They are significant, and this is an area in which one is expected not to err.

17. And a lot of colleagues. Four faculty teach in each seminar of sixteen students. This provides a student-to-teaching faculty ratio of 4-to-1. If one counts all those listed as faculty in the draft self-appraisal, there are 133 faculty for 320 students, or a ratio of 2.4-to-1.

18. Self-Appraisal (1996), Annex 6-C.

19. Note that this is for an eleven-month year, not the nine-month year of a typical civilian school.

20. Senior faculty might well be willing to come and benefit from a year or two as a visiting professor, but they would be expensive.

21. The Socratic method involves teaching by questioning, a difficult technique that is rarely well executed.

22. The composition and responsibilities of the Academic Board are discussed in Chapter 9.

23. Top administrators from the various war colleges meet regularly, and some comparison of war-college curricula is part of their discussion. Also, a variety of outside bodies may offer unsolicited advice—for example, Congressional and Department of Defense panels.

24. In the tips for new faculty, the phrase "be prepared" is repeated over and over. That is always good advice, of course, but it also seems to reflect the fact that new USAWC faculty in general are not prepared (if only because they must teach material prepared by others), and that they must invest a great deal in preparation every day. In contrast, a new civilian faculty member will have spent four to ten years of study before assuming the role of graduate instructor.

25. A course directive is a super-syllabus.

26. One knowledgeable observer said that the problem with ensuring "rigor" in the curriculum lay not in the students but in the faculty. He believed the curriculum had to be dumbed down so the faculty could teach it.

27. The best-known quotation attributed to Socrates is, "He who knows he doesn't know, knows."

28. At least abstractly there is a consciousness of the difference between training and education. But "teaching" is conventionally used to describe both successful training and successful education. Great care is taken to do a good job of teaching, but the question is not systematically raised: "Are we teaching them who, what, when, were, and how to, or are we asking why, what is the evidence, is that logical, how do you and how do we know?"

29. Retirement for a colonel is mandatory after thirty years of service. Thus, if a faculty member attended the Army War College, had another assignment, returned to teach at Carlisle, then received the college's version of tenure, it would probably cover no more than an additional five-year period.

30. For a total of twenty-three.

31. "Title 10 Civilian Faculty Manual" (n.d.), 1. A civilian institution might ask faculty to express commitment to the fearless pursuit of truth and transmission of knowledge to the next generation, but they would not be asked to place public interest over private or personal interest. Ever since Adam Smith, and reinforced by liberals such as John Stuart Mill, our national ideology has simply assumed the compatibility, the harmony, of individual and public interest.

32. Self-Appraisal (1996), Annex 6-A.

33. They are good candidates because they are more familiar and comfortable with the work to be done and the manner in which it is done—indeed, the whole context of military higher education. Also, in 2000, Congress repealed the Dual Compensation Law, so retired military can now receive full retirement benefits while employed by the federal government. One should expect that in the future even more faculty will be retired officers.

34. A female faculty member noted that, when she was a student as recently as 1990, there were only four women in her class—and that her fellow students kept confusing her, a female officer with black hair, with a blond civilian. Of the four women, one was civilian and one was a nurse. In the whole class, then, there were only two female officers in non-traditional fields, and of course none were in combat branches. Also, it did not seem to bother other class members when slides of a woman in a bikini or of two elephants copulating were slipped into a series supporting an all-college lecture.

35. In an academic institution, the usual source of "discomfort" is exams and grades. At their orientation, USAWC students were told to expect (and even welcome) discomfort. It is not clear what administrators thought would create it.

36. One suspects that the explanations offered have a good deal to do with justifying what has been an Army War College tradition. The other war colleges give grades.

37. This imposes another burden on the faculty adviser, because the adviser's responsibility is not restricted to the academic. It includes mentoring the advisee as to his or her self-development plan for the Army War College year and his or her goals for the future.

38. Which for most people probably translates into "grades."

39. The library has a remarkable current periodical collection, so staying up to date is not difficult.

40. These are part of the materials given to new faculty at orientation.

41. Note that curriculum changes for the fall will have been worked out the previous spring.

42. Professional schools, such as those in business and law, consciously train for a vocation or an occupation and are the schools that are the most likely to have good alumni lists and the means to conduct such surveys.

43. "USAWC Graduates: 1983 to 1991, Education for Strategic Leadership," Directorate of Academic Affairs, U.S. Army War College, Carlisle, Penn., n.d. A similar survey done earlier contains similar results, and the larger number of free-form "comments" make interesting reading. It also includes a discussion of whether grades should be initiated. The overwhelming response was "no." The earlier survey also discussed the differences between the in-residence and Corresponding Studies experience: See Glenda Y. Nogami, Julie Colestock, and Terry Phoenix, "U.S. Army War College Alumni Survey, Graduates from 1983–1989," U.S. Army War College, Carlisle, Penn., n.d.

44. "USAWC Graduates: 1983 to 1991," 15.

45. Military students have to pass fitness exams every six months, but responsibility for fitness is individual. The presence of the Army Fitness Research Institute means there is an emphasis on education about fitness at Carlisle. Also, at entry students are given a thorough exam and are advised on an appropriate "wellness" program.

46. Jointness would soon receive more attention, as curriculum changes would be closely monitored to insure that Goldwater–Nichols provisions were being implemented. See Chapter 9.

47. USAWC efforts to build consensus seem to have been successful.

48. There were 320 responses to 432 surveys. The study was conducted in 1991 and asked generals to think about what would be required of a general officer in the year 2000, almost a decade in the future. It should be noted that the officers would have experienced a "Cold War curriculum," but would have had as their immediate experience the collapse of the Soviet Union and the waging of the Gulf War: Glenda Nogami, Lisa J. Baum, and Judith R. Vetock, "U.S. Army War College 2000: Army Senior Officer Education," U.S. Army War College, Carlisle, Penn., 1992.

49. Ibid., 6.

50. They missed the degree to which operations would not just be joint (with other services) but would be coalition operations—that is, with allies.

51. Army War College students travel to New York and visit the United Nations; only International Fellows take a trip abroad. Students at the Air War College and National War College do take international trips. Speakers are mostly exemplary, not contrary.

52. Historians are collected from many different Army War College units. They do not have a department of their own. Thus, they are likely to be easy targets for an administrator determined to trim.

53. Pleasing students is a powerful incentive to teach well for any faculty member. In a civilian school, though, students are young, not so experienced, and not exceptionally critical. In addition, they usually want good grades. War College students can be more critical. They are self-confident, middle-aged, and unused to having their time wasted. Most of them want a brigade command when they leave—something a faculty member cannot dispense, although she or he could exercise a veto.

54. Again, teaching involves successful classroom performance by a faculty member. Evaluations tend not to distinguish between performance that trains (conveys information, elicits desired behavior) and one that educates (stimulates critical and creative thinking—at best, habitually).

55. In this discussion, Ph.D. is equated with "expert." I recognize the existence of many non-degreed experts and the inadequacies of many degree holders, but academic convention calls for Ph.D.s for those teaching in graduate programs.

56. Some will have taught previously at West Point and in ROTC programs.

57. However, the college is also competing against the Army Chief of Staff, the Chair of the Joint Chiefs of Staff, and the CINCs, all of whom are seeking the best among the graduates.

58. Nogami et al., "U.S. Army War College Alumni Survey," 10.

59. But why not? Pre-retirees represent the most experienced officers. Why would the best faculty be those eager to leave the college for a "real" job?

60. There is little of the Martin Luther spirit: "Here I stand; I cannot do otherwise."

61. Including the judgment not just of teaching partners, but also of students, graduates, and generals.

62. Being a civilian in a military institution is probably more comfortable for some than for others. In a discussion with one female civilian student, I asked whether she had had any of the "token" experiences Rosabeth Moss Kantor describes in *Men and Women of the Corporation* (New York: Basic Books, 1993). She replied that she was used to working in a largely male environment but that she found her status as a civilian created credibility difficulties. Other civilians, too, referred to the need for civilians to be appreciative of the fact that this was a military institution, not just a "college."

CHAPTER FIVE

1. There are even reserved fishing spots for the handicapped (with a supporting rail) at creekside.

2. A speech second only to Pericles' Funeral Oration in arguing the honor residing in dying on behalf of democracy.

3. The ones with no utility lines belong to the Amish.

4. Well, on the East Coast they are called "mountains"—specifically, the Appalachians and the Blue Ridge. Both ranges are within bicycling distance of Carlisle.

5. Except that the U.S. version is built of gray stone, whereas the one in England is red.

6. Three interstate highways and toll roads converge at Carlisle.

7. There is also a jail where visitors line up to visit friends and relatives.

8. Carlisle is the retirement community of choice for a large number of military personnel. Some 90,000 military retirees and their families are said to live within a fifty-mile radius of the town: *The Banner* (August 1995), 9.

9. The land now occupied by the Army War College, however, was owned by the Penn family.

10. This is not true of other nearby towns.

11. There is regular discussion, however, about how local high-school teams should incorporate "post-toasties," or student athletes who will be available for only one season because their Army War College families are in town for just one year.

12. In May 1996, a memo circulated on post noting that tattoos could denote membership in an extremist group—something that was of grave concern to the Army. Current Army War College students are not of a generation that accepted the tattoo as part of exuberant, not just alienated, youth culture. In twenty years, though, it is possible that tattoos and even pierced bodies could be a part of war-college culture, just as they are now a part of civilian youth culture. It is hard to imagine, though.

13. In general, the Army has posts, the Navy has yards, the Air Force has bases, and the Marines have camps and forts.

14. Western farmers did not want to pay federal taxes on whiskey that they were manufacturing.

15. Washington was definitely a commander-in-chief.

16. But perhaps this is not irony. A warrior may be less likely to hate his enemy than civilians who are better able to stereotype those with whom they have no contact. A soldier may also have respect for a brave opponent and can feel compassion for those he has vanquished. Some retired U.S. Vietnam veterans have actually sought "reunions" with former enemies. Also, it is not unusual for retired military personnel to seek employment with relief agencies working areas in which they served while in the military.

17. As a lieutenant, Pratt had also served as an officer with the all-Negro 10th Cavalry Regiment; thus, he was also familiar with this minority community.

18. Substantial personal and financial support for the school came from the Society of Friends.

19. Critics charged the program with kidnapping Indian children and destroying native languages and culture.

20. After it lost its cherished Fort McNair building to the National War College (see Chapter 2). Commemorative plaques, photos, and other evidence of Carlisle's multifaceted history are much in evidence throughout the post. One cannot be in residence for a year without absorbing much of the post's story.

21. However, there is no Officers' Club. Policies that discourage drinking and that require pay-your-way clubs put a virtual end to this institution, though it

is still featured in war novels and movies. The former club building is now used as a Community Center, and special and catered events are held there. The change was made in 1994, and the deficit at Carlisle decreased from $195,945 to $70,978 in the first year: "Good Times Guide" (December 1995), 1. A special problem for Carlisle is that it offers a complete array of opportunities for a small garrison. If retirees did not use the Community Center, the facility's budget would be even more difficult to balance.

22. But security is not. One can drive onto the campus and park with no questions asked. The one secure building is Collins Hall, site of the war-gaming facilities. It was not always this way. Security eased following the end of the Cold War, but it not clear whether this resulted from a belief that the Soviet Union was no longer an enemy or merely because it was no longer effectual.

23. My seminar had sixteen students. Only five lived on-post; nine lived off-post; and two were road runners, or commuters. Collectively, there were twenty-six children. Nine of the sixteen students had master's degrees. Three students and one seminar instructor were named Mike.

24. Practices that seems quaintly (or excessively) controlling can be very functional for individuals who lead a nearly nomadic existence. The ability to settle quickly into life in a new location is essential to military personnel. That is why so much attention is given to making things predictable (and to requiring name tags). Even so, a significant capacity for flexibility is also a prerequisite for success in a military career, where assignments, locations, superiors, and subordinates are constantly changing.

25. The academic program for the whole class is conducted in a single building, Root Hall. Attached to it is Bliss Hall, the main auditorium. On the other side is one of several gyms. The other principal structures are Upton Hall, once the site of the college and now the site of the Army History Institute, and Collins Hall, the war-gaming facility.

26. Carlisle is a small town. On a still summer evening, one can hear taps being played from the other side of town—usually ten minutes after the ice-cream truck has gone by.

27. This is true of the military generally. Although the military prepares for risky missions, it makes every effort to eliminate the risks of everyday accidents.

28. There are still a substantial number of athletic injuries among these expensive, middle-aged officers, for intramural competition goes on all year. The Jim Thorpe Day extramural competition especially calls forth unwise but heroic efforts.

29. Even basement service areas have paintings, photos, and trophy cases.

30. Civilians have a plaque of their own.

31. These are a favored class gift because the artist also sells prints of the painting to class members, who can then sell their prints to collectors and recoup the donation they made to the class gift. Class-gift decisions are not always easy. One year, a lengthy discussion involved whether a Civil War painting was an appropriate gift, and, if so, whether a painting that showed the Confederate flag would be acceptable.

32. The seminar table seats precisely sixteen students and is equipped with TV, video, computer projection—everything the proponent of the high-tech classroom could desire.

33. Civilians sometimes feel marginalized in a military environment. Similarly, enlisted people, who make up 85 percent of the military and dominate most posts, sometimes feel isolated at Carlisle, where they are outnumbered and surrounded not only by lieutenants and captains but also by lieutenant-colonels and colonels.

34. One more publication is "Alive," put out by the Fitness Research Center.

35. It should be noted that non-compliance is also part of military life. For instance, rules, stern warnings, and even pleadings bar the use of black-soled tennis shoes on the well-kept gym floors. To achieve zero defects in this regard, one gym even stocks dozens and dozens of tennis shoes for use (for free) by people who arrive wrongly equipped. There are still marks on the floor.

36. One officer added, "Most of us don't have that many civilian clothes, anyway."

37. Army women, Navy men and women, and Air Force men and women may use umbrellas while in uniform. An Army general may use an umbrella if it is held by an aide; he may not shelter himself. Some think that the Army cannot (or will not) change its policy for men until the Marines change theirs; this could be a long time coming.

38. Some of my distinguished academic colleagues wear sandals, shorts, and T-shirts when lecturing. (It is hot and humid in Miami.) Ironically, many of the students there come to class directly from white-collar jobs and are better dressed than their professors.

39. Carlisle's year actually lasts ten months, from August to June. This narrative is based on the "Weekly Schedules" from 1995–96.

40. Newcomers are provided with maps, informal ratings of local restaurants, and briefings on local schools and community organizations. Local businesses and organizations also hold a "fair" on-post to acquaint new class members and their families quickly with the Carlisle community.

41. The commandant and his wife give a separate welcome to spouses, who are also invited to all of the orientation presentations except the meeting of the seminars.

42. Faculty at civilian schools feel sufficiently challenged when they offer one three-hour graduate seminar a week. (They would also probably be teaching a lecture class.) USAWC faculty meet their three-hour seminars three times a week.

43. The club retains its traditional name, although most official announcements now refer to "spouse" events. There are some male spouses, some absentee wives (leaving their husbands what are called "geographic bachelors"), and some working wives with low participation rates. Still, wives' clubs do continue to exist.

44. Families can be a distraction to military personnel. In recent years, the Pentagon has recognized that the happiness of spouses and children is of great importance to the retention of senior personnel (officers and enlisted). Thus, mil-

itary family programs are given both attention and resources, and this is reflected in the active programming for families at the Army War College. The fact is that many of the students have been in jobs that required long and irregular hours as well as temporary duty (and year-long assignments) away from home. Being on a post or campus and keeping regular hours (8:30 A.M. to 4:00 P.M.) is experienced as a luxury (or by some as slacking off). Repeated admonitions by the commandant to "spend time with your family," and actually having the time to do so, were just not a part of most students' recent experience.

Family programs have two purposes beyond retention. One is readiness—to ensure that a spouse called away for an assignment can leave promptly and with confidence that the family can effectively manage necessary affairs in his or her absence. The second is to prepare students and spouses for future leadership. Thus, two rather different kinds of family programs were offered.

One covered a wide range of topics, often bringing guest speakers to Carlisle. These included sessions on the meaning of MBTI scores for relationships within the family (children older than nine were encouraged to take the profile); planning for college (many students had high-school-age children); financial management and tax preparation; caring for aging parents; health maintenance for men and for women; getting a state job; and substance-abuse awareness. One particularly important course was the "Transition Course for Seniors." Army War College students are precisely the age at which some men have what is known colloquially as a midlife crisis and academically as a midlife transition. The transition is made especially dramatic for military officers because retirement (chosen or forced) becomes an option just as they have achieved mastery of their profession and when they are much too young to imagine a life of leisure, even if they could afford it. Further, in a period of downsizing, "selective early retirement" is an unpleasant possibility. In 1995, very successful officers were facing the possibility of a limited military future. These were people who had enjoyed years of significant success but also whose skills might or might not be transferable (or seen as transferable) to the civilian sector.

A second set of programs specifically targeted the wives whose husbands might become commanders. These programs included a mock selection (promotion) to help the spouse understand the effect of major events in an officer's career; a five-day "Facilitating, Leadership and Group Skills" workshop; a senior leaders' wives idea exchange; and sessions on legal issues for spouses and customs and courtesies.

45. He is always alert to the possibility of finding publishable articles but claims not to be sanguine about the number of SRPs that will meet his standards.

46. During the year other dances will be sponsored by the Marines (a ball), the civilians (a sock hop), and, of course, the Army (a ball).

47. The leader of my seminar had a deep west Texas accent. During my first week at Carlisle, I heard him everywhere I went—in the coffee shop, at the library's photocopying machine, in the corridor. I kept turning around to say "hello," but he was nowhere in sight. Finally, I realized that his drawl was not unique in the Carlisle population.

48. They may, though, have lived in foreign countries.

49. One seminar's IF sent a postcard featuring nearly nude Brazilian women. It was diligently passed around the room, without a single comment. The three women present and respect for the international student worked to silence comments—of all varieties.

50. This ambitious event involves bringing several hundred senior citizens to the Community Center for refreshments—700 dozen homemade cookies—and putting on a musical program and skits. This is done on two different days and requires participation by every student and most spouses. It also requires raising some $4,000. This was the one event that came close to provoking a rebellion among folks accustomed to doing what was specified as "voluntary" but experienced as required.

51. "Elective" means you have choice, but you have to choose something. "Option" describes an opportunity one may or may not pursue, as one is inclined.

52. They must, however, be evenly distributed across the regions, so some may get a second or third choice.

53. It was reported that in a two-year period, class members lost 1,000 pounds.

54. I took line dancing. When I had taken a class in my hometown, the handful of men were awkward and abashed. At the Army War College, half the class was male, and they were stars. But, of course, they know their left from right; they have been marching and drilling for years.

55. Many colleges and universities provide similar and extensive optional programs, and many even have a vice president for student affairs to manage them. However, these programs are directed to young undergraduates, not to the mature undergraduates (who make up much of the student body at U.S. colleges and universities today) or to graduate students. Both of the latter groups are assumed to be focused and not to need to be entertained in order to be retained.

It is probably not appropriate to describe church or religious programs as elective or optional, or as a distraction, but it should be noted that (in a very nondenominational way) religion plays an active role in war-college life. Prayer is a part of many ceremonies; Wednesday morning prayer breakfasts are well attended; and a series of ongoing "growth" programs, as well as the expected worship services, are offered at the post chapel.

56. Particularly undergraduate students. Graduate students—at least, those pursuing doctoral degrees—hold values closer to those of faculty.

57. Who are largely engaged in training students for the workplace.

58. Academic freedom does not imply that all ideas espoused in the academic marketplace are either truthful or meritorious. The argument is that the market environment is the best possible environment for the stimulation of critical and creative thought. John Stuart Mill's *On Liberty* is usually taken as the most persuasive statement of this position.

59. New ideas, new information, and new forms of delivery may be tried the next year, but each year all students will have the same core experience. One thing is not done in one seminar and something different in another.

60. One vignette emblematic of the difference between the academy, where faculty have little expectation of control over students' attitudes and behavior, and the military, where a colonel expects respect and compliance from lieutenant-colonels, comes from the introductory remarks by an academic dean during student orientation. In the impressive Bliss Hall auditorium, and at a time that people were almost certainly on their best behavior, the dean noted that sometimes Bliss Hall was referred to as "the Red Bedroom." He said, "It is not a bedroom, nor is it a family room. Be alert."

61. Seminars have a lot of short breaks. This seems to be part of keeping students alert, but it may simply be that coffee-drinking middle-aged men need to pee a lot.

62. Feelings may be aggravated by the timing of the list's release, which occurs shortly before the Christmas holidays.

63. Assignments do not come mysteriously from on high. One can essentially apply and be interviewed for particular assignments.

64. The second feminist movement, which elevated the two-career family over that of the two-person career family, is conventionally said to have begun at the end of the 1960s. Military families have been affected. In particular, more wives work, and many are in the military themselves. Whether the military family is only lagging behind the civilian family, or whether the demands of a "total institution" mean that military families will continue to resemble a so-called traditional family—a married couple with children and only one breadwinner—remains to be seen.

CHAPTER SIX

1. For example, most members of the class were infants at the end of World War II and elementary school students at the time of the Korean War (police action).

2. More than 36,000 American troops remain in South Korea.

3. The United Nations, an institution dedicated to world peace, was created under U.S. leadership in 1945.

4. Students in the Army War College class of 1985 likely came to political consciousness about the time that Kennedy was assassinated and Johnson became president. By the end of the Johnson administration, many were in uniform, and some were in Vietnam. Members of the class, then, assumed the existence of the Cold War. In addition, many were "hot" war (Vietnam) veterans.

5. A small number of allied troops did fight in Vietnam with the United States and with the South Vietnamese.

6. Nixon was elected in 1968. The peace talks began shortly after the Tet Offensive, which included an attack on Saigon. This offensive was very costly

to the North Vietnamese. However, it also marked a shift in U.S. public opinion toward bringing our troops home.

7. This was also the period in which Nixon visited China, and later Moscow, for a summit that culminated in a strategic-arms-reduction agreement.

8. South Vietnam eventually surrendered to the North, and the American embassy was evacuated in 1975.

9. The act was passed over Nixon's veto.

10. Congress invoked the War Powers Act requiring the departure of U.S. troops after victory had been secured.

11. The list described is actually for the class of 1984. The list for the class of 1985 was not retrievable.

12. Only von Clausewitz's *On War* and Russell F. Weigley's *The American Way of War: A History of United States Military Strategy and Policy* (New York: Macmillan, 1973) would still be in the curriculum a decade later.

13. Note the emphasis on land warfare. By 1995, joint warfare would be central to the curriculum.

14. Again, the war-college curriculum is not restricted to war. Significant attention is given to values and politics, and some attention is given to the nature of U.S. society.

15. The *Curriculum Pamphlet* further noted that "your year here will likely be the only period in your career when you are encouraged to consider and challenge your own intellectual assumptions and prejudices. . . . Unexamined acceptance of assumptions and the status quo are neither expected nor desired" (p. 3). Students were warned that the expected "conceptual thinking can only result from close, detailed, reflective study . . . and it can only be done by imaginative people who have trained themselves to think logically about tough problems." In seminar discussions, students were told that they should assent and dissent "logically, tactfully, and convincingly." One could almost say that the students were being ordered to think differently—from one another and from the way they had thought in the past.

16. But remember: On entry, they were given eleven Army manuals and numerous Army regulations.

17. The informal message seemed to be that the college knew best, for the seminar system was careful to keep everyone on the same track. Although the core curriculum lasted most of the year, seminar membership was reshuffled periodically to provide fresh faces and ideas and to extend acquaintanceship within the class.

18. An eighty-one-page "Pre-Course Background Readings for Soviet Studies" was compiled by a faculty member and distributed to each student. Titles of some of the articles in this list were "How the Soviet Union Is Ruled," "The Militarization of Soviet Society," and "Soviet Military Strategy in Transition." Each came from a military or defense journal.

19. More than half the Army is in the Army National Guard or the Army Reserves. "Total Army" is a phrase that reminds active-duty officers of this.

20. Brace yourself: There are ten course directives for 1985. The directive for the first course, which lasted only three weeks, was fifty-seven pages long.

21. Of particular concern was "Type A" behavior. One full lesson was devoted to it. "Family wellness" as well as personal wellness was also included in the curriculum.

22. In later years, individual MBTI results would be made public—at least within the seminar.

23. The last topic, behavior under fire, disappeared in later years, presumably because it was part of earlier military education that focused on smaller units.

24. Seminars meet for half a day. Still, the program seems ambitious. One might learn the subject matter provided, but having the time or the tools to think critically about it seems doubtful.

25. Fewer than two years had elapsed since the bombing of the Marine barracks in Beirut.

26. "The U.S. Heritage," U.S. Army War College, Carlisle, Penn., 1984. The introduction notes: "It is in fact an intellectual TV dinner designed only to ward off starvation until the student prepares his own banquet."

27. The take-home message was not that workers should unite, but that the U.S. has enduring values and aspirations beyond those of mere interest.

28. This was the longest of the ten core courses.

29. These institutions are the presidency, Congress, the National Security Council, and the intelligence community. The study of policy was not restricted to its making, however. Course Two also considered concepts such as the "national interest" and the "moral dimension" of policy and factors such as the economy.

30. By the mid-1990s, there would still be a list, but it would look quite different.

31. As had been the introduction to ethics and the presentation on American values.

32. This is the lesson on civil–military relations.

33. There were no "hers" or "shes" in the 1984–85 curriculum, although women had attended the USAWC since 1968–69.

34. This is another topic that would later lose space in the curriculum.

35. Not as the Soviet people saw the world but as the leaders who made Soviet military and foreign policy saw it—at least, as U.S. leaders saw them seeing it. Few of the readings assigned or recommended were "academic." None questioned the premises or the seriousness of the Cold War or questioned U.S. policy versus the USSR. None let the Soviets speak for themselves.

36. Course Directive 2, 44. The need to cover curriculum without "wasting time" seemed to be an implicit theme, an informal element, of the whole curriculum, even though it was stated explicitly only with regard to strategy.

37. Hardly a bite-size topic. Note that Frederick the Great's statue graces the Army War College's grounds but in an area removed from most activity. Two

twentieth-century wars against Germany may have reduced enthusiasm for emphasizing the college's roots.

38. Harry Summers's conclusion that the problem in Vietnam was not so much political interference as the lack of a coherent military strategy was one of several analyses advanced.

39. A very full plate. The Military Reform Movement was a congressionally based civilian group that sought new formulations for strategy and military organization.

40. Things would be different ten years later.

41. Von Clausewitz distinguished carefully between preparing for and conducting war.

42. Created in 1947.

43. All systems were directly linked to resource allocation—that is, the budget. In addition to dollars, the other major restraint on military planning is manpower allocation. Ethical considerations arising from the resource-allocation process were also part of the discussion. These included budget-proposal gamesmanship and the use of exaggerated claims to support procurement goals.

44. Congress and the president, could, of course, make decisions disregarding the whole (long and arduous) planning process, if they chose.

45. These included a former member of the Joint Chiefs of Staff and a unified commander.

46. The invasion of Grenada did not go smoothly, and this acted as a stimulus for passage of the Goldwater–Nichols Act in 1986. That act was designed to promote cooperation among the services. Representative Bill Nichols, Democrat of Alabama, had proposed reorganizing legislation as early as 1983, and there was substantial discussion at the war college and in the military generally about the effectiveness of the organization of the Department of Defense and of the Joint Chiefs of Staff.

47. A full week was also spent studying Soviet organization, capabilities, and doctrine.

48. It might be noted that the use of chemical weapons was still on the agenda at the time.

49. One naval station; one Air Force base; and Quantico, the Marine training center.

50. Games serve two primary purposes. One is to train, to prepare. The other is to provide the basis for analysis and, perchance, discovery.

51. By the mid-1990s, neither installation trips nor movies would be featured.

52. The format of the "white paper" was open-ended. It could be an essay, a magazine article, a speech, and so on.

53. For each section, I have selected the first item and one other that seemed emblematic of the category.

54. An interesting companion publication that year was an "educational booklet of experience" titled "Leaders' Wives Speak Out." The booklet included twenty-four short essays by women whose husband–students had served as bat-

talion commanders. Most of them were written by women who saw themselves as participants in a two-person career. The U.S. Army Wife seal heads the introduction. Even though the booklet acknowledges that "Wives aren't in the Army, wives don't have rank" and quotes General Maxwell Thurman—"Wives should never be mentioned in a husband's OER [Official Efficiency Report]" (p. 5)—most of the wives seemed to expect and accept enormous responsibilities for social events, recruitment of volunteers, and communication to families within their husbands' command. One essay addressed the issue of a working commander's wife, noting, "While the official Army position supports the right of any spouse to work, few posts welcome the idea of a leader's wife actually doing so" (p. 42). Another essay addressed the problem of raising volunteers when so many junior officers' wives were working. One suggested response was to turn to *all* wives (that is, to include enlisted servicemen's wives) in support of the community. Some of the essays are so detailed that they resemble an Army manual.

Since 1983, the Army has become attentive to the effect of families on retention and readiness. Accordingly, a white paper was prepared in 1983, and a Family Action Plan followed. Family programs and concerns continue to be a central part of post programs.

55. The Department of Command, Leadership, and Management prepared a hefty, twenty-seven-chapter reference text on the theory and practice of Army Command and Management specifically for use in this course.

56. This is true even though the Capabilities Based Requirements System is, by policy, the initiator of organizational changes.

57. The students' major task for the course was preparation of a "strategic appraisal," a standard document used in the formulation of policy. The format usually includes a definition of U.S. defense, economic, world-order, and ideological interests; the document then considers the effects of current and projected trends on U.S. interests. It concludes with recommended courses of action, including the use of political, economic, and psychological, as well as military, elements of power.

58. Every part of every region seemed to be seen as an existing or potential arena for U.S.–USSR competition.

59. "Regional Appraisals," Course Directive, Carlisle, Penn., 1985, 18.

60. Ibid., 21.

61. Ibid., 24.

62. Ibid., 33.

63. Ibid., 41. At another time and place, it would be useful to study the antagonistic relationship between militaries and peace-action groups, both of which profess to be seeking "real" peace.

64. Remember that Courses Three, Four, and Five focused on "preparing for war."

65. This was the first course to use a substantial amount of classified information. During this course, the IFs took a field trip to several major U.S. commands. Security was a routine but important part of life at the Army War College in 1985. It became more relaxed in the 1990s.

66. Christian views on the use of force range from a tradition of pacifism, passed down from the earliest days, to the Crusades and the Inquisition, which had few qualms about supporting "right" with might. The "just war" tradition is also a long one, and much of the debate has taken place among Roman Catholic theologians. Also, the Catholic church, more than Protestant denominations, has an official view on many social issues, so it is not surprising that a member of that denomination was asked to make the address.

67. Defensive actions can be provocative if they reduce the need for mutual restraint because one side, and only one, now feels "safe." Possible destabilization is an element in the current debate about the Strategic Defense Initiative.

68. The NCA is the U.S. President and Secretary of Defense.

69. A not unusual public line taken by some authorities (civilian authorities, since military authorities may have opinions but do not usually make them public) was that peace movements were irrelevant or irresponsible and probably led by dupes or by agents of the nation's enemies.

70. Materials related to the second topic were classified. so a different program was provided for the IFs.

71. Central Command encompasses the Middle East, Southwest Asia, and North Africa. After the exercise, the commander of Central Command made a presentation on current plans related to his command.

72. And after the exercise to evaluate the planning system itself.

73. Certainly not excluding the USSR.

74. Course Directive, Common Overview, "Course 8: Conduct of War, Application of Power: Contingency Planning," 18.

75. Senior reserve officers attending a short course at the Army War College participated in this course. Two lessons were devoted to the reserves, which make up 40 percent of the U.S. Total Force. The Total Force also includes the National Guard, which is under state government. All told, one-half of the Army's combat power and two-thirds of its support capability were in the Reserves and National Guard in 1985: Course Directive, Common Overview, Conduct of War, "Course 9: Application of Power: Theater Operations," 31.

76. "Flexible response" implies a willingness to escalate to the use of nuclear weapons.

77. Who could have imagined that NATO would first employ its troops in 1999? And that it would do so not against the Soviets, but against Serbia (a remnant of the former Yugoslavia) and on behalf of Kosovo, a province of Serbia.

78. An effort was made to observe the range of problems associated with major cities. Thus, one of the debriefing questions was, "Are military professionals adequately prepared to understand the domestic pressures with which members of Congress must contend?" Course Directive, Common Overview, "Course 10: U.S. Global Military Strategy," 14.

79. Ibid., 3.

80. Many had not written papers for a very long time.

81. The commandant had listed nine "high priority" topics; all were selected for research.

82. The following year, even more materials would be included on the USSR: See the 1985 Annual Report, Appendix F, 2.

83. Ibid.

84. Note that these were the kind of wars most recently fought and were also considered the "most likely" forms of conflict in which the United States would be involved. Neither peacekeeping nor terrorism was yet on the agenda.

85. When I was young, milk arrived at the doorstep in glass bottles, with cream on top and milk below. The Carlisle texts were intended to skim the cream by not "wasting time."

86. Although students were promised that they would have to face ambiguity and complexity, as noted earlier, there was more emphasis on complexity. Moreover, in Soviet studies, which permeated the curriculum, one found little complexity *or* ambiguity. Certainty was the order of the day. The USSR was a threat, and it was important to know only what one needed to know in order to neutralize that threat.

87. One is reminded of Machiavelli's discussion of Fortuna. That most realistic of thinkers understood that fate, the unexpected, the uncontrollable sometimes would have to be faced. He recommended that one prepare for eventualities as one prepares for a flood—by building dikes. However, he noted, some things could not be prepared for. At those times, he urged the Prince to act as one does with a woman—by seizing her (the opportunity).

88. Also, seminar assignments that involved constructing an agreed-to policy from individual formulations tended to produce consensus thinking. In that context, the independent thinker was likely to be seen as disruptive, difficult, or deviant—or simply as a time waster.

89. But they do act, thus following Hume rather than Socrates, who never committed anything to writing for fear that he might record an error and thus lead others astray.

90. The Department of Command, Leadership, and Management alone sponsored five lectures in the Creighton W. Abrams Command Lecture Series (all by retired general officers); four in the Brehon Burke Somervell Management Lecture Series (three by civilians); and five in the Ethics and Professionalism Lecture Series (three by retired general officers, one by the superintendent of the U.S. Military Academy, and one by the Archbishop of New York). It also presented eleven Military Family Programs (the only series to include female speakers). The Department of National Security was not far behind, with the Elihu Root Lecture Series on Military Strategy and the Military History Lecture Series. The Department of Military Strategy, Planning, and Operations offered five lectures in its Eisenhower Lecture Series.

Chapter Seven

1. This was a complex civilian-control issue, because some of the lawbreakers were military officers working for the executive branch. Although they clearly defied Congress and were not "controlled" by the executive, they may

have had what amounted to tacit executive approval. For a portrait of the major actors, see Robert Tinberg, *The Nightingale's Song* (New York: Touchstone, 1995).

2. Mikhail Gorbachev served as general-secretary of the Soviet Communist Party from 1985 to 1991. His policies of *glasnost* and *perestroika,* his reduction of the military budget, his withdrawal of Soviet troops from Afghanistan, his acquiescence to democratization in Poland and Hungary, and, finally, his acceptance of the removal of the Berlin Wall essentially brought the Cold War to an end just as the class of 1990 was beginning its study.

3. Both will be discussed further in Chapter 9.

4. Dean Rusk, *The American Revolution and the Future* (Washington, D.C.: American Enterprise Institute, 1975); Bernard Brodie, *War and Politics* (New York: Macmillan, 1973); John Keegan, *The Face of Battle* (New York: Viking Penguin, 1983); Samuel Huntington, *The Common Defense: Strategy Programs in National Politics* (New York: Columbia University Press, 1966). Typically, the articles came from the journal *Foreign Affairs* and from *Parameters,* the college's journal, with many articles by active-duty officers. Other articles came from the *National Review* and the *American Legion* magazine. Although the selections did not adhere to a single line, they also did not represent the full range of public debate.

5. "Curriculum Pamphlet, Academic Year 1990," U.S. Army War College, Carlisle, Penn., 1989.

6. Each student was involved in a year-long research project under the Military Studies Program discussed near the end of this chapter. Most students wrote papers that were reproduced and distributed (at a minimum, through the Defense Technical Information Center), but some participated in the Oral History Program: see "Curriculum Pamphlet, 1990," 2.

7. Ibid.

8. Ibid., 2–3.

9. This message was similar to that delivered in 1985, but just as there was not much to make students "uncomfortable" then, there was not much that was "provocative" in the 1989–90 curriculum.

10. Thus, electives occupied almost four months of the year, a major change.

11. The rationale for the New York City trip evolved from an emphasis on the United Nations to seeing the city as a microcosm of the nation. The United Nations was still the first visit, and in the afternoon of the first morning students visited the missions of the IFs' countries. The whole second day, though, was spent visiting a wide range of public and private, profit and nonprofit, institutions in small groups. The morning of the third day involved an urban-affairs panel presented by New York experts: Course Directive, "Course 2: War, National Policy, and Strategy," 91.

12. The theme was consistently raised in virtually every lesson.

13. This is the Army, after all.

14. Goldwater–Nichols requirements had been defined earlier that year, and Phase I of the Joint Professional Military Education (PJE) requirement (senior level) was integrated into the curriculum for the first time. However, before

becoming a Joint Service Officer (JSO), graduates had to take PJE Phase II as a short course at the Armed Forces Staff College. They also had to serve in an appropriate joint assignment.

15. This involved development of an individual learning plan for the year at the Army War College.

16. This is not just a matter of personal ethics; it also considers the ethics involved in preparing for and executing combat. The heavy emphasis on ethics derives partly from concerns about nuclear war and is also partly the legacy of Vietnam, where senior officers were seen as "careerists" who had too long done what was asked instead of what was right (such as resign when young lives were being expended on goals that were not realizable by the means permitted).

17. This topic would disappear by 1995.

18. This could be more revelatory than one might expect. Students were encouraged not to feel presumptuous if they selected, for example, the role of Army Chief of Staff.

19. Most students were not geniuses and would not become generals, but the goal was to get them to think expansively.

20. By 1995, the mock selection board would become a Family Program billed as an opportunity to understand better the process to which a spouse is subjected, rather than as a problem in selecting senior leadership.

21. Students were engaged and made self-conscious by considering their personal results on three surveys: on Terminal Values, Instrumental Values, and Organizational Values.

22. Colonel Bill Ekhard, the Army major who prosecuted and won the conviction of Lieutenant William L. Calley for the My Lai massacre, was a member of the USAWC faculty in 1990. In May–June 1998 (thirty years later), the officers who persisted until My Lai was addressed were given medals. Although not widely known, it should be noted that 122 U.S. servicemen were convicted of war crimes for killing Vietnamese civilians: reported by Gary Solis, U.S. Military Academy, at a meeting of the Inter-University Seminar, Baltimore, Maryland, October 23, 1999.

23. Background reading included the case study "The Criminal Responsibility of Israeli Military Commanders for the Pogrom at Shatila and Sabra," in "Selected Readings: Course One, The Senior Leader." Carlisle, Penn., 1989, 213–43.

24. Dresden involved nighttime area bombing, with massive civilian casualties. Other raids involved daylight "precision" bombing—even that, though, did not avoid "collateral damage" (civilian deaths).

25. It is understood that many civilian leaders have not had military experience, more or less seen combat, but it should be noted that many military leaders have not had the "cherished" combat experience, either. This could be construed as both good and as bad news. It is good news because there were no wars in which to fight, but it is bad news because, if combat experience does matter, no one will have that experience to contribute to the decision-making process. It should be noted, too, that senior leaders have two grave responsibilities

that are not often required in junior positions: innovation and the building of consensus.

26. Staff as opposed to command. In 1990, there was much emphasis on "generalship." This was reduced by 1995, perhaps because a student's chances of actually becoming a general had been reduced as the size of the military was reduced.

27. The first lesson in Block I, "War and the International System."

28. Course Directive, "Course 2," 20. Thus, students are again told that senior leaders must be able to perform with skill in structures and organizations very different from the authoritative and hierarchal system in which they have to date been successful.

29. In this assignment, the study of military power was restricted to nonviolent military action.

30. Block II of Course 2 focuses on "Domestic and Global Environments."

31. The class trip to New York City later in the year was part of the assessment of the domestic environment.

32. It would be hard to construe this assignment as supportive of independent thinking, but it does support another war-college goal—learning to build consensus.

33. Course Directive, "Course 2," 2:1–79.

34. Even the case for legalizing drugs was made—not from a libertarian view or with the view that legalization is an individual right, but from the perspective that it is the most effective way to control the drug trade. Just as Prohibition created great profits, high crime, and corrupt government, so an antidrug policy that approaches the supply side was described as not effective: ibid., 298–325. Other articles proposed other solutions.

35. In 1989–90, the agenda was very much set by Reagan and Bush. There was little on race, and not much on poverty. No note at all was made of the fact that roughly one-third of America's youth were not even considered competent enough to join the Army as privates. There were questions such as, "Can government welfare and drug programs promote greater civic virtue and private self-discipline?" with a clearly correct answer. Again, the curriculum was in accord with the philosophy of the current executive. Was this intentional? If so, would it change with each new executive? Would it not be better to expose USAWC students to the full range of public views? Or should USAWC students entirely avoid the cursory study of domestic issues and especially avoid making policy recommendations to one another about such issues?

36. U.S. interests were described as of varying intensity. In order of declining importance, they were identified as: survival, vital, major, and peripheral interests. Another way to conceptualize interests is by their purpose: defense, economic, world order, or promotion of values: Course Directive, "Course 2," 47. Students were cautioned about how quickly the definition of interests can change, how difficult it is to reach a consensus about interests in a democracy, and how important it is to understand how other nations define their interests. The last aspect tended to get lost in discussion: ibid., 44.

37. Symbolic of the dramatic change in U.S.–USSR relations was the speech given by the Chair of the Joint Chiefs of Staff, Admiral William J. Crowe, Jr., at the General Staff Military Academy in Moscow in June 1989. This followed a 1988 visit to the U.S. of a senior Soviet officer.

38. These regional appraisals represented only a few days' work. However, students were also required to take one advanced (elective) course that involved the development of a Regional Strategic Appraisal. Thus, the military would have a set of officers with at least a rudimentary understanding of each region of the globe. The required reading was from Donald Nuechterlein's *America Overcommitted:United States National Interests in the 1980s* (Lexington: University of Kentucky Press, 1985). The regional analyses were based on an edited volume prepared at the Army War College and a volume by the Association of the United States Army: Course Directive, "Course 2," 42–43. The basics were presented, but the materials were neither provocative nor "out of the box."

39. After the Republicans gained the White House, the Democrats, who controlled Congress, become almost truculent once the Soviet Union was no longer seen as a threat. By the mid-1990s, the roles had been reversed: the Democrats held the White House and Republicans had gained control of Congress.

40. Although officers should certainly be acquainted with government institutions, and although they should be aware of the large and irresolvable issues related to those institutions, one wonders whether the question format, the small group seminar, and the impulse to reach a decision might not lead USAWC students to think they have the answers.

41. The media would get increased curriculum time in the future.

42. The readings for this lesson provided a good account of how the press works, but what is the effect of posing complex, unanswerable questions day after day? One cannot possibly come to an independent, logical, evidence-based conclusion for each of them. Is the lesson learned that "truth" doesn't matter? Or that it is unattainable? Or is the message to be open-minded? Or flexible? What effect does so much inconclusiveness have on a professional officer? Does it enhance compliance, or does it encourage officers to think their opinion is as good as anyone else's and should, therefore, be heard?

43. Until the Cold War was over, neither the United States nor the Soviet Union participated much in U.N. peacekeeping. More neutral nations were considered better contributors to those missions.

44. "Integrated" because the U.S. nuclear force is a triad composed of Army, Air Force, and Navy components.

45. No nuclear weapons have been used since 1945. A "What if?" question not asked is: "If the U.S. had successfully maintained a monopoly on nuclear weapons, would we have used them in the last fifty years? Or was the world spared nuclear warfare because the Soviets also had nuclear weapons?"

46. The services are headed by civilian secretaries who are responsible for organizing, staffing, training, equipping, resourcing, and sustaining personnel. However, when it comes to using them, troops are placed under the command of a CINC, who can be from any service. The CINCs are responsible for a

geographical area or for certain specified commands, such as special forces or transportation.

47. There seemed to be more effort to follow Sun Tzu's admonition to "know your enemy" in this curriculum than was encountered previously. The portrayal of the Soviet military as having serious deficiencies is also new.

48. Course Directive, "Course 3: Implementing National Strategy," lesson 3-10, details the strategic-planning process. It implies that planning happens as prescribed (pp. 32–33). It also describes the "gap" between requirements and capabilities as a question of ethics for a senior commander.

49. These pillars are readiness, sustainability, modernization, and force structure.

50. As in other years, the course lays out the JSPS, the JOPS, and PPBS. It also set forth the Army's methodology for translating goals and objectives into requirements and for integrating its various elements into a force that is prepared to act. The Army's budgeting process is given careful attention. The environment for these lessons included increased influence for the CINCs in determining requirements as a result of the Goldwater–Nichols Act; a congressional commitment to budget reduction and a balanced budget; the recommendations of the 1986 President's Blue Ribbon Commission on Defense Management (the Packard Commission).

51. Represented by the two houses' Armed Services, Budget, and Appropriations committees.

52. Budget requests are often supported by defense contractors and by workers employed in the defense industry.

53. This involves "Force Integration," TAP (the Army Plan), and PPBES. (The Army's Planning, Programming and Budgeting System adds an "E" for "execution.") TAP combines long-range perspectives and midrange guidance, and it establishes priorities. It is classified as a secret document.

54. One discussion question is, "Is the current methodology too complicated and cumbersome to be understood? Are we captive to a system and its associated processes?" Some would consider this black humor.

55. Remember how long it took to build up our forces in the Gulf? Of course, there were advantages to the slow but ever-increasing build-up. Unfortunately, those advantages did not deter—or stimulate a retreat.

56. For more on Special Forces, see Tom Adams, *U.S. Special Forces in Action: The Challenge of Unconventional Warfare* (London: Frank Cass, 1998).

57. Sustainment refers to the ability to sustain combat power by providing sufficient personnel, medical support, and supplies for months of combat.

58. Unity of effort is essential to a successful campaign. Unity of command is generally thought to enhance unity of effort, and "jointness " is supposed to achieve that for U.S. forces. Unified command is more difficult to achieve for combined forces because different national forces may operate in the same area under different commands and rules of engagement.

59. In the Regional Strategic Appraisal courses, at least two students from each seminar attend one of six geographically defined courses. IFs attend their

own region's course and participate in regional panels devoted to their area. Each course prepared a brief that assessed trends in the region, U.S. interests there, and challenges to U.S. interests, and recommended regional policies. At the conclusion of the course, each region's brief was presented to the seminar as a whole, which then created an overarching set of recommendations that were used in Course 4 applications.

60. From *National Security Strategy of the United States,* Course Directive, "Regional Strategic Appraisals," Carlisle, Penn., 1990, 9.

61. Once enrollment is complete, students and other people associated with the Army War College are allowed to register as auditors.

62. Some students who did not have a master's degree entered the Cooperative Degree Program with either Shippensburg University or Pennsylvania State University. The schools gave them nine credits for their Army War College work; otherwise this work, too, was an add-on. The five students who were selected for the Current Affairs Panel were able to use one elective course as a reading course to support their participation in the panel.

63. Students were cautioned that the scenarios were hypothetical.

64. By 1995, the mill had become the home of the Peacekeeping Institute, and the war-gaming and modeling functions had moved to the spectacular new Center for Strategic Leadership.

65. Some group projects are approved, and those preparing oral histories do not write a paper.

66. DNNS annual report, 1990.

67. "AY 1990 End-of-Year Evaluation," n.d.

68. The role of the military in a democracy was not the specific title of a lesson, but in addition to examining the military's formal role and the formal workings of the U.S. government, it was pointed out that in a democracy we do "what we can agree on," that the military is but one of four kinds of national power, and that the media play an important but not always soothing role in the making of policy.

69. Exercises are considered very important to adult learning, yet students do *not* give them high marks. With the Army's state-of-the-art gaming facilities then under construction at Carlisle, the prospects of reducing the number of exercises seemed poor.

CHAPTER EIGHT

1. Although the government of Iraq was left intact, and U.S. forces remain active in the area, the stated goals of the war had been to remove Iraqi troops from Kuwait and to restore that country's government. This was done.

2. Only a limited number of officers who served in Vietnam were still on active duty, but those who were held high rank.

3. Increased competition for promotion could mean that any blemish, any "defect" on one's record, could result in not being promoted and being forced out of the military for failure to progress. Thus, the need for "zero defects"

began to haunt those seeking promotion. For any organization, a widespread "zero defects" mentality creates a climate of caution and conventionality. Most healthy institutions, though, require at least some risk-taking and initiative. By the mid-1990s, the importance of encouraging a certain amount of initiative and creativity was a matter of concern within the military. By then, however, downsizing was mostly over, even if it was not forgotten. By the end of the 1990s, concern would be focused instead on "op [operations] tempo," the frequency of assignments away from one's post. Thus, a new, and opposite, concern arose: that too many officers would leave the military because of the increased demands of "op tempo."

4. Classical U.N. peacekeeping involved consent by both sides to a conflict; the neutrality of peacekeepers; action limited to observing and reporting; and the use of force only in self-defense. In the early 1990s, U.N. peacekeeping missions proliferated, and the range of peacekeeping duties increased to include humanitarian relief, human rights, de-mining, monitoring, demobilization, elections, the collection of evidence for war-crimes trials, and more. Sometimes the U.N. actions of the 1990s were, in fact, unwelcome interventions, and the peacekeeping "blue helmets" were not perceived as neutral by either side. Further, the threat of force was very much present. Some would argue that such operations, although perhaps legitimate, should not be called "peacekeeping" at all, and that participants should not wear the classic blue helmets.

5. They believe that peacekeeping's duties are so different from war fighting that formal retraining is necessary after service in a peacekeeping mission.

6. Although the military has the special responsibility of using force, its primary task is not fighting but deterring. If peacekeeping were understood as a deterrent rather than as a police or monitoring action, it might be more in accord with the military's concept of self.

7. Culminated in two senses: first, public interest turned elsewhere, and second, people began to consider the drawbacks to policies that seemed to require severe punishment for behavior that was by no means unknown and variably punished in civilian life. Although few condoned harassment, issues related to infidelity and fraternization seemed to warrant review.

8. Sometime later, the Army's highest-ranking woman, a three-star general, would accuse a fellow general of harassing her in her own office. The Army found her credible. She retired as planned. The male general had an unplanned retirement.

9. All students took the core curriculum together in the first half of the year. In the second half of the year, some elements of the curriculum also involved all students. These were the Regional Strategic Appraisals, conducted during the first two months of the second term; the two week-long Strategic Crisis Exercise; and the week-long National Security Seminar, held the week before graduation.

10. Including community and family activities reinforces the view of those who see the military as a total institution.

11. The testing continued to include an in-depth physical assessment and an introduction to Carlisle's Total Wellness Program. Communicative Arts skills were also assessed, and low scorers invited into a special program.

12. Officers experience many hierarchical relationships in the military. After twenty years of service, most have learned to relate well, up and down. An important goal for the Carlisle year is the further development of effective relationships among peers. This anticipates future staff and other assignments that will involve working with a wide range of people—some of them civilians, some from other services, some foreign—who are neither superiors nor subordinates. They may be peers, or there may be no defined hierarchical relationship.

13. See Chapter 3 for a discussion of the Myers-Briggs typology.

14. In my seminar, two-op ed pieces on gay marriage were used as a stimulus for discussion. This probably required courageous thinking by the instructor, but it did not require students to examine their own unacknowledged assumptions. They acknowledged their assumptions without a pause. It did provide an adrenaline rush and reminded students that the United States is an unusually tolerant society.

15. The two pieces that followed the text's introduction, "Leading and Managing in the Strategic Arena," were an article by the school's commandant (clearly an authoritative voice) and the draft of Field Manual 22-103, "Strategic Leadership" (also an authoritative account). Ironically, then, just after lessons on creative and critical thinking were completed, the students were instructed as to precisely how they were to define and how they were to think about strategic leadership.

16. VUCA again. Bob Woodward's *The Commanders* was recommended reading for the requirements of strategic leadership. Strategic leadership was specifically differentiated from direct leadership and from organizational leadership. It was noted, too, that at the strategic level leading or managing by consensus replaced leading or managing by control: Course Directive, "Strategic Leadership," Carlisle, Penn., 1996, 5.

17. The first introduction to U.S. politics was Chapter 13 of Admiral William J. Crowe's *The Line of Fire from Washington to the Gulf: The Politics and Battles of the New Military* (New York: Simon and Schuster, 1993). This is a realistic description of the congressional decision-making process and the limited role testimony, rationality, and information may play in it. (As Crowe describes candidates' speeches: "Look at the facts, they say, and immediately start distorting the facts.") Crowe concludes that politics is "pervasive" and that the process is "fractious and messy." (Note that this conclusion on the lack of impact of logic and evidence was presented just after students had had their lesson on the importance of critical thinking.) The other assigned reading was Robert Kaplan's "The Coming Anarchy," *Atlantic Monthly* (February 1994), 44–76. This article was almost certain to leave the reader feeling uncertain about how best to approach a complex, volatile, and dangerous future, as Kaplan described.

18. Since the people in the best position to make change are the ones who have been most successful in the existing system, it is often hard for them to see the need for change. For example, it is hard to get elected officials to believe that there is much wrong with our electoral process or the way we finance campaigns. The Army is a doctrine-driven organization that may seem particularly difficult to change, but once a change is directed—once it becomes doctrine—it may occur more rapidly and even more willingly than in other organizations.

Recent changes in the U.S. military include the all-volunteer force, race integration, more women and women in more roles, increased use of computers, and the end of the threat from the "Evil Empire." Perhaps the most conspicuous example of recent, intended change in the military, though, is the effort to create a culture of service jointness. Some would argue that there is also a new, and perhaps unintended, trend toward making force protection a high priority—that is, on fighting without the loss of American lives.

19. Because any particular performance is sure to be deficient when compared with textbook theory, critiquing the boss's lecture proved awkward. The vision statements of the Navy and Air Force were posted in the seminar room. The Navy's was "Forward . . . from the Sea"; the Air Force's was "Global Reach, Global Power"; the Marines' was "Operational Maneuver, from the Sea." Army students grimaced when they read these vision statements and lamented the Army's lack of a similarly catchy theme.

20. The West Point code not only requires honorable behavior; it requires that one "not tolerate" dishonorable behavior in others. Even at West Point, however, there is still a strong ethic of not "ratting" or "blowing the whistle." In fact, many of the difficult ethical issues for individuals may involve their responsibility versus the acts of others—particularly peers and superiors. Tailhook was an example of failure both to stop and to report others' bad behavior—or even to acknowledge it when officially questioned.

21. Here is a brief review of the doctrine as it was originally developed by St. Augustine and as it evolved in Western Christian thought: To embark on a just war (*ad bellum*) requires just cause, legitimate authority, just intention, public declaration, proportionality, last resort, and likely success. In war (*in bello*) the principles of discrimination and proportionality have also become part of just-war doctrine.

Just-war theory may act as a constraint; most believe that to be its intent. However, some argue that its actual function is justification, and that it can be stretched to support virtually any military action.

22. Although just-war theory was not new to the students, its application to interventions rather than conventional wars was timely. Some of the readings—for example, Stanley Hoffman's, "The Politics and Ethics of Military Intervention," *Survival* (Winter 1995–96), 29–51—were sophisticated and substantive. However, readings may receive short (or no) shrift in seminar discussion and may or may not be read.

23. Major John E. Shephard, Jr., "Thomas Becket, Ollie North and You," *Military Review* 71, no. 5 (May 1991): 20–33.

24. A neologism drawn from the deeds of Oliver North.

25. It was not clear whether the emphasis on second- and third-order consequences was truly an effort to weigh long-range effects correctly or intended to prepare officers for the unexpected. Or, perhaps, it simply represented an effort to ensure that negative results were systematically weighed against the positive.

26. The lesson involved a one-day negotiation session on oil pricing based on a Harvard Business School case study.

27. There appeared to be an assumption that, once made, a decision would be implemented. However, if examples had been drawn from the political sphere rather than from business—that is, after all, the alien sphere with which senior military leaders are most likely to interact—it would have to be acknowledged that decisions not only are often not made, but they are often poorly made. And even when the decisions are made, they may or may not be translated into action. When one considers political decision-making, one might even have to concede that the military and the professoriate are engaged in similar Sisyphean activities, trying to discover or impose intellectual order on a disordered world, and that professors and soldiers who look to logic and evidence as the basis for their judgements need to remember that much political behavior is driven by neither.

28. Only one comment was made about the "political correctness" of the lists. The leaders were to be studied as to the degree to which they achieved strategic leadership. Students were invited to speculate on their subjects' MBTI and KAI types and their ability to think creatively and critically. They were asked to consider their subjects' vision, the environment in which they operated, their competencies, and their ability to negotiate and create consensus. In short, their careers were to be measured against the definitions laid out in the class and in FM 22-103.

29. Large lectures followed by small discussion groups would be typical in a civilian school. All-class lectures by experts were, however, infrequent at the USAWC.

30. Summers's *On Strategy: A Critical Analysis of the Vietnam War* uses a Clausewitzian framework to analyze the American experience in Vietnam. The basic assumptions are: 1) war is a continuation of policy (purposeful); and 2) war can be conducted only when the people, the government, and the military act us a unit, as "the Remarkable Trinity." Summers argued that U.S. strategists did not learn from Korea and must learn from Vietnam. He argued that Congress must be involved; that the All Volunteer Force is connected to the people through the reserves, who must now be mobilized for any major action; and that the media, too, connect the people and the military. That connection and seeing the "big picture" were deemed all-important.

31. Course Directive, "Course 2: War, National Policy, and Strategy," Carlisle, Penn., 1996, 13.

32. Military tasks, force structure, and weaponry should vary depending on the strategy selected.

33. "Traditional Values in American Life," a report prepared for the United Nations Educational, Scientific, and Cultural Organization by Professor Emeritus Ralph Gabriel of Yale University, was the assigned reading for this topic. It is nicely rooted in history but mighty dry reading.

34. National interests were said to be "subjective, relative, and continually debated," but (almost in contradiction) the Army War College then offered a formula for defining interests and subsequently developing strategy. Long-term national interests were said to be: defense of the homeland; economic well-being; favorable world order; and promotion of values (human rights, democracy). It was said the importance (intensity, criticality) of these interests could be rated on a scale from vital to important to peripheral or humanitarian. One reason for providing a formula was that each student was responsible for preparing a strategy document. Comparability was useful because groups of students then prepared a comprehensive strategy from their separate contributions. Course Directive, "Course 2," app. 1.

35. The Supreme Court received no mention.

36. Richard Kohn's article "Out of Control: The Crisis in Civil–Military Relations," *National Interest,* no. 35 (Spring 1994), and responses to it were assigned reading. But at least in my seminar, there was not much discussion of the topic.

37. The military believes deeply in "the unity of command." However, as the Course Directive points out, our Constitution was specifically designed to fragment authority. Thus, military and political processes are almost antithetical. The readings selected for presidential–congressional relations and for the norms of bureaucratic behavior are much in line with good teaching in a civilian institution.

38. In the seminar discussion, one journalist said that the media have been lied to and that they expect to be lied to. He also noted that although journalists had little respect for the classification system, there was great respect for the necessity of keeping operations plans secret.

39. The debate on affirmative action in my seminar was real. But it was also a seminar of fourteen (plus two international students) that included three African Americans, two Caucasian women, and a Native American. One suspects the discussion in other seminars was different. To be fair, the intention behind the use of the debate format was said to be not to select a winner, but to use debate as a device for finding a compromise position informed by the exposure of each position's weaknesses as well as its strengths. This process is described by the Army as "constructive controversy."

40. The domestic environment does affect national-security policy; what is spent on domestic concerns is not available for spending on the military. That message is clearly conveyed. Concern was also expressed, however, that social problems could "threaten the very fiber of America's national-security interests." It may be important for senior officers to know that more young African American men are in the criminal justice system than in college. The question, though, is: Is getting into a debate about tough domestic issues, activity that is sure to

generate heat and to be "political," a proper part of the education of a suppos-edly nonpolitical officer?

If the point was merely for officers to understand that government officials have multiple worries and responsibilities, one lesson might suffice. If the intent was to assist officers in arriving at considered opinions about domestic policy, the lesson was not at all sufficient. The question of the appropriateness of teach-ing that may shape officers' political opinions, even if unintentionally, is a seri-ous matter and deserves more examination than can be offered here.

41. Note that students at the National War College and Air War College took trips to foreign countries. Was the New York trip just a low-budget version of an excursion for the Army? The other schools apparently felt no need to see a U.S. city or to visit the United Nations.

42. That year by an attorney, a professor at Cooper Union, and the police commissioner.

43. Some included visits to two different organizations by small groups. Examples of organizations paired for visits were: the AFL–CIO and the New York City Human Resources Administration; Mutual of America and the New York University Stern School of Business, *Forbes* Magazine and the Carnegie Commission on Preventing Deadly Conflict, and Phoenix House and the Drug Enforcement Administration. Some all-day visits were made to Harlem, Kings County Supreme Court, and the New York City Department of Corrections.

44. Boutros Boutros-Ghali, then the secretary-general, had recently issued an extremely ambitious "Agenda for Peace" proposing that preventive action, peace building, and peace enforcement be added to the United Nations' tasks.

45. Just grasping the materials on strategy was a challenge. There was really no testing of logic or of evidence, and no identifying of assumptions.

46. This was not new material for most of the students.

47. Sun Tzu was Chinese and wrote about 500 B.C.; Machiavelli, a Florentine, wrote in the early sixteenth century; and Jomini, a Swiss, was a contemporary of Clausewitz—that is, an eighteenth-century thinker. Machiavelli considered his *The Art of War* his most important work although it did not turn out to be his most famous.

48. A detailed account of the planning is found in Charles I. Kirkpatrick's *An Unknown Future and a Doubtful Present: Writing the Victory Plan of 1941* (Wash-ington, D.C.: Center of Military History, 1992).

49. This was a secret document. Was it strategic if one element of Clausewitz's trinity, the people, were left completely unaware of its existence? Was it "doc-trine" if the president was displeased with the document? Other analyses of the Cold War like George Kennan's were "suggested" but not required reading.

50. Limited wars may permit the loser's survival, avoid open conflict between superpowers, and avoid using nuclear weapons. However, limited wars are not necessarily short, nor are casualties necessarily limited. (More than 30,000 Americans died in Korea.) It should be noted that President Harry Tru-man suffered a significant loss of support when he fired General Douglas

MacArthur, who favored victory of the World War II variety, but he did establish both a strategy of containment and a commitment to the pursuit of dominance in a cold (but not a hot) war with the USSR.

51. It is not clear that these limitations were clear or accepted when Truman declared war without consulting the U.S. Congress or the United Nations, although the latter later blessed the U.S. action as a U.N. "police action."

52. The primary reading assigned on Vietnam came from Henry Kissinger's *Diplomacy* (New York: Simon and Schuster, 1994).

53. The title of the lesson on the Vietnam War.

54. And, perhaps, with the understanding that to others, *we* could be perceived as a threat.

55. We did not completely give up our hope that an internal uprising would depose a ruler we did not like, but our strategy did not depend on it. In fact, there was concern that if Iraq were totally defeated, the country would splinter and create a situation worse than one with Saddam Hussein in at least some control.

56. In discussing strategy, there was a great deal of discussion of the "American people" and what they thought, but little was done to try to assess what the American people did think. It was almost as though John Locke was being taken literally—that one (or the public as a whole) can be said to consent (tacitly) so long as one does not actively resist.

57. The vital interest at stake was really oil for our allies, who basically financed the war. The goal was to restore the government of Kuwait. Some effort was made to characterize that government as benevolent, although Kuwait was the only country in the world with an election process in which only male citizens can vote. The tide for public support seemed to turn when the United States invoked the possibility of Iraq's possession of atomic weapons.

President George Bush made executive decisions without extensive consultation, or so it seems from a reading of Woodward's *The Commanders*. His personalization of the war and mocking of Iraq's Saddam Hussein was experienced as unprofessional by some, but he did take the issue to Congress. Bush did not act unilaterally, as Truman had done, nor did he gradually slip into the war, as had occurred in Vietnam under Kennedy and Johnson.

58. The United States once saw nuclear weapons as its "equalizer" against the larger ground forces of the Soviet Union. With the proliferation of nuclear weapons, small countries can view the weapons as equalizers against the United States—hence, the importance to the United States of nonproliferation and counterproliferation strategies.

59. More specifically, to make the United States secure, to promote U.S. economic prosperity, and to promote democracy.

60. Thus, instead of establishing ends, determining ways, and then listing the requirements needed to achieve the ends, planners found themselves having to shift to plans based on capabilities rather than requirements.

61. In an all-class lecture and in an essay "Why Is Strategy Difficult?"—both by USAWC Professor David Jablonsky—students are told that "like the Romans

the United States is faced with permanent struggle in the international arena," that the military must "think beyond the military aspect of military strategy," that "the military must also help convince the American people that the United States cannot pull back from its global leadership responsibilities, that concomitantly military power will remain a requisite ingredient of national strategy," and that the U.S. military must be prepared to "go beyond Samuel Huntington's 'professional military function' of simply advising." (The essay was published by the USAWC's Institute for Strategic Studies [1995], 64–65.) These are understandable views, given the perception that civilian officials are not fulfilling their function of providing a sufficiently concrete, consensual national-security strategy. Still, even if the assuming of responsibility for tasks left undone is understandable, it is not necessarily acceptable.

62. A vision can be created by following a formula?

63. In its Strategic Assessment 1996, the National Defense University's Institute for National Strategic Studies reported that, from 1988 to 1994, U.S. overseas troop strength fell from 541,000 to 286,000. (During the Gulf War, though, we had more than 600,000 troops abroad; p. 16). Also, Department of Defense outlays as a percentage of gross national product fell from 6 percent to 4 percent (p. 5). Department of Defense budget authority fell (in constant 1995 dollars) from $352 billion to $254 billion (p. 128). Active-duty personnel fell from about 2 million to 1. 5 million. (p. 128)

64. One of the arguments for a large defense budget has been that the technological advances made by military research yield benefits to civilians.

65. In the seminar discussion of Course 2, even the two best (committed and able) students said it was "overwhelming" and "too fast." Another felt domestic issues were cursorily covered. One (not an underachiever) pointed out that, after all, generals are generalists. They are not supposed to know everything; they are supposed to know how to find out.

66. Because classified materials were used, a trip to Latin America was organized for the International Fellows.

67. A classified document.

68. There are four functional and five geographical CINCs. Each prepares plans for his area of responsibility, providing a list of requirements, priorities, and alternatives.

69. The assigned reading includes dense, lengthy official documents and pithy, critical articles by military authors.

70. The "winners" in this process (developed in the mid-1990s) were the CJCS and the CINCs. The "losers" were the service leaders who had previously been in a strong position to advocate, and Pentagon civilians who made integrative decisions in putting together the Department of Defense budget.

71. One of several learning objectives is, in a single day, to "analyze and assess Federal and Department of Defense budgets for [the fiscal years] 1997–2002."

72. The National Military Strategy is not classified. Though general in nature, its codification almost makes it function as doctrine. Often it is not distinguished

from the National Security Strategy, although it should be, because it employs only one of four kinds of national power.

73. The estimate is that it takes two to four years to change doctrine, four years to change organization, and five to seventeen years to change material. But the crucial question is *how* should the Army change? Should it prepare for urban warfare? For terrorism? For asymmetrical warfare? Should it modernize? Restructure? Reduce personnel? Will jointness create savings? And isn't jointness the opposite of current societal trends toward both competition and decentralization?

74. Congress had passed the Federal Acquisition Streamlining Act in 1994 and passed further acquisition-reform legislation in 1996. Defense Secretary William J. Perry issued a Specifications and Standards Reform memo in 1994. Both were efforts to reduce prices and enhance quality, particularly in areas related to science and technology.

75. By which was meant the defense-industrial base. Declining budgets meant that by 1995, the defense industry was shrinking, merging, and converting. It was also seeking more foreign sales and was adjusting to an increasingly globalized economy. Students also examined Clinton administration efforts to promote "dual-use" (civilian–military) technology.

76. Retired officers' organizations and contractors, whom Secretary of the Army Togo West called part of the "Army family," are two obvious stakeholders.

77. This course had twenty-nine academic days. Course 1 had seventeen, Course 2 had thirty-six, and Course 3 had eighteen, but the first and third courses were two halves of the course offered by DCLM, thus totaling thirty-five days. This unit completed the PJE Phase I learning objectives. Its faculty in 1997 was all military—50 percent Army, 50 percent other services.

The first four lessons in this course, "Module 1: Unity of Effort and Joint Planning," are described as being four lessons offered in the previous unit. These were the lessons dealing with the Unified Command Plan, the formal relationships between civilian and military leaders responsible for implementing the nation's military strategy, and the joint planning process, with emphasis on deliberate and crisis action planning.

78. Since World War II, the United States has participated with allies in most major operations. Some alliances are of long standing, such as NATO. Others are ad hoc, such as those of the Gulf War. The cases studied in 1996 were the command and control arrangements of NATO, of the Korean War, and of Desert Shield and Desert Storm.

79. A case study does not just tell a story. Students are asked to analyze the case for its geostrategic situation; the impact of economic, political, and informational factors; the security and military objectives of each side; and the centers of gravity and strategic vulnerabilities of each side. Also, they are expected to analyze operational-level issues such as readiness, planning assumptions, force protection, and the effect of asymmetry.

80. For example, the Navy's contribution to a CINC's planning could include sea control, power projection, strategic deterrence, and strategic lift. The Air

Force could offer aerospace control, strategic attack, air interdiction, close air support, and force enhancement.

81. The author's opinion.

82. The three phases of the Somalia mission were studied for lessons to be learned, but the official lessons-learned report was still classified.

83. Course Directive, "Course 4," Carlisle, Penn., 1997, 30.

84. This argument was made by Ralph Peters in "The New Warrior," *Parameters* 24, no. 2 (Summer 1994): 16–26.

85. Robert B. Killebrew provides an analysis of the game and its value in "Learning from Wargames: A Status Report," *Parameters* 28, no. 1 (Spring 1998): 122–35. A "research" exercise does not have a correct result. It is an exploration. If it is repeated many times, it may lead to the possibility of prediction, but no prediction would be based on a single playing of a game.

86. A review of one hundred of the paper titles for the class graduating in 1996 reveals a wide range of topics. A number consider proliferation, one was on Asian Americans and one on African Americans, one was on privatization, a number were on Africa, one was titled "Belief in God as a Foundation for Strategic Planners." Virtually none were on the Commonwealth of Independent States or Russia.

87. A maximum of fifteen students and two faculty were planned for each section. Enrollment required a recommendation from one's faculty adviser and approval by the commandant.

88. For example, planning could not be focused on "requirements" to meet identifiable threats. Instead, planners had to think in terms of "capabilities" that might be needed.

89. The success of the Gulf War, which largely involved a transfer of strategy, troops, and weapons to the Gulf that had been a part of a plan for the defense of Europe against a Soviet invasion, probably made it harder to think differently.

90. Wryly, it was noted that while much effort was being expended on assessing what would probably happen down the road, what would actually happen would be "the improbable."

91. The administration of President George W. Bush has begun to ask fundamental questions. However, the difficulties of instituting change are proving most difficult. And it is not just the military that resists. Congress is unenthusiastic about base closings, and a number of corporations and unions benefit from weapon production.

Chapter Nine

1. "Report of the Panel on Military Education of the One-Hundredth Congress of the Committee on Armed Services," House of Representatives, 101st Congress, First Session, April 21, 1989. Committee Print, no. 4. (Washington, D.C.: U.S. Government Printing Office, 1989) (hereafter, Skelton Report).

2. This was especially true following World War II, when unification of the services was under consideration.

3. As will be discussed later, the war colleges are now responsible not to their service chief of staff, but to the Chair of the JCS for the part of their curriculum that relates to joint professional education.

4. Most commandants are not on the spot for long, however, and only a few imprint the school the way long-serving civilian college presidents do.

5. The founder of the Army War College, Elihu Root, served as both secretary of war and secretary of state. He saw diplomacy and the military as two crucial instruments for "preserving the peace" and believed that it was important to emphasize their linkage, even if the link was more or less symbolic. Also, there are usually several members of the Foreign Service in each Army War College class.

6. Not all war colleges are alike. The dean of the College of Naval Warfare, for example, said emphatically: "The faculty owns the curriculum" (interview, December 14, 1998).

7. Some of the opponents of reform, such as Secretary of the Navy John Lehman, were formidable. For a lively account, see James Kitfield, *Prodigal Soldiers* (New York: Simon and Schuster, 1995), chaps. 31–32.

8. Its focus was on acquisition practices, but its scope was not narrowly defined. Senator William Proxmire, Democrat of Wisconsin, had managed to acquire a certain amount of publicity by regularly making "Golden Fleece" awards for apparently ridiculous or ridiculously priced military purchases.

9. Thus, the chiefs of the services were removed from the operational chain of command.

10. Two follow-on reforms were the creation of two new unified commands (CINCs): Transportation Command and Special Operations Command. Note that these reforms all came during a period of enormous peacetime defense spending. A downward turn in spending would follow—particularly after the dissolution of the Soviet Union.

11. This represented an important shift in power away from the separate service staffs to that of the JCS.

12. Also, the Marine commandant formally received full voting membership on the JCS.

13. Skelton Report, 51 f.

14. Ibid.

15. Again, the Industrial College of the Armed Forces and the National War College were the joint war colleges.

16. The Army, Naval, Marine, and Air war colleges.

17. Skelton Report, 59.

18. The chronology of this report and the war-college curricula analyzed in this volume is that the report follows the account of the 1985 war-college curriculum provided in Chapter 6 but precedes (and thus influences) the 1990 curriculum.

19. It quoted Sir William Francis Butler: "The nation that will insist on drawing a broad line of demarcation between the fighting man and the thinking man is liable to find its fighting done by fools and its thinking done by cowards" (Skelton Report, 18). The committee included three active-duty officers on its

staff. This is one of the few times military officers have served on a congressional staff.

20. Ibid., 3–4.

21. The thirds were Army, Air Force, and "sea services," which encompassed Navy, Marine, and Coast Guard officers.

22. Skelton Report. By act of Congress, service-war-college classes convening after September 1996 must have a minimum of 20 percent non-host students among their U.S. military students: Chair of the Joint Chiefs of Staff, "Officer Professional Military Education Policy," Washington, D.C., doc. no. CJCSI 1800.01 (March 1, 1996), B-2.

23. Skelton Report, 3–4, 102, 105 f.

24. Italics added.

25. Skelton Report, 27.

26. In civilian education, breadth comes first. As education becomes more and more advanced, it becomes narrower and narrower. The specialist is most prized. The Skelton Panel's formulation seems to invert this pattern. It also suggested that PME cannot provide all that is needed for a bona fide strategist—that civilian education may also be required: Ibid., 31

27. Italics in the original.

28. Skelton Report, 28.

29. As was seen in the exploration of curricula in the previous chapters, the Army War College appears to want to turn all of its students into strategic thinkers. It does not make the distinction between theoretical and applied strategists. Nor does it acknowledge that only a very few will be capable of the highest level of strategy formulation. The problem of recognizing, then using, special talent well is not confined to the military. Plato's effort to design a system to do this in *The Republic* has made delectable reading for centuries, though few advocate adoption of his model.

30. Skelton Report, 65, 136. With promotion opportunities linked to command and large numbers of staff jobs to be filled, plus more than 1,000 students in war colleges at which faculty-to-student ratios are very low (one-to-three or -four), it seems evident that there is simply not enough of "the best" to go around. Specifically, in the mid-1980s, more than 3,000 students attended the intermediate and senior military schools. Some 800 faculty were required to teach them. Great selectivity was impossible. In fact, at the Army Command and Staff College, almost half the faculty were officers who had completed that course by correspondence. They had not been selected to attend that school's residence course. In other words, they were good enough to teach there but not to go there: Skelton Report, 135.

31. In contrast, the Skelton Committee believed that the commandant did have to be a role model and an individual who was still "on his way up" but who was willing to serve as commandant for a three-year period: ibid., 148.

32. Ibid., 140–42.

33. Ibid., 142. This practice was more common at command and staff colleges, but it was not unknown at the war colleges.

34. In their present incarnation, academic-freedom issues have not been a part of the war-college landscape. It is a little hard to imagine the colleges being comfortable with the kind of independent, sometimes eccentric, faculty present at civilian colleges. But if civilian faculty were screened or selected for institutional compatibility, what benefit would accrue? Presumably, continuity only. However, the committee accepted the practice of two- or three-year contracts for civilian faculty. This does not suggest that stability was of prime importance. Because short-term contracts are not typical of civilian universities, it is hard to imagine that the war colleges could attract high-quality civilian faculty, especially if those potential faculty were doubtful about the institution's commitment to academic freedom and to providing time and resources for research. Boston College, a Jesuit institution, has endured decades with the radical feminist Mary Daly as a tenured faculty member. One would not want to wish the equivalent awkwardness on the war colleges, but one wonders whether the committee fully grasped the range of debate expected in the civilian academic marketplace, or if war-college officials would tolerate it.

35. Under Title 10, the Navy already had legal permission to hire civilians and set their pay scale. This permission was subsequently extended to the other services, but, as noted earlier, this has often meant hiring retired officers who may have doctorates but do not necessarily have the deep academic expertise that was the primary reason cited for hiring civilian faculty.

36. Skelton Report, 146.

37. Ibid., 151. In the Navy, the trick was said to be to get selected for the war college (a mark of approval), but then to avoid going.

38. As noted earlier, the committee believed that when students said, "I learned more from my fellow students," it was an indictment of the faculty and curriculum. At the same time, high marks are always given to seminar discussions—which are, after all, among students. Note, too, that in the USAWC orientation described in Chapter 3, even reading was defined as "passive."

39. There are two different kinds of lectures to consider. One is by the outside (high-ranking) guest who speaks to all the students. There may be general agreement that there are too many of these lectures, but they remain numerous. The second would involve a tightly organized academic lecture based on expertise. There are few of these, at least at the Army War College. In fact, there seems to be an ethic that the faculty should not lecture.

40. At the time of the study, only the Navy gave graded exams. It also gave 600–700 pages of reading a week. In contrast, the Army War College assigned about 250 pages of reading a week but had more scheduled classroom hours than the Naval War College: ibid., 160. The discussion of grading appears in ibid., 161–66.

41. According to the data analyzed by the committee. Further, the committee calculated that at the war colleges, the time spent in passive learning in the core curriculum ranged from 18 percent at the College of Naval Warfare to 62 percent at the Air War College, with the other schools falling somewhere between 30 and 40 percent: ibid., 159.

42. Ibid., 125 f.

43. Ibid., 183.

44. It also criticized the lack of research time available to faculty.

45. Transition Memoranda, 1996, sec. A.

46. When the commandant attends, he chairs.

47. Who was a woman in 1998—the only woman on the board then, and possibly ever.

48. These fifteen individuals are the heads of most units in the college and the representatives of the sister services. An important office that was not represented on the board in 1996 was the Concepts, Doctrine, and Joint Education Office, which manages all doctrinal matters, joint education, and accreditation. This office coordinates with both the Army Headquarters (HQDA) and TRADOC, giving it an important role is ensuring that the curriculum is up to date: Transition Memoranda, 1996, sec. W. A decision to seek graduate-degree-granting authority from the civilian regional accreditation body was made in 1995. This has become a major concern of the board.

49. See, for example, the discussion later of the content of a January 14, 1985, memo sent to department chairs and course directors by the director of academic affairs conveying the commandant's guidance.

50. Its only power.

51. Chair of the JCS, "Officer Professional Military Education Policy."

52. Ibid., B-B-3.

Conclusion

1. John W. Masland and Laurence I. Radway, *Soldiers and Scholars: Military Education and National Policy* (Princeton, N.J.: Princeton University Press, 1957), 330, 417, 420.

2. Bernard Brodie, *War and Politics* (New York: Macmillan, 1973), 448, 486–87.

3. Martin van Creveld, *The Training of Officers: From Military Professionalism to Irrelevance* (New York: Free: New York, 1990), 106 f.

4. Eliot Cohen, "Defending America in the Twenty-first Century," *Foreign Affairs* (November–December 2000): 53–55.

5. The Air War College was the most criticized and the most responsive.

6. It will probably get it. However, such accreditation is given to schools of greatly varying quality. It should not be assumed that a war college's master's program would be among the best master's programs in the country, even if the military's academies do rate high among undergraduate institutions. This is true if only because a ten-month program with distractions cannot be the equivalent of the best master's programs, which are frequently two years in duration.

7. Note that using Whitehead's definition of "creative" thought, one would expect it to follow a period of "precision." This is not the result of (romantic) brainstorming or other exercises designed to make thinking less rigid. Also, critical thought meticulously examines assumptions and the logic underlying an argument. It is not necessarily negative.

8. Even elite liberal-arts colleges, which emphasize small classes and where some believe the best education occurs, have a ratio four times that of the war colleges.

9. The class president is chosen by the department chairs and appointed by the commandant. The three vice-presidents are chosen by the Reserve Component Adviser, the International Fellows Director, and the Civilian Liaison. The position of class secretary is assigned to the Air Force and that of treasurer to the Navy or Marine Corps. So much for elections and active learning about the democratic process.

10. Note that in student evaluations, exercises do not do particularly well. However, the response has generally been to think about how to do them better rather than to reconsider their merit. Because expensive new war-gaming facilities have been built so recently at Carlisle, one should not expect a reduction in either the number or the scale of exercises.

Note, too, that even though one of the three teaching departments focuses on operations, this volume shortchanges analysis of the plans students are asked to prepare and does not give details of the content of the exercises and games in which they participate. Such an analysis would be well worth pursuing, for many revealing assumptions are built into the design of such assignments.

11. Remember that another USAWC goal is to develop skills in consensus-building, and a number of lessons require seminars to reach an agreed-on conclusion. The training for these skills would seem to work in opposition to efforts to encourage individual, creative, and critical thinking.

12. A reminder: There are, in fact, *many* lectures at the war colleges, but they are by people who hold important positions. It is academic lectures that are disdained.

13. It is true that although each USAWC class emerges with shared knowledge, that knowledge is not necessarily the same as that of any other class—even of the classes that immediately precede or follow it.

14. The feedback in general endorses the curriculum, the methodology, the total experience.

15. Again, it is important to remember that academic freedom is based not on an individual's right to be different, but on the benefit to society from having ideas in competition with one another—even though some of the ideas may be incorrect or only partially correct. Note, too, that in their evaluation of the USAWC curriculum, generals suggested that the curriculum and speakers could profit from more "contrary" views (see Chapter 4) and that in their evaluations, students have complained that speakers are too often "party men" (see Chapter 7).

16. Not so long ago, the University of Denver's doctoral program included two female students. One of them began her dissertation under Josef Korbel, Madeline Albright's father; she was Condaleezza Rice, a "realist" who is National Security Adviser to President George W. Bush. During her student days, Rice shared a library carrel with Susan Waltz, who until recently was the president of Amnesty International worldwide. It is hard to imagine a war college producing students with such divergent views.

17. Some would even say that the trademark of the best education is a graduate who, à la Socrates, "knows that he doesn't know."

18. The class now is at least as large as classes were when the Army was one-third larger. Although admission is described as highly selective, a high percentage of colonels do in fact attend a war college.

19. But, yes, they have become much more Republican. There are now eight Republicans for every Democrat among senior officers: Peter D. Feaver and Richard H. Kohn, "The Gap: Soldiers, Civilians and Their Mutual Misunderstanding, " *National Interest* (Fall 2000), 32. Also, the Army would probably be more reluctant to use force than the Navy and Air Force.

20. That debate led to a major research effort, the "Project on the Gap Between the Military and Civilian Society," based at the Triangle Institute for Security Studies and led by Peter Feaver of Duke University and Richard Kohn of the University of North Carolina. Some of these findings are cited later.

21. A message reinforced by the known misbehavior of some elected officials (both executive and legislative).

22. This theme seemed to be more prevalent at several other war colleges than it was at the Army War College.

23. An expansive discussion of the military's ability to generally serve society appears in Robert F. Hahn III, "Politics for Warriors: The Political Education of Professional Military Officers," Project on U.S. Post-Cold War Civil–Military Relations, Working Paper no. 12, John M. Olin Institute for Strategic Studies, Harvard University, Cambridge, Mass., June 1997.

24. In the United States today, there is another danger: that of civilians inviting the military to take over civilian responsibilities. For example, in December 1999 the Los Angeles Unified School District signed a contract with the Army to have it manage its school-construction program. This was the result not of an earthquake or other emergency but of civilians who were responsible for public education hiring the military to do their job for them.

25. For a more comprehensive discussion, see Judith Stiehm, "Civil–Military Relations in War College Curricula," *Armed Forces and Society* 27, no. 2 (Winter 2001): 273–94.

26. A rare but little-noted protest by early retirement of the Air Force chief of staff occurred over the issue of assigning responsibility during the Clinton administration.

27. The emphasis on an ethic of absolute truth-telling sometimes seemed to be undermined by offhand references to those who held to it as "Boy Scouts."

28. In his essay "The Widening Gap Between the Military and Society," Thomas Ricks offers several vignettes suggesting that Marines not only believe that they should speak up, but that in the future they might have to educate or even discipline American citizens: see Thomas Ricks, "The Widening Gap Between the Military and Society," *Atlantic Monthly*, vol. 280 (July 1997), 66–78.

29. Responses are from the Army War College, Naval War College, and National War College. Students at the Marine War College, Industrial College of the Armed Forces, and Air War College did not participate.

30. Saying that a course of action was appropriate did not necessarily mean an officer thought one should or would take it.

31. The one alternative overwhelmingly rejected was leaking to the press, to which 93 percent said, "Not appropriate."

32. Roughly half the students, however, thought that the commander-in-chief should have served in uniform to be respected. This is disturbing. In our democracy, the commander-in-chief is chosen by the voters. That in itself should be at least some ground for respect.

33. As did Colin Powell, then Chair of the JCS. See, among other discussions, Michael Desch, *Civilian Control of the Military: The Changing Security Environment* (Baltimore: Johns Hopkins University Press, 1999), esp. 29, 32, 35.

34. William Pfaff, "Beware of a Military Penchant for a Parallel Foreign Policy," *International Herald Tribune* (September 22, 1999), 8.

35. The test of civilian control comes when the military is asked to do something it does not want to do, not in whether it refers to civilian leaders as its masters.

36. Moreover, they have attempted to use the press for their own purposes—something most say they believe to be inappropriate.

37. The Pentagon was asked to prepare a display of military weaponry for the 2000 Republican Presidential Convention. It did so at the cost of half-a-million dollars. Recently, retired flag officers have graced the podium of presidential conventions. Officers have worked in congressional offices. All seem of doubtful propriety.

38. The atrocious attacks of September 11, 2001, proved right those security specialists who argued that conflicts do not have to be state against state, and that our expensive and well-trained military was prepared for the last war rather than for the most likely threats. Still, even the strategists who warned of potential terrorist attacks must have been numbed by the scale and the success of the attacks on the World Trade Towers and the Pentagon.

39. Many contemporary conflicts involve secession rather than aggression. Although aggression is considered unacceptable, international law and norms regarding secession are not well developed.

40. An excellent discussion and explanation of this position appears in William Langewiesche, "Peace Is Hell," *Atlantic Monthly,* vol. 288, no. 3 (October 2001), 51 f.

41. One answer is they have the resources. They have lift, they have communications, they have intelligence, they have field hospitals.

42. These criteria set a high standard for the use of force. Note that the August 1990 vote on the Gulf War was 52–47 in the Senate and 250–183 in the House of Representatives, even though Iraq clearly had committed an act of aggression and threatened a large share of the world's oil supply.

43. The victories in the Gulf and in Kosovo have not been satisfying. In the first case, the war's objective was met: Iraq left Kuwait. However, Saddam Hussein is still in office, and the U.S. military is still in the Gulf monitoring, polic-

ing, bombing, and spending resources. In the second instance, NATO has been unable to guarantee safety for Serbian residents of Kosovo, and the United States has ended up almost as an accomplice of the Kosovo Liberation Army in its efforts to make Kosovo independent.

44. Students thoroughly study war at the war college. They study wars past and wars yet to come. They study small wars and large ones. They plan for wars in the jungle, in the city, and in the mountains. A third of the core curriculum is taught by the Department of Military Strategy, Planning, and Operations. Also, the most subscribed electives are the two course on "Advanced Warfighting Studies."

There has been recent interest in "war termination." Still, there has been little examination of what it takes to create a sustained peace or of the second- and third-order effects of such institutions and processes as war-crimes trials and truth commissions.

45. Some even claim that the more than $50 billion paid represented a profit: John O'Loughlin, Tom Mayer, and Edward S. Greenberg, eds., *War and Its Consequences: Lessons from the Persian Gulf* (New York: HarperCollins, 1994), 17, 165.

46. The United States has been engaged in asymmetric conflicts in the past— for example, the kidnapping of the Panamanian head of state during the Bush administration and the invasion of Grenada during the Reagan administration. But these were small in scale, brief, and not registered officially or by U.S. public opinion as wars.

47. After the Bay of Pigs, John Kennedy repeatedly berated himself for trusting "the experts."

48. Boys' fiction stresses the importance of standing up to bullies. The message is that one does not have to win, but one must be willing and able to inflict enough damage to command respect. This means that in the future, the bully will leave you alone. In striving to make our military impugn, our civilian guardians seem to be pursuing an impossible goal rather than building a military that demands respect and does so backed by only "enough" will and capacity.

49. See Walter Russell Mead, "The Jacksonian Tradition," in *National Interest* (Winter 1999–2000), 1–25, for an account of "American ruthlessness at war."

50. As argued by William James in his classic essay "The Moral Equivalent of War," repr. in *War and Morality*, ed. Richard Wasserstrom (Belmont, Calif.: Wadsworth Publishing, 1970), 4–14.

Index